The Good Old Times; the Romance of Humble Life in England

THE GOOD OLD TIMES

JOHN BALL PREACHING.

(From an illuminated MS. of "Froissart's Chronicles" in the British Museum.)

THE GOOD OLD TIMES

THE ROMANCE OF HUMBLE
LIFE IN ENGLAND

BY

FREDERICK W. HACKWOOD

AUTHOR OF "INNS, ALES, AND DRINKING CUSTOMS OF OLD ENGLAND,"
"OLD ENGLISH SPORTS," ETC.

WITH 44 ILLUSTRATIONS

T. FISHER UNWIN
LONDON: ADELPHI TERRACE
LEIPSIC: INSELSTRASSE 20
1910

NOTE

THIS volume, it is hoped, will be found readable ; for it aims at arresting the attention of the general reader, and arousing popular interest in a highly controversial subject, not by pretending to offer any particular solution to what is really a vast economic problem, so much as by presenting the past history of the subject in its more striking and picturesque phases.

Analytical Table of Contents

Stow, the historian, a licensed beggar—A licence equivalent to a "rate in aid"—Bedesmen called "Badgemen."

The badging of paupers in receipt of out-door relief—Penalty on recalcitrant paupers who tried to escape the "badge of poverty"—Paupers in iron collars.

Poverty a source of crime—The vagabond—The rogue.

Impostors and impostures—Nothing new.

"Caveat for Cursetors" (1566)—Celebration of rich man's funeral by the "Canting Crew" (1521).

"Caveat against Cut-purses" (1614)—The tricks of Bartholomew Fair—The training of a cut-purse—John Selman and Mary Frith, experts—Their interesting careers.

The users of Cant and Flash languages—A curious catalogue of offenders.

Arrive in England in fifteenth century—Origin and name—Act of 1530 banishes them—To depart the country under their governor, Philippe Lazar (1545)—Yet found occupying a church-house in 1560.

Accounted felons 1597—Joined by English vagrants and "loyterers"—hence their English names.

Dekker's description of Egyptian "moon-men" villanies—How they forage—Dress fantastically—Thieve and poach—And tell fortunes—"Egyptian roges" described in Holinshed's Chronicles—Pedlers' French—Romany language—Arnold's "Scholar Gipsy."

North Britain gipsies—"Jonny Faa the Gypsie Laddie"—Gipsy Hill tribe—Queen Esther, of Yetholm.

Child-stealing—Maggie Tulliver's adventure—Divination—Allusions by Crabbe and Gay—The gipsy blood.

The trader who carries his stock with him—Autolycus—A pedlar's song—Pedlars' cries.

Derivation of the term "pedlar"—Pedlar's fardel—

List of Illustrations

The illustrations facing pages 148, 150, 154, 177, 200, 215, 227, 228, 230, 232, 248, 1329, 340, are from prints kindly lent by Messrs. Myers & Co, Booksellers and Printsellers, Holborn

THE GOOD OLD TIMES

I

EARLY ASPECTS

The Saxon system—Mutual dependence of master and man—Did not prevent mendicancy—Especially in bad seasons—The *hlaford* or "lord of the loaf"—The royal almoner—*Deodands* confiscated for alms—Maundy distributions—Origin and history of the ceremony—Institution of tithes—A portion of them intended for the poor—For "God's poor and the needy in thraldom"—As recognised by law—Every man to be domiciled—Yet homeless wanderers broke loose—Oblations enriched the Church—Which of its plenty gave to the poor—The monastic almoner — Daily doles — Encouraged vagabondism — The Almonry—The amount distributed—Benevolence a social necessity of the age

"YE have the poor always with you" is a New Testament dictum which certainly does not look hopefully towards the possibility of a universal socialism. Even Saxon England, under the mutuality of its manorial system, by which every man in the land had owed allegiance to a master, who, in turn, was responsible for him to the State, was not without its poor.

The Saxon law for the poor was strictly what may be termed a law of settlement; the serf was compelled to remain in one place and one service, and his lord was obliged to provide for him. Yet, such is the diver-

25

sity (or, shall we say, perversity?) of the human temperament, there were men who, under a patriarchal government like this, could escape their daily apportionment of God-given food.

There were miserable wanderers who, being unattached to any lordship, and outside the very fringe of Saxon society, had no legal provision. They therefore had to depend entirely on private benevolence, a source of sustenance sometimes drawn upon more extensively in bad seasons, when the failure of the harvest produced general or local distress.

In those far-away times, when means of intercommunication and transport were extremely limited, the laws which now regulate the distribution of supplies were inoperative. Then, in times of stress the lord and the lady distributed alms at the hall door. Indeed, etymologists tell us that in the Saxon tongue the word "lord" was *hlaford*, of which the first part was *hlaf*, or loaf, and the second half, *ward*, the whole literally signifying "breadward." Similarly, the word "lady" has loaf as its first element.

There is extant an ancient Anglo-Saxon illumination—and its authenticity is undoubted—which depicts a royal or noble house, with its attendant warriors, its priests, and its chapel, with the poor at the door receiving food, as it were in customary manner, from the hands of the lord and the lady of the household.

In this benevolent lady of the Saxon household we seem to recognise the prototype of the "Lady Bountiful"—introduced into Farquhar's play, "The Beaux Stratagem," as a traditional English character—the typical lady of the village, who scatters her charities around her with both hands, as it were.

In the best regulated baronial halls of mediæval times, every baking day a fixed proportion of the loaves produced

BEGGARY.

(From Harleian MS.)

tant se taist li contes de
vaspasyen ke il ne pole
plus. & li commenche de iose
ph. Et dist ke ioseph en uoie querre
tous ses parens & ses amis & si loe

A MENDICANT FRIAR PREACHING FROM A PORTABLE PULPIT.

(*See p.* 57.)

were allotted for alms, which were to be distributed, not by the grooms, but by an orderly division made among the poor by the lady in person.

In early times there was an officer of the king's household, called the Almoner, or Almer, whose special business it was to distribute the king's alms every day. To the royal almoner, according to law, went *deodands* —the value in money of every article which in a coroner's court was proved to be the immediate cause of an untimely death—confiscated for distribution in alms.

The office of Lord High Almoner of England was sometimes held by a bishop, and sometimes by a layman, and in connection therewith must be mentioned the ancient custom of distributing the royal alms on Maundy Thursday.

Princes and others, both laymen and ecclesiastics, were encouraged by the Church to imitate the humility of Christ in washing the feet of His disciples, by washing the feet of paupers, and to associate this menial act with the distribution of charity. As the latter took the form of giving in baskets, or maunds, the day came to be distinguished as Maundy Thursday.

After the Maundy ceremony at Christchurch, Canterbury, the "Cup of Charity" was handed round; the poor were freely invited into the cloister for a ceremonial feet-washing of weekly occurrence, and an alms of twopence each was given in each case of necessity; and the almoner was responsible for visiting the sick poor of the neighbourhood in person. Other reformed monasteries of the eleventh century similarly made almsgiving a primary duty.

In England the monarch's birthday has for long centuries past been marked in a manner not altogether dissimilar, the English custom also involving the relief of the poor and the counting of the king's years. The

Thursday in Holy Week is known as Maundy Thursday, said to be originally so called from the Latin *Mandatum novum do nobis*, for it was the day of Christ's great "mandate" at the institution of the Lord's Supper, "Love one another." It is Spelman who derives the name from *maund*, "a basket," because, in olden times, on the day before the great fast all the religious houses and good Catholics brought out their broken food in maunds (baskets to hold the mandate bread) to distribute to the poor. The royal custom here, on the day before Good Friday, was for the sovereign, in imitation of Christ washing His disciples' feet, to wash the feet of as many poor people as the years of his age, and then to make them presents of alms. The word "maunder" is a cant term for a beggar.

The King of England was accustomed to bring together for this ceremony as many poor men as he was years old. Queen Elizabeth in her thirty-ninth year performed the ceremony at Greenwich Palace, attended by thirty-nine ladies of the Court. From 1714 to 1890 the custom was observed in the Chapel Royal, Whitehall; since the latter date the venue has been Westminster Abbey.

The last monarch to do the washing personally was James II., in the old chapel at Whitehall. In Hanoverian times the duty devolved on one of the archbishops; but after 1736 the ceremony was shorn of its religious significance by omitting the washing of feet. The alms distributed generally consisted of a purse containing silver pence of the number of the years celebrated, some clothing, a loaf of bread, a platter of fish, and a bowl of ale, or meat and drink in some form. At the beginning of Queen Victoria's reign an additional sum of money was substituted in lieu of the provisions; and the coins still used include silver pennies, and silver pieces of two-pence, three-pence, and four-pence.

Reverting to Saxon times, after the royal alms came the benevolences of the Church, in which connection we have to consider the institution known as "tithes." Tithes, or tenths, were commanded by the Mosaic law to be given to the priestly tribe of Levi. Anterior to that, as we read in Genesis, Abraham, returning from his victory over the kings, gave tithes of the spoil to Melchisedeck, King of Salem and priest of the Most High God.

So in the early days of the Saxon Church the practice of tithe-giving was introduced. It became the custom for a certain part of the fruit or increase of the earth, and of beasts and of men's labour, to be given to the parish priest in recompense for his office. Gifts of wood, corn, and hay came to be usually designated the *great tithes*.

It was at first purely a freewill offering. St. Augustine addressed a question to Pope Gregory referring to the offerings of the faithful upon the altar, and the Pope replied, in effect, that it would be well to turn the offerings into something more settled, if possible. He wrote (according to our authority, Bede, in the year 596 A.D.), reciting that it was the custom to charge bishops, when they were ordained, that the whole income be divided into four parts—one for the bishop, one for the clergy, *a third for the poor*, and a fourth for the repair of the church.

In the primitive British Church the practice did not obtain. The clergy, says Bede, took of them whom they instructed, only so much as might serve their necessities; the monks of Bangor lived strictly by the labour of their own hands, like Paul of Tarsus.

On the other hand, in a letter from Bede to Egbert, written in 734, mention is made of priests, in remote Northumbrian villages, taking tribute without rendering any sort of service.

By the year 670 the clergy collected tribute as a right, and the canonical law by this time enjoined payment of tithes. Payment, indeed, was enforced ; as by personal collection, by the infliction of a fine for non-payment, or by the thunders of the Church, even to the extremity of anathematising the defaulter.

One shameful transaction recorded by history was the pardon granted by the Pope to Offa, King of Mercia, for the murder of Ethelbert of East Anglia, on condition that he would make the tithe a legal enactment in his kingdom.

It was St. Swithin who earned for himself the enduring distinction of getting introduced the system of tithes as a provision for the clergy. This was during the reign of Ethelwulf, who was induced by Swithin, a monk of Winchester, to set apart a tenth of his lands for religious purposes. The payment of tithes did not become a legal obligation till the reign of Athelstan, who enforced the payment of tithes of live-stock as well as of produce.

The great point to observe about tithes was their original apportionment among the clergy, the fabric of the church, and the poor—"one-third to God's poor and the needy in thraldom," was the exact letter of the law of Ethelred.

It is to be feared that when the tithes had been regularized by law, but a very small fraction of them fell to the share of the poor. But the promptings of Christianity, which had recognised these fellow-creatures as "God's poor," were not slow to open up other sources of relief.

By the law of Athelstan (A.D. 924) it was ordained respecting the "lordless man, of whom no law can be got, the kindred be commanded that they domicile him to folkright, and find him a lord in the folkmote," or general assembly of the people. In those days every householder was responsible for the individuals of his household, whether bond or free, as also for the stranger he admitted within his gates. Notwithstanding, there was always a section of society outside the settled household, masterless men who were homeless wanderers.

In the early days of the Saxon Church there seemed to have been a pious contention among our ancestors who should first bring their offerings to church ; and the bishop, to whom the charge of souls was committed, was for that reason thought the fittest person to be intrusted with the administration of these oblations.

By these and other superabundant offerings at altars, sepulchres, and shrines of martyrs, the Church in time became extremely rich ; and as a result numbers of monasteries, priories, hospitals and religious houses of different orders were founded and plentifully endowed ; all of which supported and fed a very numerous body of idle poor, whose daily sustenance depended mainly, if not wholly, on the alms regularly distributed at the hospitable gates of these foundations.

Vagrant wanderers, among other wayfarers, were freely received each night at the monasteries, and given food and refreshment by the good monks, as a mere matter of course becoming to a charitable Christian community. Naturally such an easy-going system of relief was a direct encouragement to vagabondism.

In an ancient monastery there was no more responsible officer than the almoner, the good monk who distributed the alms of the house ; he was, to all intents and purposes, the relieving officer of the Middle Ages. Each morning food was freely and bountifully handed out to all applicants, and in special cases doles of money were sometimes added.

The Church, as it organised itself, evolved a moral consciousness, and bestirred itself actively in well-meant endeavours to relieve want and mitigate the evils of chronic poverty; and as we shall see presently, among its other good influences was early instrumental in discrediting the traffic in slaves.

> "The priesthood, like a tower
> Stood between the poor and power,
> And the wronged and trodden down
> Blessed the abbot's shaven crown."

Convents regarded hospitality as a religious duty; for the Order of St. John of Jerusalem it was the first of duties. Travellers and wayfarers were received, and treated according to their rank, the poor always gratuitously. Only visitors of high rank were received into the monastery itself; the mass of travellers, pilgrims, and wayfarers were housed and fed in a building specially provided for the purpose, and known as the guest-house. This building stood by itself, and was sometimes outside the precincts of the monastery, as may be seen at Battle Abbey to this day, where the guest-house stands outside the big entrance gates. These edifices usually consisted of a hall, with doors opening on each side into dormitories; and when the guests were over-numerous, beds were laid out in the entrance hall itself. Some monastic establishments had an almonry, or aumbry, a special apartment in which the distribution of alms was regularly made; it was usually a stone building near the chapel, and on the north side of the quadrangle; or sometimes, for greater convenience, it was placed near the gate-house.

The amount systematically distributed was in value supposed to represent one-tenth of the monastery's entire income. "John the Almoner" was the title of affection bestowed on St. Chrysostom, because he had first set the example of bestowing a large portion of his income "upon hospitals and charities"—at least, so said the monkish tradition.

For the more convenient discharge of the duties of hospitality many monastic establishments were planned with the guest-chamber for the reception of distinguished visitors, together with the kitchens and cellars, and other necessary offices for dispensing their bounties, at the west end of the buildings.

Though monasteries were not intended to be benevolent institutions, all of them had practically become such, owing to the social necessities of the age.

The brethren found their reward often enough in the bequests and endowments with which wealthy wayfarers acknowledged their obligation to these religious establishments, which served them so handsomely as hostels when they were on their travels; but every day of the year provision had to be made for the relief of a crowd of half-famished beggars and footsore tramps, so that the aggregate cost of the hospitality dispensed by a large abbey was enormous.

II

SAXON THRALLS AND NORMAN VILLEINS

"The needy in thraldom"—Origin of thralls—Their market value—
The comparative comfort of the freeman—To the thrall who
was not "law worthy"—Moral influence of the Church—Slave
trading forbidden (1102)—Bristol slave market—Cessation of
the Irish traffic—Effect of Norman invasion—Unfree "natives"
become villeins—"Villeins regardant"—"Villeins in gross"—
"Ancillæ"—Scott's picture of Gurth the Swineherd—The serf
of the Middle Ages—Recorded sales and selling-prices

Now to consider the lowest stratum of society, as it
was then organized. The Saxon state included thralls,
or slaves.

From the phrase "God's poor and the needy in
thraldom," quoted in the previous chapter from the law
of Ethelred, it is clear that admirable as the Saxon system
was in theory, it failed to work out satisfactorily in
practice. There was a ragged fringe to Saxon society.

Though every man was required to be settled and
domiciled, there were "masterless men" wandering about
the country in a state of destitution—these were "God's
poor."

But why there should have been any "needy in thraldom" it is, at first sight, difficult to see. Thralls were a
species of property owned like goods and chattels, and
beasts of burden, and therefore possessing a commercial
value—so long as they remained in health and strength.

But a slave who was old and decrepit, or incapacitated in any way, was just as liable to be neglected and cast off as a broken-down horse left to wander about a common ; to become, in fact, as "needy" of Christian-charity as the homeless freeman.

In Anglo-Saxon society below the three great ranks into which the people were divided—the noble, the freeman, and the dependent workman who cultivated his lord's land—were the actual slaves.

These were known as ceorls and theows, thews, or thralls, who consisted of men who had lost their liberty either as criminals, as captives taken in war, or for debt, or for some other easily conceivable cause.

It is not at all improbable that the theows originally were members of a conquered race, and their numbers were perhaps added to from time to time by criminals, outlaws, and others who had lost every vestige of their rights as freemen. Whatever minor rights were enjoyed by the bondsmen called ceorls, there can be no doubt that the theows were absolute slaves.

No old tale in the history books is better known than that of the golden-haired English slaves exposed for sale in the markets of Rome, who attracted the attention of Gregory the Great ; an episode which led to the Christianizing of the Anglo-Saxons.

In the reign of Ethelred the price of a sound man slave was two pounds sixteen shillings, the price of a good hawk, three times the value of a horse, eight times the value of an ox.

Slaves were bred like cattle on the farms, and formed a large part of the exports. For the Anglo-Saxon free-man, when he became settled in the towns, was a trader or a craftsman. The wealthy merchant lived in a fair amount of comfort, but the craftsmen fared very roughly. Their houses were crowded in narrow lanes, and they

endured, no doubt unconsciously, many domestic hardships, though they cared nothing for the dirt, the mud,
and the stench with which they were surrounded. There
was work for all, they lived in plenty, they throve, they
were independent; and having no feudal lord to harass
them, they rejoiced in their freedom, occasionally to the
verge of turbulence, whenever their rights of self-govern-
ment, in folkmote or in wardmote, were in the least
ways threatened. Being free, well fed, and prosperous,
they were cheerful and contented.

As free citizens they were "law worthy," and in those
days "every child was his father's heir, after his father's
day." But the serfs were not accounted "law worthy";
for instance, they could not claim, as the freemen did, the
rights of inheritance, or the right in a court of justice, to
be tried by a jury of their equals. The serfs were practically without rights; their lords had full power of limb
and liberty over them, though not of life and death.

In the Code of Ina there was one section containing
an important provision. Concerning work on Sundays
it directed that if a bondsman worked on that day by
order of his master, he should be free; and if a freeman
worked on that day without the order of his superior,
he should lose his liberty, or forfeit sixty shillings.

In 816 it was decreed in a Synod that English slaves
belonging to a bishop, if they had been made slaves
during his lifetime, should be set free at his death.

If we are to credit monkish legends, the great and the
mighty were sometimes, by the reverses of fortune, consigned to slavery. In 883, as we learn from this source,
King Alfred had slain the two great Danish generals of
the north, and begun to cultivate the wastes of Northum-
bria. At that time St. Cuthbert by a vision revealed to
the Abbot Edred that the Bishop, and all the English and
Danes, should be commanded to ransom Guthred, the

son of Ardecanute, who had been sold to slavery to a
widow at Whittingham (which is situated eight miles
from Alnwick), and should make him king of Northum-
bria. "Which was done," says the monkish chronicle,
"and he reigned over York, but Egbert beyond the Tyne."
From slave to king is an extraordinary turn of the wheel
of fortune; but, true or not, the legend throws a strong
light on the spirit of the age.

It is to the credit of the Church, as the chief civilizing
agent of the time, that by the Synod of Westminster
(1102) it was strictly forbidden that men should be sold
as slaves. The wording of the canon was as significant as
it was direct :—

"Let no man presume from henceforth to carry on that wicked
traffic by which men of England have hitherto been sold like brute
animals."

There is no shadow of a doubt that the thralls who
were menials and domestics, ignorant of either agriculture
or hand-craft, the lowest order of society, were veritable
slaves in every sense of the word, and as such were regularly bought and sold, Bristol being a famous slave market,
trafficking in this commodity with Ireland, Scotland, and
Denmark.

The story of Bristol as a slave emporium is rather interesting. When it was the chief port for the shipping of
English slaves to foreign lands, young persons of both
sexes, some of the girls being of great beauty, were daily
to be seen in the market-place tied together with ropes,
exposed for sale. Parents even sold their own children,
till Wulfstan, Bishop of Worcestor, came to Bristol and
preached against the cruel practice. He and Archbishop
Lanfranc petitioned the king, who derived a considerable
revenue from the traffic, in the shape of a poll-tax on
each slave sold, to put a stop to the practice, but without

success. Upon the failure of this effort, the lower orders of the city, inflamed by Wulfstan's preaching, and knowing full well that most of the slaves marted came from their own class, rose up in a frenzy, fell upon one of the leading slave merchants, and put out his eyes. "Thus," says the old writer who tells the story, "the citizens of Bristol abandoned that wicked trade, and set an example to the rest of the kingdom."

William of Malmesbury (1095–1143) roundly accuses the Anglo-Saxon nobility of selling their female servants as slaves to foreigners. Giraldus Cambrensis (1147–1223) says the English before the Conquest sold their children and other relations as slaves to the Irish.

After the Norman Conquest the export of slaves to Ireland was long continued, till, in the reign of Henry II., the Irish came to a non-importation agreement which stopped the practice.

It has been surmised that the Normans, strangers to any other than a feudal state, may have given some sparks of enfranchisement to the "natives" or cultivating serfs on the folk-land, admitting them to the oath of fealty, which conferred a right of protection, and raised them to a position just superior to downright slavery. Some change took place in the condition of this lowest class which had the effect of wiping them out of existence as a slave caste in little more than a century from the Conquest.

Under the Normans the ceorls became villeins, and villenage was not finally and completely abolished till the accession of the Tudors. A villein had no rights except that his lord might not kill or maim him ; he could acquire or hold no property except according to his master's will, and was only tenant-at-will of the cottage and plot of land on which he lived and which he held on a servile tenure. The term "villein" at first signified a serf, but in long process of time it came gradually to mean a rustic employed on the soil. "Villeins regardant" belonged to the soil and were transferred as mere chattels to the new proprietor when the estate changed hands; "villeins in gross" belonged to their masters, who could sell or transfer them at will. Similarly, the women servants of the household, called "ancillæ," could be disposed of at the pleasure of their lord, though the laws protected their chastity. In the reign of Henry III. an English female serf could be bought for eighteen shillings, the current price of a lady's palfrey.

A verbal picture of the serf has been painted for us by Sir Walter Scott in the opening chapter of "Ivanhoe." Gurth, the swineherd, is there described as a stern man, savage and bold of aspect, clad in garments of the simplest form and make, composed of the tanned skin of some animal, on which the hair had been originally left, but which had worn off in many places, leaving patches of bare leather. His feet were cased in sandals, bound with thongs of boar's hide; thin leather thongs were twined round the lower part of his legs, and his knees were left bare like those of a modern Highlander. His head was protected by no covering beyond his own thick and matted hair, and an overgrown beard covered his two cheeks. A conspicuous part of his dress was a brass ring resembling a dog's collar, but without any opening, and soldered fast round his neck, so loose as to form no impediment to his breathing, yet so tight as to be incapable of being removed, excepting by the use of the file. On this singular gorget was engraved in Saxon characters an inscription of the following purport —"Gurth, the son of Beowulph, is the born thrall of Cedric of Rotherwood." The picture is somewhat fanciful; but it will serve.

Thus, it will be seen there were several grades of

villeins, some attached to the soil, some to the person of the lord, some possessing a few trifling privileges ; but all might be legally sold or transferred with the estate.

That the serf of the Middle Ages was regarded as the absolute property of his master, if not "body and soul," to the very utmost degree, there is clear and indisputable evidence. It is recorded that in 1309 the Abbot of Whalley sold a "native," with all his family and effects, for the sum of one hundred shillings.

In the Cottonian Library is a manuscript deed which is thus translated :—

"Know all men by these presents that I, Katerna d'Engayne, who was wife of Sir Thomas Engayne, Knt., have given, granted, and delivered for a certain sum of money to Sir Edward Courtney, Earl of Devon, Thomas Wattiz, my born thrall of Schaldewell, with all his goods and chattels wheresoever found, together with all his posterity and progeny, by him begotten. Given at Exminster, on Sunday next after the Feast of All Saints. In the eighth year of Richard II. after the Conquest."

In the Advocate's Library, Edinburgh, is preserved a twelfth-century grant of a slave and his children made by William the Lion to the monks of Dunfermline ; it is from the chartulary of that abbey.

The records of Lewes Priory contain proofs of the transference of human beings from one proprietor to another, both by gift and sale, in the thirteenth century. A deed of the reign of John sets forth that Godfrey de Glende hath "given and quitclaimed to God and to St. Pancras of Lewes, and to the monks there serving, in pure and perpetual alms, for myself and my heirs, Gwarinn de hamgate, my man and native (*hominem et nativum meum*), with all his chattels and with all his following."

Similarly, by another deed, dated 1235, Gilbert de Say

gave to the monks of this Priory "Reginald, son of William de Ditchling, his man and native with all his chattels and all his following," sealing the deed in open court at the county of Lewes, for that "the Prior and Convent have given me ten shillings sterling." Both deeds were attested by the sheriff of the county.

Either the monks secured a great bargain in William de Ditchling or they paid too dear a price for their soap-maker, Alwyn. Or perhaps the high price named in the next deed of transfer indicates the man's value for his remarkable skill as an artisan.

William de Kaines, says the document, gives up to the Priory all claim to "Alwin their man of Seaford sur-named Le Soper" (*hominem illorum de Selford cognomento Le Soper*), receiving from them in payment 100 shillings sterling, "in the presence of Eustace, the Archdeacon of Lewes," &c., &c.

Reference is made in "The Annals of Dunstable" to this phase of life in 1283: "This year we sold our slave by birth, William Pike, and all his family, and received one mark from the buyer."

In the Memorandum Roll of the Irish Exchequer (20 *Hy. VI.*) is a copy of an order of the King for the sale of an Irish enemy named Neil O'Durnym to John FitzHenry, for the sum of twenty shillings, the said Neil having been taken prisoner by Sir John Dartas.

To traffic in human flesh and blood was not, at this period, alien to the spirit of the English people. Still, as subsequent chapters will disclose, there was abroad a spirit of revolt which asked—

> " If I'm yon mighty lordling's slave,
> By Nature's law designed,
> Why was an independent thought
> E'er planted in my mind ?"

III

THE CONDITIONS OF ENGLISH SERFDOM

Ceorls become villeins—Thralls, or *servi*, disappear—Escapes from
villenage—The transfer of villeins—A villein's limited rights—
Quasi-independence of copyholders—Frankpledge, *murdrum*,
and "presentment of Englishery"—Apologies for serfdom—
The "free-tenant"—The "bondsman in blood" and the "neif"
—Corporal punishment and restraint—"Merchetum" (*jus
primæ noctis*)—Abrogation of austerities—"Chevage"—Methods
of freeing a serf—Ceremony of manumission—Freedom demanded for serf's posterity—Decay of villenage—Last recorded
case—Not abolished by statute.

UNDER Norman rule the lower classes were regarded as
of less value than "the good red deer," though there is
reason to believe the people loosened the chains of their
bondage very considerably during the warlike period of
the earlier Plantagenets.

The species of slave known to the Saxons as ceorls
were entered in Domesday Book as *villani,* and the
Saxon theows, or thralls, were written down by the
Norman scribes as *servi.*

Whether the latter, the lowest grade of society, were
descendants of aboriginal natives, and therefore non-
Teutonic, has not been determined; but as a distinct
class these genuine slaves certainly did not at the Conquest constitute the mass of the labouring population.
The Domesday record shows the proportion to have

been about one *servus* to four *villani*. Sir Francis Palgrave, in his authoritative work on the English Commonwealth, declares that the *servi* had ceased to exist as a distinct class prior to the commencement of our legal records. The description "native," given in the ancient Court Rolls, cannot be accepted as applicable to the original servile class; it no doubt signified any one in a state of feudal bondage.

The policy of the Conqueror in offering freedom to every one residing a year and a day within any of his walled towns had not only diminished the numbers of the *servi*, but had quite obliterated the faint line of demarcation between their bondage and that of the villein. For who would remain unfree when by an easy escape from swine-tending or wood-cutting in the forest to the shelter of the neighbouring town one could enjoy the privileges of the "king's own freemen"? Barons and feudal lords were too preoccupied with war and preparations for war, to heed and count all the serfs who lived on their wide-reaching domains. Whether Elfric the Redhaired was still burning charcoal in the forest or Godsune the son of Snelling was still cutting wood in the copse, or whether they had transferred themselves to the liberty of the nearest city, was not likely to come within the personal knowledge of their lord till long after the law had condoned the offence.

From the fact that the attainment of freedom was comparatively so easy that the *servi* entirely disappeared from society, presumably by taking advantage of the facility, while the villeins were apparently contented to remain in serfdom, and did so remain till the fifteenth century, it has been argued that villenage, after all, was not so degrading or so hard to endure as generally supposed.

"Although," says Sir Francis Palgrave, "according to

legal language, the villein might be given, bequeathed, or sold, these expressions, which sound so harsh and seem so inconsistent with any degree of personal liberty, bore a meaning essentially different from that which we should now assign them. In no instance do we find the ceorl (or villein) separate from his land. He was always a *villein appurtenant;* and notwithstanding the language employed, the gift, bequest, or sale was the disposition of the land, and his services with it "—the services rendered in lieu of rent, it may be added.

This weighty opinion notwithstanding, the specific instances of the transference of property in human flesh and blood adduced in the last chapter do not bear the construction that they were in every case merely incidental to a transfer of real estate.

Other arguments in the contention that villenage was an easy yoke to bear include reference to frankpledge, concerning which there is a mass of recorded testimony which proves either that the great mass of the agricultural population was not in a state of villenage, or that villenage was compatible with "all the rights of freemen." The word "all" is clearly overreaching. The villein certainly possessed the right to own and till his land as a copyholder so long as he rendered the customary services to his lord for the privilege. But he was not recognised in the courts of law as the equal of the freeman and the freeholder. He was still a bond-servant, and as such the few rights he possessed were strictly limited. He might even vindicate his rights, but if he happened to lose his holding where would he be allowed another tenure ? In all his goings out and all his comings in he was the creature of his lord, dominated soul and body. Where economic independence did not exist was any form of independence, social or political, possible ?

A lord's serfs had to do what he told them, but with

his freemen he bargained one by one. With his villagers he did not bargain, but taking the villeins of each vill as a group he required from them not less than his predecessor had demanded.

In numbers of cases of litigation villeins were sentenced to pecuniary mulct, from which it is argued that the law recognised their right to property. Quite so ; or how was a villein to buy his freedom, which he often did by the sweat of his brow, endured in that portion of his time he was permitted to devote to his own interests, and which was not consecrated to the service of his lord and master ?

Again, in the case of the Hundred being amerced for every person found dead through want or cold, it has been claimed that the principle of each man in a community being answerable for his fellow strikes at the very root of slavery. It does, no doubt; but there were reasons for imposing this mutual responsibility other than a solicitude for the sanctity of human life—the death of a serf meant the loss of valuable property.

In *murdrum*, the fine imposed on the Hundred for the crime of homicide or murder, a rather frequent offence in those barbarous times, we are compelled to recognise the mutual distrust and jealousy with which Norman and Saxon regarded each other for more than two centuries after the Conquest, inasmuch that if it were proved to the jury that the dead victim was an Englishman and not a Norman—not one of the governing class, but a low-bred native fellow—the fine was averted. This process was known in the courts as the "presentment of Englishery."

There is scarcely a villain who has strutted across the pages of history but has had his character "whitewashed" by some apologist ; the same special pleading has been made on behalf of the most degrading customs of feudalism. It is urged that though some of the prescribed villein services may have been onerous and the personal ones doubly severe, it is wrong to apply to the Middle Ages the standard of life which obtains at the present day.

"Let it be borne in mind," says the apologist, "that if the villein ploughed and sowed he did it in lieu of rent, or in part of it; and that even if he, the possessor perchance of two or three score acres, were required to perform those services himself (of which, however, there is no proof), personal service was considered no degradation in an age when some of the noblest estates and some of the highest offices of the land were held by 'grand serjeantry,' no other than *personal* services."

It would seem that there is not an injustice or a wrong standing up under the scorn of God that does not find some defender.

It may be conceded that the villeins who prosecuted appeals against the lords (often enough successfully, too) were in a position to obtain money as well as subsistence and were very far from a state of pauperism. But they were in a state of bondage, nevertheless, and they did not constitute the bulk of the labouring population. Because they bore their servitude uncomplainingly that did not make it any the less a state of servitude.

It may also be granted that the bondage of the "free-tenant," who held his land on condition of performing certain fixed services, was comparatively slight as compared with that of the villein who was bound to perform services which were often undefined and not infrequently base in their nature. Here, undoubtedly, was real servitude. Differing from the "free-tenants" of the manor, who were bound by the tenure of their land to do certain work annually for their lord, he had to do practically what he was told to do, and was granted with the manor or other property, as one of its appurtenances. Shortly before 1162, for example, when the mill of Worthing, near Dereham, was granted to the monks of Castle Acre, the deed specified that Turstan the miller, his mother, and brothers, and all their land and substance went with it. The mention of their "land" seems to show that even the *servi* had some sort of fixity of tenure.

The position of the villein, or "bondsman in blood," and of the female villein, or "neif," on a manor in very early days, was essentially of that degree of slavery formerly imposed on the negroes in North America, except that they could not be alienated from their native soil. They were subject to physical restraint always, and to corporal punishment in field work, for we read of the reapers at Shouldam Thorpe, in Norfolk, in 1270, being supervised by a man armed with a "rod" or "wand."

At Tormarton, in Gloucestershire, which was anciently the seat of the Rivers family, there is a dungeon thirteen or fourteen feet deep, and about four feet from the floor are iron rings fastened into the wall. This was used for the incarceration of refractory serfs and retainers, and is a vestige of the arbitrary power once exercised by territorial lords over their wretched soccage tenants.

When it is remembered that feudal servitude is yet scarcely abolished in Russia, it should not be difficult to realise the depths of barbarism which anciently prevailed in feudal England. The barons at one time held absolute sway over their bondsmen, and there were occasions when their tyranny allowed itself to go beyond the dictates of common humanity.

There was the custom of "merchetum" (*jus primae noctis*), for instance, whereby the lord enjoyed the maiden-rights of his retainers' daughters, a shameful institution only redeemed in the eleventh century by a quit-rent. Absolute dominion hardens the human heart, and as the barons were accustomed to command their bondmen in all things, customary servitude was not infrequently intensified by caprice. That the lord of Coventry compelled his wife to ride naked on a white pad through the streets of the city, that by the sacrifice he might be induced to restore to the inhabitants those privileges of which his wantonness had deprived them, is quite in keeping with the ferocious barbarism of the times. And if this was the treatment a "noble" meted out to his equal, what consideration could be expected for those inferiors whom he held in the palm of his hand?

Authorities of standing have denied that "*merchetum*," or "the maid's fee," was in England anything more than a lewd mediæval jest, whilst admitting the historical evidence that the custom prevailed in Scotland till its abrogation by Malcolm III. at the instance of his queen.

Villeins undoubtedly paid fines if they married without the lord's licence, which was often withheld when they married a "foreigner" from another manor, and sometimes the father was fined for his daughter's marriage.

The spirit of the English people and the equality of the common law became the just corrective of the degrading institutions and barbarous customs imported from other countries. Villenage was known in France till near the end of the eighteenth century, in Russia it cannot be said to be extinct yet, and more than a suspicion of it lingers in other European states.

How soon the austerities of serfdom began to be abrogated we know not; but we are told by Sir Thomas Smith, who was secretary to Edward VI. and Queen Elizabeth, that in all his time he never knew any instance of a villein in gross—that is, of a villein transferable by sale and not attached to the soil—in the kingdom; and that the few villeins attached to the soil who remained were such only as had belonged to bishops, monasteries, and other ecclesiastical corporations.

Right to freedom could be successfully pleaded by a man who proved he had been born within a city or borough, or had lived in any such town for a year and a day without paying "chevage." Chevage was the fine paid by a villein to his lord for liberty to live outside the manor, and operated as an admission of his vassalage so long as it was paid. Later on, in some manors, those who paid it were called *aulepimen*, perhaps because they were exempt from service in the *aula*, or manorial court.

There were several ways in which a villein attached to the soil could obtain his freedom. He might be manumitted. Or if his lord brought an action against him it was supposed to allow his freedom. Or if he went into a town and settled there he, in a certain time, enjoyed its immunities and became free. Or, lastly, if he could show that, for time out of mind, he and his ancestors had been registered in the roll of the lord's court as having possession of the land he held, he obtained a prescriptive right against his lord. This was done by producing a copy of the court-roll, and hence the term copyholder. It has been supposed by some that copyhold was known before the Conquest. At whatever time it originated, the early prevalence of claims to freedom is perhaps characteristic of the English nation.

As to the form or ceremonial observed at the manumission of a serf, it may be recalled that Sir Walter Scott gives us a pen-picture of such an incident in his famous historical novel, "Ivanhoe." It is after the siege of Torquilstone, and the victors are in happy mood; merely premising that the term "esne" signifies *thrall* or *bondsman*, and "sacless" is synonymous with a *lawful freeman*, the scene is painted thus :—

"'Nay,' said the Jester, . . 'if you would indeed pleasure me, I pray you to pardon my playfellow Gurth.

4

"'Pardon him!' exclaimed Cedric, 'I will both pardon and reward him—Kneel down, Gurth.' The swineherd was in an instant at his master's feet. 'Theow and Esne art thou no longer,' said Cedric, touching him with a wand; 'Folkfree and Sacless art thou in town and from town, in the forest as in the field.'

"No longer a serf, but a freeman, Gurth sprung upon his feet, and twice bounded aloft to almost his own height from the ground. 'A smith and a file,' he cried, 'to do away the collar from the neck of a freeman. Noble master! doubled is my strength by your gift!'"

This description of the procedure in freeing a serf is romantic if not strictly historical.

From the Norman Rolls we learn that Nicholas, prior of St. Thomas's, Stafford, did manumit Richard Norman, Ralph Norman, and John Norman, sons of William Norman, *nativos suos, temp.* 18 Ric. II.

In 1514 Henry VIII. manumitted some of his villeins in this form—"Whereas God created all men free, but afterwards the laws and customs of nations subjected some under the yoke of servitude, we think it pious and meritorious to manumit."

It was the custom, probably for the purpose of giving it greater publicity, to perform the manumission, or setting free of a serf, at four cross-roads.

One of the demands of the revolted peasants in the reign of Richard II. was that serfs should be set free, and that their posterity should not be villeins or bondsmen in any degree. During the Wars of the Roses, when the bonds of society were loosened, villenage decayed rapidly; during those prolonged civil wars there was the necessity of conciliating the people. When arms were put in a man's hands he was enfranchised. Yet prisoners of war were sometimes sold, as was instanced in the previous chapters.

The Cornish men who revolted in the twelfth year of Henry VII., and were defeated at Blackheath, were sold for two shillings each. This incited a second evolt, and led to the common people inviting Perkin Warbeck to raise his standard. Civilisation, even though inspired by the genius of the English people, had not abolished slavery as an institution at the Renaissance.

Villenage fell into rapid decay towards the close of the Tudor period, not so much through the growth of liberal principles as through its having been discovered that free labourers were less expensive than villeins. The law insisted upon the latter being fed, clothed, and lodged at the expense of their owners; the former lived in the eye of heaven, and when not required had to shift for themselves. The decay of villenage contributed largely, with the destruction of the monasteries, to the establishment of the Poor Law system.

The last claim of villenage recorded in our courts was in the fifteenth year of James I.

Villenage was never abolished by statute; it fell into desuetude and died a natural death. Lord Mansfield said a man "may be a villein in England, but not a slave;" and startling as the dictum may appear, the English law on that point is in such a condition that, although *de facto* villenage by birth ceased some time in the days of the Stuarts, a man may still make himself a villein by acknowledgment in a court of record.

Serfdom is an institution founded on falsehood. The sentiment expressed by the Provost of Bruges in the old play, on the subject of human bondage, crystallizes the moral of this chapter :—

> " Fie ! fie !
> A man's a man; nor can another claim
> The right to buy, sell, or inherit him,
> Because he sprang from off a lower branch
> Of the great tree .—yet this is but a part.
> He who would have *one* fellow for his slave,
> Soon, step by step, would fetter all mankind."

IV

THE GENESIS OF MENDICANCY

Rise of the free labourer—Accompanied by increase of vagrancy
—The aged and impotent regarded as incumbrances in a
fighting age—Highways beset with thieves—Statute of Winchester (1285)—The "trailebastons," or English bravos—
Gravitation of "masterless men" to the towns—The underworld of destitution, filth, and disease—Advent of the friars
(1220)—"The apostles of the poor"—Their relationship to the
parish clergy—Their eventual corruption—And degeneration
into "dangerous vagabonds"—Chaucer's picture of the wandering friar—A semi-barbarous age.

As the centuries after the Conquest wore on, the number
of the poor steadily increased, both relatively and absolutely. The chief cause of these large accessions to the
ranks of the poor was the continual breaking loose of
free labourers from the bonds of feudal villenage. The
appearance of the free labourers in this country was syn-
chronous with the growth of vagrancy and destitution.

The more serious movement, the rise of the free
labourer, had been preceded by a lesser social revolution, the rise of a farmer-class. This latter originated in
a modification of the manorial system, whereby the
wealthier among the tenantry were enabled to rise to a
position of apparent equality with their former masters and
to form an intermediate class. This was by a system of
leasing, the Old English term for the rent being "feorm,"

from which the words "farm" and "farmer" are derived.

The derivation of the word "villain" is not without interest in this connection. A villein was in feudal times the serf on the soil, or the peasant ; he was "villanus," because attached to the "villa" or farm. When he wilfully broke away from this social anchorage to make himself a freeman, his action was regarded by his master as dishonest, and hence the term "villain" came to be opprobriously applied to one of wilfully dishonest or immoral habits.

Under Saxon rule the great body of the labouring class had remained partly slaves of the household and partly serfs attached to the soil The feudal system, as developed by William the Conqueror, intensified the serf-dom, which hitherto had been a comparatively easy yoke to bear, into a system of grinding despotism. The bulk of the population were serfs born, and described by the chroniclers as "nativi." The Norman system was one which depressed the many and elevated the few, creating great military chieftains who regarded the aged and impotent as incumbrances, to be quietly neglected and left to starvation if they could not eke out a subsistence for themselves by begging or stealing.

As none but freemen were allowed to serve in war, the more militant a king, the greater the number of villeins to be manumitted to recruit his exhausted armies.

Thousands of sturdy English serfs, held in hereditary bondage to the soil on which they were born, ran away from their feudal lords, on purpose to escape that bondage, most of them hoping to take service as free labourers in some distant part of the country where they, and their social status, would be unknown. The bolder spirits of a more adventurous type would join themselves to the band of some noble plunderer in the hope of sharing in his successes. The failures naturally fell into destitution.

The number of vagrants and professed mendicants became truly appalling; they were to be met on every highway in the country, moving from one district to the next, generally from one religious house to another. Even had work been obtainable, the rewards of industry at that period were scarcely worth striving for; while the incentives to the idle, roving life of a freebooter were many and powerful. It [was this alarming state of the country, infested from one end to the other with footpads and highway robbers, which was partly responsible for the passing of the Statute of Winchester (1285). Highway robberies, murder, and outrage were everywhere rampant.

By this piece of Edwardian legislation came about a pleasant feature which still distinguishes many of our rural highways: those wide grass margins which often run on either side of the hard road, mile after mile. The country in many parts being then thickly wooded, thousands of robbers and footpads lurked in the dense cover by which the narrow roads were often bordered. It was therefore ordered that all highways between market towns should be cleared of cover which might hide brigands, to the extent of 200 feet on either side. There was to be no dyke, tree, or bush that might afford a lurking place to criminals.

A century or two later hedges and ditches encroached upon this statutory width, and many of the clearings disappeared altogether; but where these grassy margins remained the sheep-drovers of interested landowners in Tudor times found them highly convenient when moving their vast flocks from one place to another.

This statute of 1285 (which also put the defence of the country on a national basis), while directing the widening and clearing of the edges of the public high-roads, laid upon the counties, under heavy penalties, the duty of indicting felons and robbers, ordered the police arrangements of walled towns, and expressly appointed constables and justices to carry all its provisions into effect. Yet twenty years later England was overrun by bands of riotous outlaws who, when not plying their trade of highway robbers, were to be hired for the purpose of private outrage. These companies of desperadoes came to be known as "trailebastons," from the long staffs they carried; and the measures the order-loving king took for their suppression were so rigorous that in the political songs of the day it was said to be impossible to beat your children without being punished as a *trail-bâton*.

Naturally these "masterless men," as the runaways were called, would mostly gravitate to the towns where there was better chance of lying hidden for "a year and a day," the condition legally requisite to constitute them free men for ever. Though better fitted for employment on the land outside the towns, some few were thus either absorbed into the crafts and trades, while the bulk of them sank into destitution in the purlieus of the large towns. Outsiders were carefully excluded from any participation in the privileges of the trade guilds, which, by their system of apprenticeship and other jealous devices, organised the craftsmen of the towns into close corporations.

The poverty-stricken condition of a portion of the populace of some of the towns in the thirteenth century must have been deplorable in the extreme. Crowded together on the outskirts of many of the larger of them were to be found festering masses of humanity, living huddled together in wretched hovels, which were not only filthy and verminous, but, as often as not, pestilential.

The dwellers in this underworld were the workless and the destitute, the helpless widow and orphan, the depraved and the outcast, the leper and the pariah, all of them except, perhaps, the predatory and criminally depraved, dependent, when no longer content to feed on the garbage of the streets, on the almsgiver's dole.

The condition of the lower orders of society during these centuries can scarcely be realised ; the level of it was far below anything that exists nowadays among the poor. They were not only less prosperous in their prosperity six hundred years ago, says Dr. Jessopp, but they were worse clad, worse fed, worse housed, worse taught, worse tended, worse governed ; they were sufferers from loathsome diseases of which we knew nothing. The death-rate among children was enormous ; periodical plagues decimated the population ; and the disregard for human life was so callous we can hardly conceive it.

Such was the condition of society when, in the thirteenth century, a new element in the Church's work for the care and relief of the poor made its appearance in this country. As on the Continent, there existed here, as we have seen, in all the larger towns and boroughs those weltering masses of human misery, for the relief of which this new machinery of the Church was specially designed.

To seek out the submerged sufferers of an imperfect, if not a vicious, system of society came those mediæval apostles of poverty, the Franciscan friars, whose mission was to labour amongst the lowest and the poorest of the population. Their founder, St. Francis of Assisi, had called " Poverty " his bride. They were themselves barefooted beggars, who spent their whole time in visiting, nursing, and begging the bread they shared with their humble flocks. These itinerant evangelists, penniless and heroic, sought only to minister to those in misery, to comfort those in distress. Their first appearance in England was made in 1220, the Dominicans and the Carmelites, two other mendicant orders, appearing a few decades later.

Words of hope, homely, fervent, and sympathetic, from the lips of these mendicant missionaries must have brought peace and comfort to many despairing hearts among those dwellers in the hovels outside Lynn, and York, and Bristol, in the mud huts at Shrewsbury, in the filthy, undrained swamp at Norwich, and in the "Stinking alley" in London—for it was always amidst the horrible squalor of such social sloughs as these that the Franciscans took up their mission.

These new preachers practised all the stratagems of itinerancy, and thirty years after their advent the parish churches were almost deserted; for by the favour of Rome the privilege of performing all sacerdotal functions was conceded to the new mendicant orders, both Franciscan and Dominican. Preaching in the public streets, where they practised their self-denial before all men, and administering the Communion from a portable altar to the poor and afflicted, whose bodies they had relieved, what wonder that their popularity grew enormously and always to the detriment of the secular clergy.

That the mendicant orders afterwards fell away from their first principles, became corrupt, and deservedly suffered spoliation with the others, does not detract from the good work they performed during the first century or two of their existence in this country. Their founders saw clearly enough that the parochial system might be fairly workable in a village, but was totally inadequate to meet the exigencies of town life. The disciples of St. Francis and St. Dominic going forth

as missionaries to those whom the town clergy had come
to regard as mere pariahs, became in fact the helpers
of those clergy in a task which they themselves had
almost given up as hopeless.

In the days of their degeneracy the friars came to
be despised as much as ever the monks had been ; as
a term of reproach "a jolly fat friar" came to be used
as frequently as "a lazy monk." The newer orders
thus fell under the severe lash of Wycliffe; and
Chaucer has left us a contemptuous picture of the
mendicant friar. He was "ful wel beloved and
familier" with all the franklins in the country ; that is,
in the district in which he was authorised to beg and
preach. He was "a wanton and a merry," gifted with
more "daliance and fayre language" than any of his
brethren of all the four orders. "He was an esy man
to give penance" where he knew he should receive a
good pittance, and he could tell a man's repentance by
the "silver" he gave to "the poure freres." His tippet
was stuffed "ful of knives and pinnes for to given fayre
wives." "He hadde a mery note," could sing well, and
play on a rote (a kind of hurdy-gurdy), when "his eyen
twinkeled in his hed aright, as don the sterres in a frosty
night." At "yeddings" or story-tellings he could gain
the prize, so that he was in great request on lovedays,
where he behaved "nat like cloisterere with thredbare
cope," but like "a maister or a pope." He "knew wel
the tavernes in every toun, and every hosteler and gay
tapstere, better than a lazar or a beggere" ; for with such
"pouraille," or offal, he would have no acquaintance,
but only "with riche and sellers of vitaille," with whom
he was courteous and "lowly of servise" because he
could get profit from them. "He was the beste begger
in all his hous," and "though a widewe hadde but a shoo,"
"yet wold he have a ferthing or he went."

In their later era Sir Thomas More regarded the friars as being nothing less than dangerous vagabonds, and in his "Utopia" (1518) he relates a dispute between a friar and a fool on the question of pauperism. "You will never," said the friar, "get rid of beggars, unless you also make an edict against us friars." "Well," said the fool, "it is already made; the cardinal passed a very good law against you when he decreed that all vagabonds should be seized and made to work, for you are the greatest vagabonds that be." From this it is perfectly clear that the reputation of the friars had grown worse as the centuries passed by; they still tramped their rounds through the farms and villages, but it had come about they now practised their mendicancy not so much to assist the poor as to further the material interests of their order. Their abysmal fall from the high purpose of their founders was too well known to Sir Thomas More.

Viewing the people as a whole, it must be remembered that the finer feelings of humanity were not cultivated in the Early English period. The people were ruder, their habits were rougher, and their whole moral fibre coarser. The most superficial study of the practices and customs of the period reveals a lack of refinement in every direction. The everyday environment was against a proper observance of what we now recognise as the common decencies of life. Personal cleanliness, as we understand it, was practically impossible, owing to deficiencies in the construction of the dwellings; the same cause, lack of convenience, was responsible for the herding together of the sexes at night time; and from the thirteenth to the fifteenth century no one ever wore a night-dress, everybody sleeping "naked-bed," as it was called. Fine ladies endeavoured to make up for the shortcomings of personal cleanliness by an extravagant use of perfume. Indecencies of language were common to every grade of society, moderation of it being affected but little by the presence of women and children, as any one reading an old author can scarcely ever fail to observe. Many of the games and pastimes in which the common people indulged expressed the prevalent coarseness of mind, and where the sexes intermixed in them immodesty of behaviour was often enough part of the sport. Indeed, there were customs in daily practice—as witness the Lincolnshire practice of washing with the excrement of the pig—which are positively revolting to the modern mind. Looked at from any point of view, this was an age in which the masses were but little removed, mentally or morally, from primitive barbarism.

V

CHURCH VOLUNTARYISM

The Church's recognition of its responsibility to the poor—By the Common Law the poor were to be sustained by the parson and parishioners—How the poor came to be largely deprived of their shares in the tithes—By appropriations and impropriations—The "Church Store" instituted in the fourteenth century—Supported and managed by churchwardens—For which office capable business men were chosen—The use of "Church Ales" —A parish cow—The poor-box—The alms-dish—Alms distributed at low side-windows—Mendicants begging at crosses —Gifts made to the poor at weddings and funerals—The "voider" for distribution of broken food—No legalised system of relief till 1535—Church doles—Their history—The resources of the Church—The Church as an employer of labour.

THE native Church, notwithstanding the importation of those alien auxiliaries, the friars, had not been altogether neglectful of its duties towards the poor and distressed. It had invented a system for each parish, which had worked with comparative adequacy in the small and closely organised villages, if it had failed to meet the requirements of the boroughs and cities.

As we have seen, the Church from the earliest times had gradually come to recognise its responsibility to the indigent and the impotent; and from this recognition of the Church, in theory and in practice, the great principle of making the poor a charge upon the public purse has been slowly evolved. But as yet the principle was non-existent, and the almsgiving encouraged by the Church but aggravated the fault its efforts ought to have eliminated.

A tithe of the food which came to the table of Henry II. was distributed to the poor; King John sought to make up for his life's irregularities by regular and liberal almsgiving; and most of the other mediæval monarchs distributed alms on an extensive scale in the hope that the prayers of the beggars who had dined might release the souls of their ancestors from purgatory—a royal practice encouraged by the Church which created an army of paupers.

Begging, indeed, has become an attribute of the Latin races, as visitors to the Continent are well aware; it has been contended that this weakness owes its origin to the mediæval ecclesiasticism which encouraged indiscriminate almsgiving as a duty of the faithful. In France, in Spain, in Italy the way in which the tourist is constantly pestered for *pourboires* and tips is at times almost enough to mar the pleasure of a holiday excursion. In this country, although the Protestant Church has not fostered actual mendicancy, a relic of the bad old system is the prevalence of Church doles, which are sometimes sufficient to pauperize half a village.

At no time has the Church failed to acquiesce in the social gradations which are ordinarily consequent upon an unequal distribution of wealth. For "Dives and Lazarus," for "Richman and Poorman," there is always a recognised place and a duty. Yet the "Miser and the Prodigal" are, by the same universal consent, included among the typical fools of the world. As types they are found among the passengers with which Barclay freights his "Ship of Fools," that remarkable sixteenth-century satire which reviews the innumerable dull and tedious follies of frail humanity. In the accompanying illus-

MISER AND PRODIGAL
(From Barclay's 'Ship of Fools, 1509)

RICHMAN AND POORMAN (SIXTEENTH CENTURY)

tration the foolishness of both miser and prodigal is satirised by the artful introduction of Poorman to show that poverty is always happier than either avarice or prodigality.

In the "good old times" no biblical subject was in greater favour, for the enforcement of moral duty and social obligations, than "Dives and Lazarus."

According to Fitz-Stephen, who wrote an account of London in the reign of Henry II., there was not a church in the city which was not commendable to God for its great hospitality and almsgiving.

But this, after all, was only temporising, attempting to make works of charity suffice, instead of fearlessly proclaiming the gospel of social justice. Inconsistent with the Christian axiom that in the sight of God all men are equal, the Church recognised and supported all class distinctions, and in its own hierarchy maintained a temporal system at the head of which were cardinal princes and a sovereign pontiff.

While the great ones of the earth lived in palaces and fared sumptuously, the poor were taught, not that the world was man's natural home, but that it was a wretched place to be endured, and that man's destiny was to suffer; if the poor could be induced to do so, in pious resignation, so much the more to the comfort of their "betters."

The old Latin chroniclers, it is interesting to observe, sometimes used the same word *misellus* to designate "the poor" and "the dead"; the former, like the latter, "being appointed unto punishment and judgment."

What was the parochial system which had broken down so lamentably? First it must be understood that by the common law of the land the poor were to be sustained "by parsons, rectors of the Church, and parishioners, so that none should die by default of sustenance;" and by an enactment of *15 Richard II.* impropriators of tithe were obliged to distribute a yearly sum to the poor. For it was by an alienation of the tithes, either by the process known as "appropriation," or that called "impropriation," that the poor were being robbed of their ancient rights. By the term "parson," be it noted, was meant the parish priest who was in full enjoyment of the whole rectorial tithes.

The history of tithes from the time of Magna Charta to the reign of Henry VIII. was a series of exasperating struggles between an avaricious Church and a sullen and rebellious people, to whom the Franciscans and the Dominicans continuously preached, in season and out of season, that tithes were mere alms. Then suddenly, as is well known, all the wealth which the cupidity of the Church had wrung from the wealthy in the name of religion was at one swoop quietly appropriated by this imperious monarch, who, having first satisfied his own rapacity, graciously distributed a vast amount among his favourites, and with the remainder of the ecclesiastical revenue accruing from tithe proceeded to endow a Church which grounded its right to exist on its opposition to the Church which had been disendowed.

For centuries a most iniquitous practice had been favoured, under one specious pretext or another, of depriving the parish parsons of their tithes and other ecclesiastical dues; if, as sometimes happened, these Church revenues fell "improperly" into the hands of a layman, they were said to be impropriated; but if, as was usually the case, they fell into the grip of a monastery or other powerful spiritual corporation, then they were said to be appropriated. Of course the patron who secured these revenues made provision, as by the appointment of a vicar, for the spiritual care and oversight of the parish which had been so plausibly plundered.

Every vicarage in England represents the spoliation of of a church, the rectorial tithes of which have been appropriated by a religious house, or otherwise alienated.

At the accession of Henry VIII. the appropriations made by the monasteries and other religious houses amounted to more than one-third of all the parishes in England; in these the incumbent in charge was not in the full enjoyment of all the spiritual dues rightly belonging to his parish, but was merely a vicar (*vicarius*, "a substitute") whose stipend consisted of the smaller tithes. To make an appropriation, a king's licence was always necessary, and by the Act of Richard II. aforementioned, it was ordained that the bishop or "diocesan of the place should provide a convenient sum of money to be yearly paid out of the fruits towards the sustenance of the poor in that parish," while at the same time the vicar was to be sufficiently and well endowed. If tithes could be thus dealt with by Parliament, it may be properly contended that they were looked upon as public property.

As the interest of the poor in a fair share of the parish tithes became more and more remote, the parochial clergy devised a more direct system for the relief of local distress—but still one in which the poor were left to the humanity of their neighbours.

It was in the fourteenth century that the parochial clergy, perhaps stirred to action by the keen rivalry of the friars, first instituted their voluntary fund. In some of the richer and better organised parishes this "Church Store" was fed by money put out at interest, and by rearing and selling live-stock—a business element in parochial work specifically undertaken by the church-reeve or churchwarden. This early connection of the churchwarden with the relief of the poor was recognised in later times when the law associated this Church official by Act of Parliament with the overseers of the poor in

5

such duties as the making of the poor's rates, the setting up of trades for employing the poor, the placing out of parish apprentices, the settling of poor persons in their own parishes, and so on.

The rule was to choose only men of proved business capacity to serve in the office of churchwarden, the necessity for which is emphasised by that eminent authority on the subject, Humphrey Prideaux :—

" In the City of London, by special custom, the churchwardens, with the minister, make a corporation for lands as well as for goods, and may, as such, hold, purchase, take, and devise lands for the use of the church, and sue and be sued on account thereof, as well as for goods and chattels , and this is alleged as a reason for that other custom, which hath also obtained in London, for the parishioners there to choose both churchwardens exclusive of the minister , for, say they, if the minister should there choose one of the church-wardens according to canon, he, with the said churchwarden as the major part of the corporation, may dispose of lands to the damage of the parish, and therefore it is not safe there to lodge so great a trust in him."

Hence, in the City of London the leases of houses and lands, being parish property, often run in the names of the rector and churchwardens as lessors.

Among the ancient documents belonging to Walsall is a'code of laws for "the goode rule and governaunce of the boroughe," drawn up in the year 1440 by the "maior and his bredren," one regulation of which relates to the churchwardens :—

" Also, it is ordeyned that the churchwardens, both of the body of the Churche of Our Ladye, Saynt Clement, Saynt Kateyn, and Saynt Nicholas, with alle other members, shall com to theyr accomptes uppon Saynt Kateryn's-day, before the mayor and five or six of his brethren, by the said mayor to be appoynted, and before such other of the brethren as will be there , and if they or any of them be not at the said day redy to make theyr accomptes, then they shall be so in defaute, to forfeit six shillings and eightpence, to be levyed as is before said, and to be put to the Burges Boxe."

It was the recognised duty of the wardens to look after the material as well as the spiritual and moral welfare of the parishioners.

Every parish where poverty was found to prevail, and where there was any clerical activity, anciently had its Church fund for helping the poor and for other charitable purposes. The fund was maintained in a variety of ways, some just enumerated; another, not the least popular, being the old English institution known as "Church Ales." For these parochial festivals the churchwardens begged the malt and all other ingredients of a special brew, the liquor of which they sold in the churchyard to their own parishioners, and to invited patrons from all the surrounding parishes; the money proceeds being devoted to the relief of the poor, the repair of the church, and other parochial purposes.

In old Blind Audelay's Poems this form of Church revenue is thus apportioned out :—

> "The furst princypale part lungus to your levying ;
>   The ij part to holé church to hold his honesté ;
>   The iij part to your parechyngs [parishioners] that all to youe
>   bryng ;
>   To hom that faylun the fode [food] and fallen in poverté."

At Lapworth, in Warwickshire, the churchwardens in 1580 hired a cow, the profit on which was devoted to the relief of the poor of the parish, although according to a later record (1605) some of the profit was diverted to the cost of parochial road-mending. At Preston Candover, Hants, the churchwardens are recorded to have managed a flock of sheep for the purpose of poor relief.

Says John Aubrey, the seventeenth-century antiquary :
" Before the Reformation there were no poor-rates ; the
charitable doles given at religious houses, and the church
ale in every parish, did the business. In every parish
there was a church house, to which belonged spits, pots,
crocks, &c., for dressing provisions. Here the house-
keepers met and were merry, and gave their charity.
Mr. Anthony Wood assures me there were few or no
almshouses before the time of King Henry VIII. ; that
at Oxford, opposite Christ Church, is one of the most
ancient in England. In every church was a poor man's
box, and the like at great inns."

" Poor's boxes, " according to the same authority,
Anthony Wood, the Oxford antiquary, were to be found
in every church previously to the Reformation, and they
are frequently mentioned in ancient records. Some of
them lasted till after the Reformation, and engravings
of them are given in Hone's " Table Book." Ben
Jonson, in his " Masque of the Metamorphosed Gipsies,"
produced in 1621, makes a gipsy tell Tom Ticklefoot,
a rustic musician—

> "On Sundays you rob the poor's box with your tabor,
> The Collectors would do it—you save them a labour."

Church poor-boxes very frequently bore some suitable
inscription, as " Remember the Poor." Carved on one
was " Forget not to give, but give and forget ; " and
on another was " This Boxe is Frelie given to receave
almes for ye Poore. 1629 ; " and so on.

For security a box was often provided with three keys,
one for the clergyman, and one each for the churchwardens. It was generally bound with strong iron
bands, and some of them had an ingenious contrivance,
something like an inverted iron cup, for preventing the
extraction of the coins through the slit in the top.

How neglected the poor-boxes came to be may be gathered from a picture in Hogarth's "Rake's Progress," where the box is depicted as being covered with cobweb.

In the structure and equipment of the church may still be recognised the various features which the system of parochial voluntaryism called into existence. Besides the poor-box there was the ecclesiastical alms-dish, in which were received the congregations' collection of oblations and offertories.

There was the almery, literally "the place of alms," a cupboard or locker in a church, usually by the side of the altar, where the sacred vessels, including the collecting-dish, were kept.

As to the distribution of the alms, besides the more business-like divisions regularly made by the church-wardens among their own parishioners, there were probably other and less discriminate distributions on festivals and holiday occasions. This theory is upheld by those who, disputing that the low side-windows found in so many ancient churches were leper windows, contend that the real use of these apertures was the convenient distribution of alms or doles to crowds of clamorous paupers standing outside in the churchyard.

A pious practice in olden times was to erect crosses in churchyards, markets, highways, and other places. Whatever their purpose may have been, for prayer or for penance, as memorials or as reminders, it is a fact that beggars made good use of them. Wayside crosses were often made resting-places for corpses being carried to burial ; market-crosses served to remind assembled traders of the Christian duty of honesty ; at weeping-crosses penitents expiated their sins ; many crosses were erected at corners and cross-roads, and as they were all generally places of public concourse, it became customary for mendicants to station themselves at such places, where they could importune people, in a favourable frame of mind for bestowing alms, in the name of the Christ who died on the cross. Hence in the North Country they still say of a person who is urgent and vehement in preferring a request, " He begs like a cripple at a cross."

A number of old customs may be attributed to the teaching of the Church with regard to the poor. In the seventeenth century, and probably in much earlier times, it was customary to make gifts to the poor at weddings and at funerals. (*See* pp. 199 and 251.)

As late as Hogarth's time, as may be gathered from the sixth plate of his " Industry and Idleness" series, which depicts the day after the wedding of the Industrious Apprentice (who naturally married his master's daughter), almsgiving was a recognised part of a marriage cele- bration. While the cartoonist places in the background the drummers who, according to ancient custom, attend with their thundering gratulations, he gives foremost place to the figure of the mendicant who receives the broken food from the plentiful table of the happy pair. The crippled ballad-singer whom Hogarth also introduces into this picture as rendering " Jessie, or the Happy Pair," is a portrait of a well-known character of the time, a professional mendicant called " Philip in the Tub," who had begged all over the three kingdoms, and was a regular attendant at important weddings.

Then in the home life of the rich and well-to-do there was the ancient practice of placing the domestic alms- dish on the table at mealtimes, which about the sixteenth century gave way to the less refined one of removing broken victuals by means of the " voiding knife " and the " voider." A voider (otherwise a " maund ") was a basket or tray used in rich men's houses for collecting the broken food, which was swept into it by a wand, or " voiding

knife," as it was called. Somewhat in the manner as a crumb scoop is used in modern houses, this wooden knife was used to gather all the bones and scraps left on the trenchers or scattered about the tables into the alms-basket, for distribution to the poor. Alms-drink was the name given to the leavings in the drinking-cups which were all collected and served out to the poor and needy.

In the time of Charles II. it was a royal household ordinance that no gentleman should send away meat or wine from the table or out of the chamber upon any pretence whatever, and that the gentlemen ushers should take particular care that all meat "be taken off the table upon trencher plates to be put in a basket for the poore and not indecently eaten by any servant in the room."

In the Middle Ages, it will be seen, no properly legalised scheme for the relief of the poor had as yet been devised; and during that period the ranks of the vast army of the poor never ceased to receive accessions. Then, as now, private benevolence, ever indiscriminate and indiscreet, gave encouragement to imposition; even the vigorous enactment of Edward III. (1349), that none should give alms to a beggar able to work, failed as an effective deterrent.

So that, speaking generally, it may be said that previously to the Reformation no regular or adequate provision was made for the poor of the land. And notwithstanding the responsibility of the Church clergy, and their parochial machinery, implied by the common law in consonance with the ethics of Christianity, the poor were in a great measure left to such relief as the humanity of their neighbours would afford them.

It was not till the reign of Henry VIII. (1535) that any statute of a compulsory nature came into force. As to the old-time Church merrymakings in the sacred cause of charity, the justices of the Puritan era (which followed close upon the introduction of compulsory laws) waged an incessant war against them. In 1607 they ordered the suppression of Church Ales everywhere; but for a long time these orders had little or no effect, for twenty years later it was reported that these parochial revelries were as rife as ever; and it is to be feared that their survival was attributable more to a gross self-indulgence than to any benevolent intentions.

The voluntary parochial system, as any voluntary system was bound to do, failed to relieve the mass of poverty with any degree of effectiveness. How it was in due time succeeded by a compulsory system will be seen in a later chapter; but one present-day survival, the system of parish doles, had its rise in the activity of the Church for the relief of the poor.

Benefactions seem to have accrued to churches on the warranty of St. Chrysostom, who observed, "Doles are used at funerals to procure the rest of the soul of the deceased, that he might find his Judge propitious." In expounding this further (which is really the old pagan doctrine of the propitiation of an angry deity) he also said in one of his homilies, "Would you honour the dead? Give alms."

St. Thomas's Day, December 21st, the shortest day in the year, is the most popular date, because considered as midwinter the most appropriate, for the distribution of parish doles. In fact, this day was known in some parts of the country as Doling Day; and in others, where the poor went about begging corn, as Mumping (begging) Day.

In Derbyshire the custom was known as "going a-Thomasing," children and adults going from house to house carrying baskets and cans to beg corn, oatmeal, flour, and milk; in many other parts of England it was called "going a-gooding," the common practice being to carry round a two-handled pot in which to collect the wheat which was afterwards to be made into furmety.

The moral effect of doles is by no means good, especially in the villages where the population is small. In these places a wealth of doles is sufficient to pauperise a whole parish, and to undermine the people's independence to a grievous extent.

Till the institution of Poor Laws and the imposition of Poor Rates, at the close of Elizabeth's reign, the poor, it has been shown, were supported as far as it was possible by the exertions of the Church. But it must not be forgotten that till Henry VIII. stripped the Church of some of its immense wealth, the proportion of the soil of this realm in the possession of the Church was so enormous it amply justified the calls of the poor upon its resources.

The Church in those days, it may be added, was a large employer of labour; a cathedral establishment supported an army of workpeople as well as a hundred or so of priests, to say nothing of singing-men and choir-boys. Such an establishment maintained its own bakers and brewers and other household servants, and included scribes, illuminators, copyists, librarians, musicians, book-binders, messengers, and other officials.

A great monastery also provided employment for a very large number of people. For every separate estate that belonged to it the monastery wanted stewards and bailiffs, tenant farmers and labourers, foresters and hunters. At the house itself, where nearly everything was produced that was needed for home consumption, men were employed about the bake-house, the brew-house, the kitchen, the cellar, the stables, and the offices; it had its own architects, surveyors, masons, and carpenters for the upkeep and repair of the buildings; its

lawyers and clerks to administer the estates and safeguard its legal rights.   The Church, too, was amongst
the best customers of the merchants who imported
wines, silks, spices, and other foreign produce.   The
Church was a power in the industrial and commercial
world as it was in the State.

VI

VAGRANCY AND OUTLAWRY

Alarming increase of vagrancy—Statutes multiplied in vain—
Severities against sturdy beggars—Struggles for liberty—
Pretended pilgrimages of devotion—Undertaken with pass-
ports—Seals of these "testimonial" letters fabricated—University students placed in the same category as beggars—
Fugitives from bondage take to the woods—Become freebooters—Emulating the popular hero, Robin Hood—John
Love Peacock's description of life beneath the greenwood tree
—The hardships of woodland life—Confessed in the ballad
of "The Nut-brown Maid"—Legislative restrictions on food
and apparel — Significant of growing emancipation — Laws
against vagrancy mitigated in cases of infirmity (1504).

DURING the Middle Ages vagrancy was ever on the
increase, and by the law of Richard II. it became
synonymous with crime, and therefore to be rigorously
suppressed by the stocks and the prison.

Feudal serfdom or villenage was only a modification
of slavery, and the history of events in the nation's
steady march towards freedom shows that as the evil
of serfdom was left behind, the evil of vagrancy grew
even larger and more formidable.   And moreover the
legislation which the newer conditions called into
existence aimed only at the repression of the wandering
vagabond, and never once attempted a solution of the
problem by making provision for the real poor.

Statutes were multiplied in vain ; it was prohibited to give alms to this sort of person, and the law directed that "their bodies be put in the stocks or taken to the next gaol." Edward III. in 1349 had condemned to prison those persons who, under pretext of charity, gave assistance to these sturdy beggars, described as " vagabonds going through the country, giving themselves to idleness and vice, and sometimes to theft and other abominations." Similar complaints recur again and again throughout the reign of Richard II., and that king was compelled to recognise in his ordinance of 1383 that the "feitors" (idlers) and vagrants " overran the country" more abundantly than they were formerly accustomed. In 1388 renewed orders were issued to mayors of towns, bailiffs, and stewards of manors, and all parish constables, reminding them of their duties, and especially to keep their stocks in repair, ready for the reception of these idle and dissolute wanderers. The Act of 1388 insisted that persons setting out on pilgrimages as beggars were to be treated as vagabonds according to the statute of 1383.

Threats of stocks and prisons—and in most towns the gaols were horrible fetid dungeons in which ofttimes the prisoners literally rotted — did not deter or hold back the workers who were weary of being attached to the soil. Escaped peasants brought the largest number of recruits to the wandering class. Every pretext for getting away from the manor to which they were born was eagerly seized upon. Not the least welcome was the pretence of making a journey of devotion.

From the tenth to the fifteenth century there was a rage for going on pilgrimages. Everybody wanted to be a pilgrim. No money was required, for alms could be begged, and every night a bed and a supper were unfailingly to be found at some monastery or other. To sit round the fire in the strangers' room of a monastery was a pleasant change from the monotony of life and the hard work of the village.

Here came in another phase of the difficulty with which lawmakers were beset. No "base-born" native of feudal England but possessed a soul that hungered and thirsted for the liberty of the freeborn; and many of them, under colour of going on a pilgrimage, set off staff in hand, secretly resolved never to return to their native village. Then a new restraint was imposed; every one was ordered to provide himself with a passport or letter of travel before he could move from one county to another; generally with a bishop's licence which set forth the cause of his going and the date of his return. Such letters were sealed by an appointed officer of the justices in each town or hundred; the seal used was specially designed, having the king's arms in the centre, and the name of the issuing city, borough, or hundred right across it.

These seals in time were fabricated, and the widespread revolt against thraldom still filled the highways with rovers, most of them bearing "testimonial letters" of one sort or other. As to the beggars who were maimed and halt, and physically incapable of working, they were ordered to cease frequenting the high-roads; it was ordered they should end their life in the city or place where they were found at the time of the proclamation, or else in some town near to that in which they were born; "they will be taken there," says the statute of Richard II., "within forty days," and must "remain there for the rest of their lives."

It was even demanded of students going to the Universities—and surely it is significant of the class to which so many students then belonged—that they should carry the regulation letter. Not only were poor scholars then placed in the same category as beggars, but if they had not furnished themselves with the necessary document, they were just as unceremoniously to be put in irons. To such a pass as this had our statute law been brought by the Englishman's whole-souled revolt against hereditary serfdom, fired perhaps by the taint of nomadism in his blood. But the remedy was not to be found in repression.

Seeking a little relief from the sombre side of our subject, we may for the moment turn aside here, and leaving the open highway for the forest shade, find a more picturesque form of life in the outlawry of the woodland. The brigand is a more interesting character than the vagrant, and there were not a few forest freebooters in England at that time.

Of those who broke away from the bonds of society, many of them criminals and outlaws, but not a few of them fugitives from the oppressiveness of bondage, thousands took to the woodlands. Every forest in England was infested with bands of robbers, all of them living more or less in emulation of the traditional merry men of Sherwood.

For no hero of romance ever seized upon the popular imagination as did that English bandit, Robin Hood. The number of old ballads in which he figures as first favourite is legion. Even Piers Plowman cannot restrain his pen on a subject so enticing :—

> ." I cannot parfitly my paternoster as the priest it singeth,
> But I can rhyme of Robyn Hood "

No modern writer has exalted the joys of a freebooting life beneath the spreading greenwood tree so happily as John Love Peacock. In picturesque language he tells of the delights of the free rover who finds himself in the very best of company in the high court of Nature; where the goodly grove is his palace, of which the oak and the beech are its colonnade and its canopy; the. sun, the moon, and the stars its everlasting lamps; the grass and the flowers its many-coloured carpet; the woodbine, the eglantine, and the ivy its curtains and its tapestry; the lark, the thrush, the linnet, and the nightingale its un-hired minstrels.

Robin Hood (continues the lively author of " Maid Marian ") is king of the forest both by dignity of birth, and by virtue of his standing army, and the free choice of his people. He holds his dominion over the forest and its horned multitude of citizen-deer, and its swinish multitude or peasantry of wild boars, by right of conquest and force of arms. He levies contributions amongst them by the free consent of his archers, their representatives. Is it not written that the fat ribs of the herd shall be fed upon by the mighty in the land? Does not the freeman of the forest give thanks for them when they are well roasted and smoking under his nose? What title had William of Normandy to England that Robin of Locksley has not to merry Sherwood? William fought for his claim. So does Robin. From whom both? From all that they could or can make pay them. They differ indeed in this, that William took from the poor and gave to the rich, and Robin takes from the rich and gives to poor. Scarlet and John, are they not peers of the forest—lords temporal of Sherwood? . . .

And so on, in merry strain, the novelist paints the charms, the irresistible fascinations of the forest free-booter's life, as viewed through the rosy spectacles of romance and idealism.

Within the freedom of the forest, according to most balladists and romancers, life would seem to flow ever pleasantly along in a sort of perennial summertime; and very seldom indeed do we hear anything of the actual discomforts which must be inevitable to a life lived always in the open, in a climate so villainously ungenial as that of England. An exception to this rule, however, is found in "The Nut-brown Maid," a famous old ballad which tells how Henry, Lord Clifford, driven from home by a miserly father and an ill-natured step-mother, took to the woods and became the head of a band of robbers. As an outlaw he meets and woos the Nut-brown Maid, and to test her love paints the hardships she would have to undergo if she became his wife. Suffice it here to quote the stanza which depicts life beneath the greenwood tree with some approach to realism. In congruous terms he warns the confiding damsel—

> "Yet take good heed, for ever I dread
>   That ye could not sustain
> The thorny ways, the deep valleys,
>   The snow, the frost, the rain,
> The cold, the heat; for dry or wet,
>   We must lodge on the plain,
> And us above, none other roof
>   But a brake bush or twain;
> Which soon would grieve you, I believe
>   And ye would gladly than
> That I had to the greenwood go
>   Alone, a banished man."

Her constancy being proof against all this, the supposed outlaw reveals himself as no banished man, but an earl's son, fit to mate with his loving nut-brown maid, whom all the time he had known to be the Lady Margaret Percy, daughter of the baron whose estates lay so near his own.

The woodland chieftains of old ballad lore were often men of birth and position, but the "merry men" who followed them were drawn from the lower orders, though

not necessarily criminals. Life beneath the greenwood
tree was rough ; and the *gentle* seldom got near the actu-
alities of life without finding the *simple* indispensable to
them. Thousands of the woodland population were
escaped serfs ; for the feudal customs and the harsh
legislation of the time led to outlawry as well as to
vagrancy.

In 1363 another piece of legislation attempted a further
interference with the freedom of the industrial classes.
This was the Statute of Apparel, which sought to regulate
their dress and their diet. It directed that artificers and
servants should be served only once a day with meat and
fish, or the waste of other victuals, as milk and cheese ;
and that they should wear cloth of the value of twelvepence a yard ; farm labourers were to wear no kind of
cloth save that called black russet at twelvepence the
yard. There were other provisions relating to yeomen
and others which need not be quoted here ; the significance of these remarkable provisions being that the
labourer had so completely emancipated himself from the
grasp of his feudal master, the latter, being unable to
exercise his arbitrary will upon him any longer, had now
to appeal to the powers of Parliament to compel him to
work at all, and at the same time tried to dictate what he
should eat and what he should wear.

The emancipation of the serf had been going on,
gradually and almost imperceptibly, for two or three
centuries. How that progressive movement was checked
at an inopportune stage of its development, and then
precipitated by ill-considered enactments, will be dis-
closed with more detail in a subsequent chapter.

It is evident from the tone of the legislation of Henry
VII. that the indigent classes were by that time regarded
with a little more consideration than previously. By an
Act of 1504 the penalties were somewhat mitigated, and

6

discretion was given as to the amount of punishment in cases of sickness and old age. It was set forth that the king's grace now leaned more to pity than extreme rigour in seeking the restfulness of his land.

Yet the cruelty of the laws against vagrancy, however modified, were thus seen by More: "They be cast into prisons as vagabonds, because they go about and work not, whom no man will set to work, though they never so willingly proffer themselves thereto."

VII

OUTCAST LEPERS

THE abject misery in which the poor lived in olden times
can scarcely be compared with any standard known to us
in modern times. They lived in foul hovels, unventilated
and ill-lighted, clothed in filthy rags, their bodies alive
with vermin, breathing a stench-laden atmosphere, and
disregarding every law known to modern sanitary science.
Their scanty food consisted mainly of barley-bread, black
and gritty, occasionally eked out with garbage, and the
refuse food of their "betters."

Moral degradation could not but accompany this material degradation ; the poor were brutal in their habits and
coarse in their speech ; inured to physical discomfort

and callous to actual suffering. With dirt everywhere supreme, it was inevitable that many loathsome diseases should add to their appalling misery. The outbreak of plague and pestilence was of constant occurrence, sometimes general, sometimes merely local.

The repeated use of the epithet "scurvy knave" in Shakespeare's historical plays discovers to us the prevalence of at least one uncleanly disease. Then leprosy was also rife. Outside the walls of most towns and cities were lazar-houses, in which scores of lepers, many of them too horrible for the sight to dwell upon, might be seen and heard, cursing and howling, and calling clamorously for alms upon the passers-by. Outside London alone were some half-dozen of these establishments, the best known of them being St. Giles's Hospital, Cripplegate, founded by Maud, queen of Henry I., in a field a mile outside the west gate of the city.

It was a common result of leprosy to make the sufferer lame, and perhaps to earn for him the nickname "Hobbling Giles"; hence the connection. Generally, however, Lazarus, whom Christ raised from the dead, was esteemed the saint of lepers, whence a hospital for lepers was always called a Lazar-house. There was some confusion between the Lazarus who was the friend of Jesus and the Lazarus of the parable.

In 1129 were founded the Knights of St. Lazarus, instituted for the cure of persons infected with leprosy, and to them was assigned the famous hospital in Jerusalem for the reception of lepers. It was a military order, open only to men of gentle birth; they took vows of obedience, poverty, and charity. In the sixteenth century the existing members of the fraternity were merged into the Knights of Rhodes, or other kindred orders in the different countries to which they belonged.

The patron saint of cripples and beggars was St. Giles,

himself a cripple. Churches dedicated to this saint in olden times were generally to be found on the outskirts of the large towns and cities, as at London and Norwich, Cambridge and Salisbury. Cripplegate, London, near St. Giles's Church, was so called before the Conquest from the number of cripples who resorted there to beg.

By the Church, lepers were committed to the care of the faithful; and so prevalent was the scourge there was scarcely a town of any size without its lazar-house, great or small. In Kent there were thirteen; and though commonly known as leper hospitals, the inmates often included a preponderance of the aged, sick and infirm, and sufferers from a number of contagious or incurable diseases, such as cancer Suspected lepers had to submit themselves to the examination of the parish priest, to an unscientific diagnosis which was more frequently wrong than right.

Scrofulous persons, or "scroyles" as Shakespeare calls them, all those suffering with *lues venerea*, those who were "full of sores" from any loathsome form of skin eruption —malignant and disfiguring disorders were then all too painfully prevalent — even the mangy and dirty, were all of them very often included under the elastic and convenient name of lepers.

It was no inconsiderable proportion of the population which was afflicted by either scurvy or leprosy; and as the former was always found to be more prevalent in the spring of the year, it has generally been attributed to the extensive use of a salted diet throughout the long winter season. The existence of leprosy cannot be traced to intercourse with the East; in fact, the English mediæval variety of this disease was more serious than the biblical. The skin thickened, became discoloured, and ulcerated; the limbs swelled, fingers and toes dropped off, the voice sank to a whisper, and the mind gradually weakened under the awful affliction. The disease may have been communicated in some cases by a person with abraded skin coming into actual contact with a leper.

Whether the leprosy was infectious, or contagious, or hereditary, it is quite certain that the malady was greatly aggravated by the habits of the time ; and especially contributary to its prevalence has been considered the consumption, during long and compulsory fasts, of fish that was unsound, this stock food being always imperfectly cured, and not infrequently half-putrid.

A person smitten with leprosy was sternly shunned by society, and practically died a civil death. The horrible and revolting appearance of the lepers, partly eaten away by disease, excited loathing and disgust, rather than pity. People either turned horror-stricken from the sight of them, or drove them fiercely and mercilessly away. If the poor afflicted creatures broke the least of the rules of separation, they were liable to the most cruel punishments ; any citizen who harboured one was imprisoned ; and bailiffs were stationed at the gates of London and other large cities to prevent their entering.

In fact, every effort was made to isolate the sufferers ; they were regarded as unclean, thrust out of the community, and forced to live apart by themselves. If a leper walked abroad he wore a grey gown for distinction, and carried a bell or clapper which he sounded as he went along, crying out at the same time the warning words, " Unclean, unclean !" so that the people might stand aside, and not so much as touch the hem of his garment. And as he was not able to work for wage or hire, he was permitted to carry into the market a " clap-dish," which was a bowl or basin in which to receive food and alms, and which he beat loudly to attract attention to his wants, calling out, says the old chronicle, the piteous cry, " Sum good, my gentyll mayster, for God's sake ! "

It is curious to note, by the way, that the earliest door-knockers were known as "lazar clappers."

In the regular leper-houses the inmates were compelled to wear a distinctive dress, of which the shoes were not the least important item. No leper was ever allowed to go unshod, or even to wear low-cut shoes; he was required to wear high boots that reached well up the leg nearly to the knee. At Harbledown both sexes were shod in foot-gear of strong ox-hide, and at Sherbourne each inmate was allowed fourpence a year for grease with which to dress the boots.

Lepers were not allowed to worship with the rest of the congregation; in some churches were separate chapels or chambers from which, through a hole in the wall, they could look upon the celebration of the Mass; and in a great many other churches were "low-side windows," always placed lower than the other windows, generally on the south side of the chancel, and commonly supposed to be for the purpose of allowing communication between the priest inside and these afflicted creatures so strictly relegated to the outside. Many of these apertures would certainly permit of a leper, or other communicant considered too loathsome to come in contact with the congregation, to witness the elevation of the Host at the altar inside, while kneeling in the churchyard outside.

According to a local legend Patrishow Church, an ancient edifice of considerable architectural interest, situated in a remote spot among the Black Mountains of Breconshire, was erected by a "foreigner" who had been cured of leprosy through the waters of a neighbouring well, and had left "a capful of money" to build a church as a thankoffering for his marvellous recovery.

Of the more ancient leper-houses St. John the Baptist's Spital at Ripon, St. Mary Magdalene's at

Exeter, and St. Mary Magdalene's at Colchester, are all claimed to have been in existence before the Norman invasion.

It is stated that a lazar-house stood on the site of St. James's Palace long before the Conquest; so that for six centuries at least the mysterious disease was an ever-present terror in the land. Other plagues appeared at intervals, and disappeared. Leprosy remained—it never left the land. No class or condition could escape its clutches. Though most prevalent amongst the lowest orders, it sometimes seized the monarch on his throne, the bishop in his cathedral, the nun in her cell, the soldier in camp, the sailor on board his ship, the workman at his bench, the merchant in his counting-house. Robert the Bruce died of it (1326), so did Orivalle, Bishop of London.

Among royal lepers were alleged to have been Henry III., Henry IV., and Adelicia of Louvaine, second wife of Henry I. Of Robert the Bruce's leprosy Sir Walter Scott says it was a scorbutic disorder rather than that called leprosy. It is clear the disease was not always properly diagnosed. Margaret of Anjou is said to have been a leper, but the evidence in several of these cases is conflicting; in the lower orders of society a person was not unfrequently reported to be a leper in order to get him removed and deprive him of his property. Henry IV. was for a time a patient at a "leprosery" at Bermondsey; not the abbey there, but a special "stone house" in charge of monkish nurses.

The name "spittle," according to one authority, was reserved for a lazar-house, while the word "spital" was given to an almshouse. Such distinctions, when orthography was unsettled, were impossible. Another writer, less dogmatic and nearer the truth, writing in 1580, says: "A spittle or hospitall for poore folkes diseased; a spittle, hospitall, or lazar-house for lepres." Some hospitals for the treatment of "leapery," others for the reception of almsmen or other deserving poor, were all indifferently known as *Maisons Dieu*; one such ancient institution at Newcastle went by the name of "Maison-dewe" till quite recent times.

Stow, the historian of London, enumerates those "built without the city some good distance; to wit, the Lock without Southwark; one between Miles-End and Stratford near Bow; one other at Kingsland, betwixt Shoreditch and Stoke Newington." There were also several others round London, namely, at Highgate, Hammersmith, Finchley, Ilford, and one at Knightsbridge.

The last named, which was a lazar-house till the Reformation, was converted in the reign of James I. to "a hospital for sick, lame, and impotent folk"; during the Great Plague of 1665 it was extensively used for the reception of those stricken with the disorder.

The one at Highgate was founded in 1473 by a yeoman named Pole, who had himself been stricken with leprosy. It was dedicated to St. Anthony, and was subsequently benefited by other bequests, the last one, in 1517, by William Cloudesley, of Islington, in these terms: " I bequeath to the poor lazars of Hyegate, to pray for me by name in their bede role, 6/8." Appointments to the governorship of this " Spytyl Howse of Holowey " were made under the Privy Seal, and the office seems to have been one of some emolument. After the Reformation the establishment lost its character as a leper-house, as well as its religious associations.

A mile westward of Charing Cross there stood in very early times a hospital for leprous women; although the endowment was for " fourteen maidens that were leprous" only, eight brethren were attached to the house for the purpose of conducting the religious services and to discharge "the cure of souls." It was from this establishment, dedicated to St. James the Less, that the present St. James's Palace, which stands on its site, obtained its name.

Every mediæval town of any pretensions (as the old county towns and market towns, the cities and seaports) had its leper hospital; or a village near it was utilized for the isolation of these sufferers. Frequently the lazar-house, in the form of a group of cottages with a chapel attached, was outside the walls. There were upwards of two hundred of these institutions in England; there were three in and around Canterbury, six in or near Norwich, and five near King's Lynn; others were to be found at St. Albans (two), Stafford (two), Lincoln (several), High Wycombe, Ilford, Nottingham, Newcastle, Pontefract, Reading, Stamford, Sudbury, Maldon, Chichester, Colchester, New Romney, Faversham, Kingswood, Maiden Bradley, and Fuggleton (Wilts). Rochester and Harbledown claim to be the two oldest of these institutions; the latter and St. John's, Canterbury, were built by Lanfranc. At Cranbrook the lazar-house remained till later times as the pest-house; and that at Newport (Essex), built in the reign of King John, has only been demolished in recent years. Honiton leper-house and St. Catherine's leper-house at Rochester are still standing.

The chief establishment of them all, a remarkably large and noble provision for the lepers of the country, was the great house at Burton Lazars in Leicestershire. It was erected in the reign of Stephen, largely from the efforts of a national subscription, though the main wealth for its support had been derived from the Mowbray family. The Abbot of Burton Lazars held some sort of authority over all the other leper hospitals in the country —the Hospital of St. Giles in London, for instance, was a "cell" or dependency of this establishment—and in his turn the Master of Burton Lazars was under the control of the Master of the Lazar House in Jerusalem.

The larger and better managed establishments had a regular staff, which included, besides the warden, a chaplain, a clerk, servants, and attendants. The discipline in some was extremely rigorous, but this depended mainly on the character of the warden, who had the power of inflicting penalties, from fasting and penance to a severe flogging. Quarrelling and rioting and the secreting of money from the warden were among the offences most severely visited.

The lepers of Freford, Lichfield, were supplied with venison from Cannock Chase, by royal favour.

By an enactment of Edward I. each lazar-house was permitted to appoint two proctors to go about collecting the alms of the charitable. By Elizabeth's reign these begging proctors had become a far greater nuisance than the disease, and the legislature classed them among the "rogues and vagabonds"; indeed, so low and degraded were they that they were not accepted to lodge with the tramps in the Watts' Almshouses at Rochester.

This is the inscription over the door of "The Poor Travellers' House," the well-known charity in the High Street of Rochester, which was the scene of Dickens's Christmas story entitled "The Seven Poor Travellers":—

"Richard Watts, Esq.
by his will, dated 22 Aug. 1579
founded this charity
for six poor travellers
who not being Rogues or Proctors
may receive gratis for one night
lodging, entertainment
and fourpence each."

Starvation was declared by some to be a cure for leprosy, but it is not improbable that this was but a sinister suggestion. Early in the fourteenth century (1320) a number of lepers having a malignant form of the disease were burnt alive. They were charged with going about the country as well-poisoners. In the twentieth year of the reign of Edward III. (1347) the number of lepers in the country had increased so alarmingly, that specially strong measures were taken for the suppression of the plague, and it was peremptorily ordered that they be removed to "out-places in the fields from the haunts and company of sound people."

The most esteemed specific for leprosy was garlic, so that garlic and leprosy became inseparably associated. From this fact we get the term "pil-garlic," signifying one who is shunned like a leper, because lepers were compelled (by the force of circumstances) to peel, or pil, their own garlic—and commonly these outcasts were dubbed "pil-garlics." Leeks were also supposed, when fortified with other remedies, to have curative virtues.

By the more superstitious, human blood was regarded as the special and only cure for leprosy, a disease supposed by them to be the type and symbol of sin. One legendary tale declares the miraculous powers of the holy well at Canterbury, in which a single drop of the blood of St. Thomas had been dissolved, and how its virtues triumphed in a monkish contest over those of the highly reputed sulphur springs of Bath.

The superstitions connected with the subject were very numerous. It was believed that the disease could be conveyed to a person by witchcraft. In fact, it was believed that all infectious diseases could be conveyed by an infected person breathing in the face of another ; it is noteworthy that one of the articles exhibited in Parliament against Wolsey (1529) was a charge that he, knowing himself to be suffering from an infectious disease, "came dayly to your Grace [the King], rounding in your ears and blowing upon your most noble Grace with his perilous and infective breath to the marvellous danger of your Highness." On the other hand, it was believed that leprosy, among other kindred complaints, could be cured by a priest breathing on the face of the afflicted, and at the same time exorcising the wicked spirit dwelling in the afflicted body.

In the accounts of St. Bartholomew's Hospital, in the middle of the sixteenth century, appears an item of expenditure incurred by the removal of some patients to "the lazar-house at Holloway," the prevalence of the disease having then considerably diminished. Leprosy is therein referred to as "the linenless disease." The explanation is that "the true cause of the disorder" was supposed to be "the wearing of woollen garments next the skin;" for "through the habit of not having these garments regularly changed and washed, but wearing them till saturated with perspiration, the skin became diseased." The theory is, that with the introduction of linen, and the more frequent washing, this loathsome disease rapidly disappeared.

Different writers have assigned different reasons for the decline and ultimate disappearance of leprosy from these shores. One disputant attributes it to the change of diet with which its banishment synchronised. Till the time of Henry VIII. the country had produced no salads, carrots, turnips, or other edible roots; and this controversialist contends that it was the introduction of garden vegetables which did more to get rid of leprosy than the medical art of all the previous centuries had accomplished; he argues that the food in use previously had given an excess of phosphates, but practically no alkalies, to the blood. Another wrangler asserts that the antidote was found in the tea, coffee, and other astringent drinks which were introduced about that period!

Leprosy was said to have been cured in Ireland with whiskey distilled from potatoes. It was called, not without reason, says this authority, *aqua vitæ*, or, in Irish, *uisge beaga*, otherwise usquebaugh.

Leprosy raged in this country from the eleventh to the thirteenth century, after which period it began to abate, and as the leper-houses were not always full, some of them gradually came to be adapted to other purposes.

At the Dissolution all the endowed lazar-houses were suppressed, and as no more were established, and as, indeed, we hear little more of lepers in this country after that period, it is certain that leprosy had practically disappeared from the country by the middle of the sixteenth century.

It is singular the disease should have lingered longest at the two extremities of the country—Cornwall and the Shetland Isles. In the latter there was a case as late as 1798.

After the Reformation certain of the London lazar-houses seem to have been called Lock Hospitals, and converted to the treatment of peculiar patients. The first one was the "Loke" in Kent Street, Southwark, and is said to have derived its name from the French *loques*, "rags," referring to the linen rags applied to the sores ; or it may have been from the Saxon *log* or *loc*, equivalent to "shut," in reference to the "closed" or isolated condition of the leper. The latter is the commonly accepted derivation of the term.

VIII

THE PEASANT REVOLT

Revolt against serfdom—"Head money" paid for leave to go
in search of work—Labour services commuted for money
payments—Conditions of English bondage—Commutations in-
opportunely interrupted by a terrible visitation of plague (1349)
—The Black Death—A devastated land—Society disintegrated
—Labour market upset—Landowners hard hit—Scarcity of
labour—Higher wages demanded—A clumsy expedient—Rate
of wages fixed by Statute of Labourers—Origin of hiring fairs
—Dear food and impossible wages—Landlords' expedients—
Origin of the English farmer—Attempted reversion to labour-
rents—A poll-tax precipitates the revolt (1381)—Outbreaks in
various parts—Wat Tyler's insurrection—Socialistic teaching of
John Ball—The labourer confined to his own parish—Second
Statute of Labourers (1388)—Wandering labourers—Become
sturdy beggars or bandits—Jack Cade's outbreak—The spirit of
revolt—Was it fostered by the poverty of the people?—The
opinion of Sir John Fortescue on the causes of discontents and
armed risings—Paston letters—Strained relations between
landlords and peasants—Rents and wages—Sumptuary laws.

WE have to consider now that period in our history
which probably presented the England of direst poverty
and deepest misery.

The revolt of the English peasant, coming as he did
mainly of a freedom-loving Saxon stock, was inevitable.
His innate love of liberty had been held in check so far,
pending the fusion of the two races, the blending of
Saxon and Norman, by the repressive severities of the

feudal system. Early in the reign of Richard II. the revolt was precipitated by the imposition of a poll-tax, the payment of which, in an age when money was always scarce, fell upon the poor with oppressive incidence.

As neither villein nor serf had any choice either of a master or a sphere of toil, the peasant revolt which made itself felt at the end of the fourteenth century is not difficult to understand. He occasionally paid head-money for licence to remove from the estate in search of trade or hire, but if he refused to return on the recall of his owner he was pursued as a fugitive outlaw.

Another step towards freedom was made by the growing tendency to commute labour services for money payments, and with the advance of society a labour-rent was every year becoming more difficult to enforce. Also the luxury of the castle-hall, the splendour and pomp of chivalry, the cost of campaigns, all tended to drain the purses of knight and baron, and the sale of freedom to a serf, or the commutation of villein services, was an easy and tempting mode of refilling them.

The growth of money-rents was very gradual, but in time it became part of a land-steward's duties to visit the various manors of his stewardship at least twice a year, to receive money payments from his lord's tenants, to enquire strictly into the customs of the manor and the other services due, and to take every precaution for preserving the rights of lordship.

By the conditions of English bondage the serfs were bound to the land, having to render their lord so many days' work each week, and certain extra days' work at busy seasons of ploughing, harvesting, and hay-making. Aiming at economic liberty, by commutation, supposing a man's labour was reckoned at a penny a day, he would arrange to pay threepence a week if he owed three days' work, and further pennies for extra days.

TENANT PAYING RENT
(From Fitzherbert's ' Boke of Surveying ' 1523)

AGRICULTURAL LABOURERS

To add to the many miseries of the poor in olden times was the ever-present and oft-recurring terror of plague and pestilence, sometimes local, sometimes national; periodical calamities which were equally destructive of living comfort both in their cause and their effect. Of the former were the filth, squalor, and unwholesome dietary; the foul and insanitary surroundings of daily life; among the latter the decimation of the population, the dereliction of widows and orphans left without bread-winners, the suspension of tilth, and the temporary stoppage of trade, to the not infrequent accompaniment of famine.

The social progress of the English bondman was interrupted in 1348, when the terrible pestilence called the Black Death burst over Europe, ushered in on the Continent by a succession of appalling earthquakes. It first appeared in England in Dorsetshire in the month of August, and it was not long ere corruption smelt to heaven in the fierce summer sun all through that country-side. By November the Plague had reached London, and thence advanced to the north.

The outbreak could not have occurred at a more inopportune time. The practice of commuting services for money payments had been gradually spreading over the country, and its interruption by this visitation was nothing less than a national calamity.

This scourge was probably a variety of the Oriental plague, a putrid typhus, which obtained the name of Black Death because the rapid putrefaction of the dead turned the bodies black. It generally attacked the victim in the head and the stomach, appearing first in the groin or under the arm-pits as a small boil or blain, called a plague-sore. These symptoms were accompanied by a devouring fever, with the occasional spitting and vomiting of blood. Some succumbed within six hours,

7

some lingered two or three days. Victims were found in castle and in hall, but the most fearful ravages of the dread destroyer were committed in the huts and hovels of the rural population, in the filthy dens of the noisome city alleys. So fast they died, the dead-carts could not overtake the stalking pestilence, and soon towns and villages were littered with blackened carcases lying about in huddled heaps of fetid putrefaction.

> "So they died! the dead were slaying the dying;
> There were none to love, and none to wed,
> And pity and joy and hope had fled,
> And grief had spent her passion in sighing."

It has been estimated that at least two million of the population were swept away that dreadful year; distress and penury naturally followed, although it is not impossible that the country, man for man, with about half the number to share the existing wealth, may have found itself richer.

Lords of manors certainly found themselves richer for the time being, because extraordinary amounts had been paid in heriots and fees, and not a small portion of their estates had escheated for lack of heirs. The common people in the first year of the Plague found provisions extraordinarily cheap, owing to the excessive mortality; but the next year they rose alarmingly, owing to the scarcity of labour and the consequent neglect of agriculture. There had been a general disintegration of society during that awful visitation; the labourer had left the fields, the courts of law had been closed, Parliament repeatedly prorogued, families had broken up, and the loudest calls of honour, duty, and humanity appealed to ears of stone.

> "Frantic with fear, they sought by flight to shun
> The fierce contagion. O er the mournful land .

The infected city poured her hurrying swarms;
Roused by the flames that fired her seats around
The infected country rushed into the town.
Some sad at home, and in the desert some
Abjured the fatal commerce of mankind.
In vain! Where'er they fled the fates pursued!"

The superstition of the age attributed the terrible visitation to the anger of God at the prevailing extravagance in dress, and a sect of fanatics arose, called "Flagellants," who sought to release themselves from sin by severe scourgings.

Above all, the labour market was completely upset; wages had been rising for ten years previously, and when in 1349 it was realised that the dearth of labour was something phenomenal, the labourer not unnaturally became somewhat insolent in his demands.

It easily may be seen that the landowners were hard hit in various directions. They lost the payments for commuted services, so many of their tenants having succumbed to the pestilence, and the remainder being impoverished through neglected cultivation. What had paid for a day's labour before the Black Death would no longer pay for it. It was a common complaint that whereas a woman's labour had formerly cost a halfpenny a day, now it cost twopence or threepence. Hence a lord who was expected to receive at the old rates, and to pay at the new ones, saw nothing but ruin staring him in the face.

The policy of the landowner, who was largely represented in Parliament, may be easily traced by the course of legislation. The first idea was to check the rise in wages by legal enactment; then, in order to be perfectly just, it was intended to check the rise in prices as well; if prices remained the same, it was argued, there was no need for wages to rise.

This meddling interference with economic laws was but an extension of the prevalent practice of every trade guild in the country, which artificially fixed the prices at which its wares should be sold. Parliament was only attempting to do for the whole country what every craft guild did for the towns. The task, however, proved beyond the strength of the Government.

It was a clumsy expedient by which the legislature attempted to meet these economic difficulties. By the Statute of Labourers, passed immediately after the subsidence of the Plague, valiant beggars who "live by begging and do refuse to work" were not to be relieved "under colour of pity or alms"; but in view of the scarcity of labourers and the urgent need for cultivating the land, pressure had to be brought to bear on the labouring population. The labourers, practically acquainted with the natural law which regulates wages, had demanded unusual terms. The Government, therefore, issued an ordinance which fixed the price of labour, and enforced obedience by fines and corporal punishment. A mower, after the subsidence of the pestilence, had demanded a shilling a day, and a reaper eightpence with food, a wage equal to fifteen shillings and ten shillings a day respectively, when compared with modern money values. This was exorbitant. The statute therefore enacted that labourers should be content with such liveries and wages as they had received before the Plague; that where they had been paid in wheat they should receive wheat; that mowers should receive fivepence a day, reapers twopence and threepence a day, without food, and weeders and hay-makers a penny a day. It was further enacted that farm labourers were to be hired by the year and not by the day, and that they were to carry their implements of husbandry openly in their hands to market towns, and apply for hire in a public quarter of the town.   This, be it noted, was the origin of the statute fairs and hirings which are still held in the remoter country towns (see p. 365).

It is worth remembering in this connection that the law-makers of the period had not been above fixing the rate of recompense due to themselves as legislators; in the reign of Edward III. Parliament had fixed the rate of wages payable to its members at four shillings a day for a knight of the shire, and two shillings for a citizen or burgess representative.

Enforcement of the law was found impossible because corn had risen to such a price that a day's labour at the old wages would not have purchased wheat enough for the man's support.   Landowners, however, persisted in the attempt to apply the law, and runaway labourers were ordered to be branded with a hot iron on the forehead, while the harbouring of serfs in the towns was rigorously dealt with.

With so much distress and misery accompanying a rise in wages it came gradually to be realised that the prices of commodities could be high, not through any lack of gold and silver, but for the want of those things which gold and silver are only used to buy.

Some landowners dispensed with labour by turning their gardens and farms into sheepwalks; others spitefully levied harsh tolls and dues, and all the various private taxes of feudal lordship; while practically all of them enforced the old cruel laws against the taking of game in the parks and forests; till the country was seething with resentment, ill-feeling, and bitter discontent.

Wiser lords granted land on lease to tenants for a rent, giving them stock as well as land.   Thus the tenant had to find labour; the lord was free of the difficulty.

Here we have the beginnings of the modern farmer—a person who stands between the labourer and the landowner. The land soon became full of these "plough-men"—humble tenants no longer at the bidding of their lords. The best of these acquired their holdings in time, and became "yeomen," as we shall see presently. Chaucer's "Ploughman" was a man of "goods and chattels" who, though he had spread many a load of dung, and would thresh and ditch, yet paid his tithes and was kind to the poor.

Of the landowners who met the difficulty by converting their arable into pasture more will be said in a subsequent chapter. There was a great demand for wool at that time, and English wool was the best that could be had. Besides, as sheep-farming needed less labour than arable farming, it paid the landowner better.

In spite of all the ferocious penalties of imprisonment and branding, of slavery, and even death, wages continued to rise, because men could not live on the old wages. For as the lords could not afford to see their estates fall out of cultivation, they were tempted to break the very laws they had made for their own protection, and offered higher wages than the law allowed to serve their own private ends.

One section of the landowners, more retrograde than their fellows, tried to put back the hands of the clock still further. Wages being at the root of all the trouble, why not abolish wages? There had been a time when no wages were paid or needed ; when obligations were paid for by services, and the land was cultivated by serfs. Why not go back to this system? It seemed easy ; all that was needed was to refuse the commutation payments, and insist upon the rendering of labour-rents once more.

But in entertaining a proposal of this nature the landlords had vastly mistaken the temper of the English peasant. Men who had partly gained their freedom were

RICHARD II. IN HIS BARGE MEETING THE REBELS.

A miniature in the British Museum.

Reproduced from "Froissart in England," by Henry Newbolt, by permission of Messrs. James Nisbet & Co., Ltd.

To face p. 103.

not likely to consent to give it up again; and soon the peasants everywhere were infuriated with their lords; it needed only the imposition of a poll-tax, which pressed very unfairly on the poor, to cause the smouldering discontent to break into flame. It was the shameful way in which the tax was collected which brought matters to a head. Risings broke out, first in East Anglia and then in the counties around London.

In Essex the people, led by Thomas the Baker of Fobbing, slew the jury called to assess the tax. The flame spread like wildfire through the Eastern and Midland counties, and other leaders sprang up under such assumed names as Jack Straw, Jack Trueman, and Jack the Miller. "Jack Straw's Castle," an inn on Hampstead Heath, is supposed to mark the site where this revolutionary priest made his headquarters. How the revolt was organized, and how communication passed between the different sections so rapidly is a mystery —possibly by Wycliffe's poor priests, although there was a vast wandering population in England at that period. In some way or other the word was passed quietly round to be ready at Whitsuntide; and early in July (1381) everywhere south of York the labourers, workmen, and farmers flocked to the gathering-places armed with clubs, rusty swords, axes, bill-hooks, scythes, old bows that had hung many a day in the smoke of the chimney corner, and odd arrows with two or three of their feathers gone. In good order the muster was made, and the march on London commenced.

On the morning of Corpus Christi Day, the king went by barge to Rotherhithe, where ten thousand of the rebels were assembled, and shouting (as Froissart says) "as though all the devils of hell had been among them." Not daring to land, the King demanded of them what they would, and the mob replied with one voice, "We would that ye should come a-land, and then we shall shew you what we lack." Richard, however, was counselled by his courtiers to return to the Tower, which without more delay he very wisely did.

The struggle was stubborn, and fiercely contested on both sides, the free labourers finding allies in the villeins whose manumissions (or freedom from manorial service) were now being questioned. Organised resistance was made in various parts of the country by large gatherings of fugitive serfs, supported by villeins who had freed themselves from the ancient and obnoxious customary services due to their manorial lords. The cry of the poor found expression through the preachings of John Ball, "the mad priest of Kent," who joined the revolted peasants there under Wat Tyler (1381), though strangely enough villein services had long been unknown in Kent.

The tyranny of landlordism had roused the spirit of Socialism to a dangerous point; the levelling doctrine was condensed by John Ball, formerly a priest at St. Mary's, York, into the popular rhyme of the day—

> "When Adam dalf and Eve span
> Who was then the gentleman?"

"Good people," cried the preacher, "things will never go well in England so long as goods be not in common, and so long as there be villeins and gentlemen. By what right are they whom we call lords greater folk than we? On what grounds have they deserved it? Why do they hold us in serfage? If we all came of the same father and mother, of Adam and Eve, how can they say or prove that they are better than we, if it be not that they make us gain for them by our toil what they spend in their pride? They are clothed in velvet, and warm in their furs and their ermines, while we are covered with rags. They have wine and spices and fair bread, and we oat-cake and

ADAM AND EVE AS PEASANTS *c.* 1250.

(From Mr. Yates Thompson's Carehowe Psalter.)

straw, and water to drink. They have leisure and fine houses ; we have pain and labour, the rain and the wind in the fields. And yet it is of us and our toil that these men hold their state."

John Ball had a terse and pithy way of putting things, and was a man not to be silenced even by repeated imprisonments. Here is an extract from one of his Letters to the Labourers :

"Let your Mill go right, with its four Sails dight,
  And let the Post stand in Steadfastness,
Let Right help Might, and Skill go before Will,
  Then shall our Mill go aright.
But if Might go before Right, and Will go before Skill,
  Then is our Mill mis-a-dight.
Beware ere ye be woe,
Know your friend from your foe,
Take enough and cry ' Ho,'
And do well and better, and flee from Sin,
And seek out Peace and dwell therein."

Though serfdom never again recovered itself, gradually dying out within the next century, this preacher of equality, like his leader, Wat Tyler, forfeited his life in his defence of the "rights of man."

A summary suppression of the economic trouble was attempted by the issue of a royal ordinance, which was subsequently thus embodied in the famous Statute of Labourers : "Every man or woman of whatsoever condition, bond or free, able in body and within the age of three-score years, and not having of his own whereof he may live, nor land of his own about the tillage of which he may occupy himself, and not serving any other, shall be bound to serve the employer who shall require him to do so, and shall take only the wages which were accustomed to be taken in the neighbourhood where he is bound to serve" two years before the Plague began. Though refusal to obey was punishable by imprisonment, sterner measures were soon found to be necessary, and the labourer was next forbidden to quit the parish where he lived in search of better-paid employment.

A second Statute of Labourers, passed in 1388, attempted to confine labourers to one locality—exceptions being made in favour of the men of Staffordshire, Derbyshire, Lancashire, Craven, and the border districts of Scotland and Wales—a principle which was subsequently exemplified further in the "law of settlement"; and by this enactment justices were empowered to fix the price of labour by proclamation every Easter and Michaelmas.

It had been authoritatively set forth in the year 1376 that "these wandering labourers become mere beggars in order to lead an idle life, and betake themselves out of their district commonly to the cities, boroughs, and other good towns to beg, and they are able-bodied and might well ease the community if they would serve."

As already indicated, the wandering labourer or artisan easily turned into the sturdy beggar or the bandit of the woods.

In the poem of "Piers the Plowman" we are shown how the shameless beggar, with bag on shoulder, goes from door to door, asking alms, when all the time he knows a trade by which he might gain his bread and beer, yet prefers not to exercise it.

> "And can som manere craft in cas he wolde hit vse,
>   Throgh whiche crafte he couthe come to bred and to ale."

The political rising of Jack Cade in 1450 was really another outbreak of the commons against the social injustices under which they laboured.

"You that love the commons, follow me ;
   Now show yourselves men ; 'tis for liberty.
   We will not leave one lord, one gentleman ;
   Spare none but such as go in clouted shoon,"

says that demagogue to his twenty thousand armed followers.

In the Norfolk rebellion of 1549, of which a tanner named Robert Kett was leader, the petition of the peasantry to the king for the removal of grievances makes this mention of villenage : "That all bondmen made be made free, for God made all free, with His precious bloodshedding."

Was the spirit of revolt (manifested not infrequently in minor isolated outbreaks) fostered by the poverty of the people ? Ere another half-century had passed the great bulk of the English constituencies consisted of those who had recently passed from the servile state into the free, and many were men of small substance. During the Wars of the Roses the populace shouted one day for the White Rose and the next for the Red ; and the question of the relationship between poverty and passivity was discussed by a contemporary writer who, upon such a subject was no mean authority—Sir John Fortesque, Chief Justice of the King's Bench under Henry VI. He writes :—

"Some men have said that it were good for the King that the Commons of England were made poor, as be the Commons of France. For then they would not rebel, as now they done often-times, which the Commons of France do not, nor may do ; for they have no weapon, nor armour, nor gold to buy it withal. . . . If they were made poorer than they be, they should not have wherewith to buy them bows, arrows, jacks, or any other armour of defence, whereby they might be able to resist our enemies when they list to come upon us, which they may do on every side, considering that we be an island. . . . Wherefore we should be a prey to all other enemies . . . Also they needen to be much exercised in shooting, which may not be done without right great expenses, as every man, expert therein, knoweth right well. Wherefore the making poor of the

Commons, which is the making poor of our archers, should be the destruction of the greatest might of our realm. . . . When any rising hath been made in this land before these days by Commons, the poorest men thereof hath been the greatest causers and doers therein. And thrifty men have been loth thereto, for dread of losing of their goods, yet oftentimes they have gone with them through menaces, or else the same poor men would have taken their goods ; wherein it seemeth that poverty hath been the whole and chief cause of all such rising . . . What then would befall if all the Commons were poor?"

The fifteenth century saw a great increase in trading, and it was from the increased profits made in trade that the great English middle-class took its rise ; while at the same time labour problems of a more complicated nature began to make themselves felt.

From the Paston Letters we learn that there were frequent complaints even in those days of the earth hunger of land-grabbing landlords, and interminable litigations and disputes about rights of way between the peasants and their landlords.

The value of land is mentioned as fourpence an acre yearly rent. On the whole the people were prosperous ; or, at least, no mention is made of poverty among the lower classes. They were certainly not so abjectly poor as in some neighbouring countries. The prices paid according to statute during the fourteenth century and until the year 1495, when the statutory wages were raised, were for a bailiff, £1 4s. 4d. per annum, with meat and drink ; for a common servant in husbandry when food was found, 15s., and 3s. 4d. for clothes. After the pestilence, from the scarcity of labourers, the statutory wages were held in abeyance. The ordinary wages of an artisan were fourpence a day without food and drink. One penny then commanded as much of the necessaries of life as about 1s. 3d. of our present money. According to the " Liber Albus," any one overpaying a workman is to be fined forty pence; and the workman taking more than is due according to statute is to be imprisoned for forty days. From the same authority we learn that the prices of nearly everything were regulated by statute, especially articles of wearing apparel, even to boots, shoes, and gloves. Every one was supposed to dress according to his class.

Distinctions of rank were rigidly enforced in every direction. The Statute of Apparel (1363) regulated the diet of servants, called grooms, and of artificers and tradesmen. They and their wives were to wear cloths of a certain low price, with no gold, or silver, or embroidery. This, of course, shows that there was at least some amount of luxury amongst the artisan and trading classes. The first clause of the enactment about dress regulates mechanics and commercial servants; the last regulates the labourers in husbandry—carters, ploughmen, shepherds, cowherds. If they had not forty shillings of goods or chattels, they were to wear only blanket and russet, and girdles of linen.

These Sumptuary Laws were passed down to the Reformation; most of them were repealed in the reign of James I., though the last was not expunged from the statute book till 1856.

IX

INCLOSURE OF THE COMMON-LANDS

From scarcity of labour to a scarcity of labourers—Origin of
English hedgerow scenery—Act of 1488 against " the pulling
down of towns"—Decay of tillage and conversion to pasture—
Wholesale appropriation of public lands—Profits of sheep-
farming—Wool becomes the national staple—The Woolsack—Wiltshire, the English Arcadia—The irregular tiller
of "waste"— The yeoman — Markets, wages, rents (*temp.*
Henry VIII.)—Sir Thomas More's complaint against the nobles
and their "devouring" sheep—English peasants driven to
distant lands—Disappearance of small holdings—Elizabethan
Act against large farms—Every cottage to have four acres.

THE economic disturbances consequent upon the deple-
tion of the population by the Black Death in 1349 were
characterized by a scarcity of labourers; in the following century a dislocation of industry occurred which
was attributable to an entirely opposite cause — the
scarcity of work consequent upon the inclosure of the
common-lands, and the conversion of thousands of
acres of arable land into pasture. A pastoral land
needed little labour expended upon it; everywhere
ploughmen and other farm labourers were discharged
by the hundred. Incidentally England became a country
pre-eminent for its hedgerow scenery.

It is not generally borne in mind that mediæval England was practically without hedges; that the whole

country was open and uninclosed ; that thousands of acres of grassland afforded free pasturage everywhere to the cattle of lord and tenant alike ; while even the arable lands of every village and township were communistic and unfenced strips, practically as unappropriated as the common fields themselves. The beautiful green hedges so characteristic of English scenery, which—with their charm of hawthorn and dog-rose, of trailing bramble and climbing honeysuckle—distinguish the English landscape from every other in the world, date only from the Tudor period.

It was early in the reign of Henry VII., to wit, in 1488, Parliament passed an act "agaynst pullyng down of Tounes." This sounds rather startling. Who were pulling towns down ? and for what purpose ? By towns we are not to understand walled towns, nor yet the larger aggregations of houses that went to make up the denser centres of population. But the Act specifically mentioned "towns, villages, borrowes, and hamlettes, tythyng houses, and other enhabitations," which "used to be occupied for tillage and husbandry ; " and all of which were ordered to be rebuilt within one year. The offenders who had brought about this "decay of houses" were the great landowners ; and the cause of this agricultural revolution was the consolidation of their holdings, and the conversion of tilled lands to pasture, with the consequent dismissal of the farm labourers. It had been discovered by the territorial magnates of this country of limited acres, that the quickest way to wealth was by wool farming. So sheep flocks were largely increased, and fields were for the first time inclosed to keep in the flocks. "Towns" in which two hundred persons had lived, occupied by their lawful labours in tillage, were now deserted except for a couple of shepherds or a herdsman or two. In all parts of England the desolation was the same ; and hence the sudden attention given by the legislature to the "late decay of the people."

Various reasons were put forward for making inclosures; as the reclamation of marsh and fen, and the necessity of subjecting such wastes to the use of man. One Act of Parliament for the inclosure of 4,293 acres of Hounslow Heath, including areas in the parishes of Brentford, Isleworth, Twickenham, and Teddington, attributed "the barrenness and infertility thereof" to the "want of diligence and industry of men." Portions were to be allotted to the inhabitants of the various parishes, to be held in severalty as copyholds, to be converted into both tillage and pasture. This sounds fair enough ; and what the king could do with Hounslow Heath, could be done by the lords of manors throughout the country, and there were many cases of a similar division of the lands of the suppressed monasteries.

But it was not the division of the large feudal properties, so much as the inclosures, both of which processes had been going on since the accession of Henry VII., which filled the land with discontent.

The inclosures were so general and so extensive, that taken in conjunction with the break-up of the monastic establishments at this time, such a revolution in the distribution of property had never before occurred in England. Taking the whole of the transactions, from that time to the present, no country has witnessed a more wholesale appropriation of public property to private uses.

If, at this re-distribution of the land, the people had come into a fair share of their own, the ultimate results might have proved a national blessing. But for a very lengthy season the distress amongst the humblest classes was enormous; so many "towns"—villages and hamlets —were reported to be "desolate and unpeopled."

" A time there was, ere England's woes began,
When every rood of ground maintained its man."

For the landowners—otherwise the capitalists—it has been pleaded that the capital of the country sought employment in an extension of cultivation, and that such extension could come only through the system of Inclosures. The increasing population demanded increased clothing, and one of the greatest exports of native produce being wool, immense flocks of sheep were now being kept on newly inclosed land, as well as upon many of the farms where the old cottier tenants had given place to a farmer or grazier who conducted the business on a larger scale.

Before the close of the Tudor period wool had become the staple of England—the number of vast churches found in the now deserted villages of the Cotswolds and the southern counties testify to a different distribution of the population in bygone times—and the most prosperous employers in the country were the graziers and flockmasters. Perhaps we may therefore be permitted to turn aside here to enjoy Aubrey's description of the Wiltshire shepherd. This famous antiquary was a native of that county, and wrote in 1671, when the sheepmasters paid their shepherds no fixed wages, but *pro rata* according to the size of the flock, " soe that the shepherd's lambs doe never miscarry." Evidently the system of payment by results is no new thing.

As painted by Aubrey, the delightful country round about Wilton and Chalke, with its rich and verdant turf, " intermixt with boscages," was a perfect Arcadia, to be compared with the classical land of the Golden Age ; when, as in the days of Ovid—

" His own small flock each senator did keep."

The innocent lives led by the shepherds here, recalled

8

to the antiquary those of Abel and Esau, of Joseph and
David, and all the shepherd princes of the East, with
their sheep-shearing festivals and other pastoral sports of
the antique world.   They had always a sheep-crook,
as described by Virgil ; a sling, a scrip, their tar-box, a
pipe or flute, and their dog.   As delineated earlier, by
Michael Drayton in Elizabeth's days, they wore a long
white cloak with a very deep cape reaching half-way down
their backs, "made of the locks of the sheep." Straw
hats and coarse stockings completed the attire, although
immediately after Aubrey's time it is lamented that the
shepherdesses—for there was a Phyllis to every Strephon—
had begun to make point lace, whereas before "they did
only knitt coarse stockings."   A later antiquary, Evelyn,
also notes (1680) that instead of slings the shepherds had
come to use a hollow iron or piece of horn, not unlike a
shoeing-horn, fastened to the other end of the crosier, by
which they took up stones and kept their flocks in
order.

In Aubrey's time these shepherds invariably took part
with other villagers in welcoming royalty and other distinguished visitors, with the performance of rustic music,
pastoral singing, and bucolic entertainments of a like
simple nature.   Indeed, if partiality has not painted this
writer's view with too roseate a tint, the Wiltshire shepherd had a recognised status and lived quite an idyllic
life in the "merrie England" of great Elizabeth's palmy
days.

In 1509 Alexander Barclay published his "Fifte Eglog"
which, in the form of a dialogue between a citizen and a
peasant, is intended to show the delights of a country life.
The accompanying illustration borrowed from that old
work treats the subject emblematically. The plants shown
under the two figures, with the segment of the earth
under the right one, indicate the fruitfulness of the earth.

But this fruitfulness comes only of a conjunction of labour, with the starry influences, the heat of the sun, the dews of night, and the rain of heaven. For this reason the celestial bodies are introduced into the picture. The left-hand figure is that of the labourer going to work in the morning, carrying his spade with him; that on the right is the labourer returning; the rod which each figure holds in the left hand symbolizes the union between earth and heaven, the "golden chain" which, in the idealism of the mediæval poets, united the whole cosmogony. The eclogue, however, does not lose sight of the Adamic curse :—

> "Ye shall be plowmen and tillers of the grounde
> To payne and labour shall ye alway be bounde
>
>   *   *   *   *   *
>
> To digge and to delve, to hedge and to dike,
> Take this for your lot, and other labour like;
> To drudge, and to dwell in workes vile and rude,
> This wise shall ye live in endless servitude"

To resume. By the appropriation of the common-lands the course of industry was changed with serious damage to the living generation. The effects became more alarming when the growing system of inclosures dis-possessed the irregular labourer of his hovel and his patch of waste; and flocks of sheep were fed where his half-starved cow had browsed upon the heath, and his scanty crop of cabbages and parsnips had eked out his miserable existence. But the squatter upon the commons clung to his life of penury and freedom, and when the system of inclosures forcibly applied the land to more profitable uses, he deliberately became a vagabond and a thief.

The miserable labourers who had eked out a scanty subsistence upon a barren heath were not the only people who were necessarily hostile to inclosures. The ancient race of small farmers had a deep interest in the preservation of unallotted land. Bishop Latimer, who was perfectly acquainted with country affairs, tells us of the old time he knew in his childhood, in that well-known passage in his "First Sermon before Edward VI.": " My father was a yeoman, and had no lands of his own, only he had a farm of three or four pound by year at the uttermost, and hereupon he tilled so much as kept half a dozen men. He had walk for a hundred sheep ; and my mother milked thirty kine. The kine and the sheep were fed on the common pasture-land." In another passage he describes how a "ploughman" must have sheep to manure the ground ; the turnip and winter root crop husbandry was then undreamt of. He must also have hogs, and horses, and kine for milk and cheese. "These cattle must have pasture, which pasture if they lack, the rest must needs fail them. And pasture they cannot have if the land be taken in, inclosed from them." That was the position of the small yeoman farmer.

A somewhat more favourable view of the situation has been taken by Froude, who gives some interesting figures as to the markets and wages at this period. The price of wheat fluctuated with the harvests, the average being 6s. 8d. a quarter, above which figure the merchants generally imported to bring it down again. Beef and pork were a halfpenny a pound, and mutton three-farthings—these prices being fixed by Parliament, 24 *Henry VIII.* Needless to say the Act was unpopular both with buyers and sellers. The butchers objected to sell by weight (says Stow), for at that time—

"fat oxen sold for six-and-twenty shillings and eightpence the piece ; fat wethers for three shillings and fourpence the piece ; fat calves at a like price ; and fat lambs for twelvepence. . . . The butchers of London sold penny pieces of beef for the relief of the poor, every piece two pounds and a half, sometimes three pounds; and thirteen and sometimes fourteen of these pieces for twelvepence; mutton eightpence the quarter."

The Act was repealed in consequence of the complaints against it, but the prices never fell again to what they had been, although beef sold in the gross could be had for a halfpenny a pound in 1570. Rent cannot be gauged so accurately, though Bishop Latimer, in the foregoing quotation, has left us some data to work upon. In estimating these prices it is below the truth to assume that the penny, in the terms of a labourer's necessities, was equal to the present shilling.

For at that time the penny would buy the labourer more bread, beef, and beer—he could certainly do more towards finding lodging for himself and his family, such as it was —than the labourer of the present day can purchase for a shilling.

An earlier Act (6 *Henry VIII.*) ordered that master carpenters, masons, bricklayers, tylers, plummers, glaziers, joiners, and other employers of such skilled workmen, should pay their journeymen, if no meat or drink was allowed, sixpence a day for half the year, and fivepence a day for the other half. The common labourers were to receive fourpence a day for half the year; for the remaining half threepence. In the harvest-time they were allowed to work by the piece, and might then earn considerably more. They were engaged by contract for not less than a year, and could not be thrown out of employment except through some gross fault of their own, and their offence proved before two magistrates.

Froude reckons, by allowing a deduction of one day a week for a saint's day or a holiday, that a well-conducted man received an equivalent of a modern twenty shillings a week wage. And the day a week was not the full account of his advantages, as the eminent historian goes on to take cognizance of the common-lands upon which, if he were not dispossessed, his ducks and geese, or even his cow, if he had one, might graze; the open forest lands where his pig might range, and where he might gather his fuel gratis; and similar advantages not unknown to the primitive lives led by English rustics.

In the early decades of Henry VIII.'s reign Sir Thomas More complains bitterly in his writings of the process then going on throughout rural England. He tells the nobles that "their sheep are no longer meek and gentle, but have become so great devourers they swallow up men!"

Thus began the system of inclosures, and the development of the wool trade into the staple of England; of which the Lord Chancellor's woolsack is the emblem to this day, and has been since the reign of Elizabeth, when wool was regarded as the source of the national wealth, and its exportation strictly forbidden. In 1548 the Protector, Somerset, appointed a Commission to inquire into the decay of tillage and the excessive inclosure of land for pasturage. Neither legislation nor inquiry seems to have had any deterrent effect; with the result that in 1548 "lewd persons" assembled in many counties to pull down the inclosures, and were almost in a state of rebellion demanding the redress of their agrarian grievances. In 1551, when a tax on sheep was proposed, it was estimated that there were a million and a half of these animals in inclosed pastures, and a similar number on the commons. For this was only the beginning of the inclosure movement, which has been going on ever since. A million acres have been inclosed since 1845; in the previous half-century even more land than this had been filched from the people by means of four thousand private Acts of Parliament.

The extraordinary provisions of the first statute of Edward VI., for making slaves of unwilling labourers, has been interpreted as a distinct proof of a demand for labour. It has been suggested that the lowest of the rural population, so long accustomed to an unsettled and irregular industry, which had about it a sort of wild independence, would not work for the masters who pulled down their hovels and made the waste lands profitable. Some few of the wiser and more prudent of these, however, emigrated, "and sought to live in other countries, as France, Germany, Barbary, India, Muscovy, and very Calicut; complaining of no room to be left for them at home."

It has been contended that the application of the commercial principle which drove English peasants to distant lands, came in due time to provide profitable employment for five times the population which had been displaced; a population which at best had derived but a meagre subsistence from the land.

No avenue to new forms of employment was open in the towns, even supposing these displaced agriculturists could have changed their mode of earning a living. The rigid system of exclusiveness under which the artificers banded themselves together in guilds, with hard conditions of apprenticeship and other like restrictions, effectively shut out ambitious farm-hands, had there been any, from the trading communities. Little wonder, therefore, that so many of these unfortunates fell away from the ranks of the industrious, and that Edward VI. was constrained to write, in allusion to this unhappy condition of his kingdom, "For idle persons, there were never, I think, more than be now."

The changing from arable to pasture had caused an industrial disturbance which was of national magnitude; and when small holdings were thrown into large farms agricultural conditions were not bettered, lessening as it did the yeomen class, in which the strength of England was, in Elizabeth's days, supposed to reside.   Acts were passed against the formation of large farms.   One anticipated by three centuries the once-popular cry of the Right Hon. Jesse Collings, M.P., for "three acres and a cow."   No cottage was allowed to be built without a plot of four acres attached; while wages, which had begun to be treated as a matter to be settled by the law of supply and demand, were yearly regulated to suit the varying value of the precious metals.   This delicate operation was left in the hands of the county magistrates, who, as we shall see, manipulated the scale of wages to suit their own ends.

In 1551 the legislature betrayed its anxiety by passing an Act to encourage the very desirable increase in tillage, particularly in an extension of the corn lands for the upkeep of the national supply of corn.

The Act of 1589, which prohibited the building of cottages unless four acres of land were attached to each, also forbade more than one family to live in each house, and the Courts Leet were, consequently, most inquisitorial in searching out illegal inmates of any dwelling-house. It is worth noting, too, that the old manorial system of Wales required four acres to every tenement.

One effect of this was to drive the population from the country into the towns.

Going back only to 1685, there were still in existence eighteen million acres of open country, consisting of moorland, forest, and fen.

The remnants of the common-lands still left around London and the other populous towns of the country— often glorious stretches of heath and fern, furze and moss—serve now mostly as breathing-spaces and open resorts for recreative purposes only; in former times their purposes were far more utilitarian. In some the people had right of turbary, and other privileges, then regarded as valuable; in all they had the right of grazing. Where are now those ancient rights in the stolen inclosures ?

> "A sin it is in man or woman
> To steal a goose from off a common ;
> But he may steal without excuse
> Who steals the common off a goose."

X

AFTER THE DISSOLUTION

Closing of the monasteries—Results in a multitude of destitute—
An increase of vagabondage—And decay of pilgrim towns like
Walsingham—"Pilgrimage of Grace"—New statute against
vagabonds (1 *Ed VI*.)—Impotent licensed to beg (1531)—
Vagabonds whipped—Ordered to beg their way straight home
and remain there.—Milder punishments proposed—Relief works
suggested at Dover—Provision for the real poor.—Valiant
beggars punished by whipping, branding, mutilation, and
death—Outrages by the unemployed (1545)—Thousands of
victims for the gallows—Statute of Vagabonds (1547)—Vagabonds branded with V—And made the slaves of their "pre-
sentors" for two years—A runaway slave to be branded S—And
made a slave for life—These severities called for repeal two
years later—Gigge-mills and threatened insurrection.

AFTER the Conquest the number of religious houses
increased largely, till the whole country was dotted with
them. And when the monasteries were suppressed by
Henry VIII., there was an utter obliteration of an order
of things which had existed in this country for a thousand
years.

The attitude of the Church at this crisis is not always
clearly understood. It must be remembered that the
secular clergy had a long-standing grievance against the
monks for their greedy, grasping appropriation of
Church property; consequently, when the fall of the
monasteries occurred, the very last people to lament it
were the parochial clergy.

After the dissolution of all the religious houses the immense inconvenience of a large and helpless section of the community, who had hitherto been supported in habits of indolence and beggary, being suddenly brought face to face with destitution, was immediately felt throughout the length and breadth of the land. As a direct consequence, in this reign and the succeeding ones we find a plentiful crop of new statutes attempting to make some sort of provision for the poor and impotent, the preambles of most of them reciting the ever-increasing evil of pauperism.

The effect of the dissolution of the abbeys upon this increase of misery, clamouring for aid, has been usually limited to the supposed absence of the relief which those houses afforded to the local poor, by doles out of the monastic abundance. Upon this it has been argued that the monasteries encouraged idle and improvident habits, and that their suppression was a real benefit to the labourer. This was true to the extent that it tended to make him more self-reliant.

When the tenure of these great properties was wholly changed ; when the monastic domains fell into the hands of those who only sought to obtain the best rents ; there was a disturbance of the labouring population, of which we have ample evidence in the extraordinary increase of pauperism and vagabondage.

In a case like that of the town of Walsingham the local distress must indeed have been terrible for the time being. The shrine of Our Lady in its famous abbey had for generations attracted countless numbers of pilgrims with their never-failing votive offerings—no less distinguished a one was King Henry VIII. himself—and now this great source of revenue was suddenly cut off, leaving nothing to replace it.

Pitiable is the report of how this town had fallen into

decay, "by sundry occasions of late happened," when no pilgrims resorted hither ; when the monks ceased to employ artisans about their house, labourers to dig, retailers to provide many comforts and luxuries, servants to wait upon them, and when every inn and hostelry on the road was deserted.

The monks themselves wandered about the country asking the alms which they formerly bestowed ; and their former servants and labourers swelled the numbers of the roving population.

A great wave of discontent spread over the land, and in the northern counties forty thousand men rose in arms under a gentleman named Robert Aske. This rising, which occurred in 1536–7, was known as the "Pilgrimage of Grace," and its chief object was the re-establishment of the Roman faith and the restoration of the monasteries. Some of the leaders, among them the last Abbot of Whalley, who adopted the title of "the Earl of Poverty," were promptly executed, and the movement collapsed.

In the Salt Library at Stafford is an extremely rare old tract recording a presentation once made to Queen Anne Boleyn by her "most bou'den bedeman, William Marshall," that there might be found "wayes and means most comodious" to deal in a "gratiouse" manner with the poor ; for at that time (it is dated about the time of the birth of Queen Elizabeth) "so great a multytude of poore and nedy folkes, the which in every strete and chyrche and at everyman's dore, yea and in every place within the realme, idly lacyuoyously and dissolutely ar wonte and have been accustomed to go ronne and wander about lyke vacaboundes."

The Statute of Vagabonds of the first year of his Protestant Majesty, Edward VI., like similar statutes directed against beggars and vagabonds in the previous century, seems in its ferocity to have been written in letters of blood. During the hundred and forty-seven years between 1384 (7 *Richard II.*) and 1531 (22 *Henry VII.*) vagabonds were to be put in the stocks. (The prison came to be dispensed with as too expensive.) Then the whip was added to the stocks.

The law of 1531 had authorized justices to give a licence to impotent persons to beg, within certain specified limits; but those who solicited alms without such letter under seal, were to be whipped and set in the stocks.

It was ordered that any idle person being whole in body and able to labour, if found begging, should be whipped at the end of a cart, and then enjoined to return to the place where he was born, or where he last dwelt, for a space of three years, "there to put himself to labour, as a true man oweth to do." He was permitted to beg his way home, but if he wandered from the direct path, or exceeded the prescribed time, he was in every place to be taken and whipped.

It will be observed there was no provision for sustaining the weak and helpless, no attempt to provide the strong and able-bodied with employment. But truly at that time the labour market was full, and there was no surplus capital wherewith to stimulate employment; and the legislators must therefore be exonerated. All punishments were devised in those times with peculiar ferocity—poisoners were actually boiled in a cauldron! If the organisation of feudalism had gone, at least some of its spirit remained.

Five years later, however, a newer if not a milder spirit begins to manifest itself, though but as a passing gleam. The "king's grace" delivered a Bill among the burgesses in Parliament, bidding them weigh well in their conscience its provisions, which at last proposed "There shall be a provision made for poor people. The gaols shall be rid; the faulty shall die; and the others shall be acquit by proclamation or by jury, and shall be set at liberty, and pay no fees; and sturdy beggars and such prisoners as cannot be set to work, shall be set a work at the king's charges, some at Dover, and some at the place where the water hath broken in on the land, and other more places. Then if they fall to idleness, the idler shall be had before a justice of the peace, and his fault written. Then if he be taken idle again in another place he shall be known where his dwelling is, and so at the second mention he shall be burned in the hand, and if he fail the third time he shall die for it." The Act of 1536, indeed, varies somewhat from this draft proposal, although its most striking feature was the salutary regulation making some provision for poor people. It contained clauses, directed as of old, with extreme severity against "rufflers, sturdy vagabonds, and valiant beggars."

For the first offence, whipping; for the second, whipping again, and "the upper part of the gristle of the right ear cut clean off." If apprehended a third time so mutilated, the incorrigible offender was to be committed to gaol, and at the next quarter-sessions indicted for wandering, loitering, and idleness, and upon conviction to be adjudged "to suffer the pains and execution of death as a felon, and as an enemy of the commonwealth." The awful wickedness which, while recognising the futility of similar correctives in the past, could design a punishment so drastic for an economic evil, reflects but too clearly the condition of society at the time, and the state of the public conscience. To the whip and the butcher's knife the penalty of a felon's death was now added; yet all alike signally failed to correct the evil. In all this we see evidenced the uncompromising spirit of the old rhyme :—

> "He that will not live by toil
> Has no right on English soil."

This barbarous law held good for ten years, from Henry VIII. to Edward VI. As for the real poor, "those poor in very deed," semi-voluntary collections were to be levied in church, appointed collectors were to "gently ask every man and woman" for alms on behalf of the deserving poor. This system never realized the expectations of its framers ; no measure of success attended the effort even after defaulters had been visited by the admonitions of their bishop. This subject will be referred to in the next chapter.

Labourers displaced by the inclosure of the commons, and all other out-of-works, claimed what they called their "liberty," and wandered heedlessly up and down the country, even under the terror of the whip; and not a few of them, we may read, "did continue stark thieves, till the gallows did eat them up." In 1545 a disposition manifested itself in those who imagined themselves wronged under the new agrarian system, not very dissimilar to that which, three centuries later, exhibited itself in rick-burnings. Fresh legislation was called for to check those malicious persons who gave vent to their feelings in the wanton destruction of property. "The secret burning of frames of timber, prepared and made by the owners thereof, ready to be set up and edified for houses, was the malicious assertion of the imaginary rights of the squatters to hold their own hovels of sticks and dirt." Carts laden with charcoal, and heaps of felled timber, were set on fire ; fruit trees were barked ; cattle were maimed. "It was the war of the savage against the settler," says the historian of the period, "a war which always contains some rude principle of imaginary right, but which had to be repressed with heavy penalties, unless a barrier be set up against human progress."

That seventy-two thousand thieves and vagabonds were hanged during the reign of Henry VIII. is scarcely a correct statement; but it is quite possible that in one year of the thirty-seven, some two thousand of these offenders found their way to the gallows. Towards the end of the reign a kind of thieves' guild came into existence; it was a professional organisation of thieves, robbers, and cheats.

The reforming Government of Edward VI. were confronted with the fact that the system of terrorism had utterly failed in its object. The cart's tail, the butcher's knife, and the hangman's noose had manifestly inspired no dread. By the rural population the accession of the boy king, it was said, was looked upon with considerable hopefulness of better things in store. " The people confess themselves most bound to God that He hath sent them such a king, in whose so tender age so much good is intended towards them; and have a great hope that the Iron world is now at an end, and the Golden is returning again." Unfortunately these hopes were unrealised. The tender mind of the young king was taught to consider the thriftless poor—"those who ran to and fro over all the realm, chiefly keeping the champain soils in summer to avoid the scorching heat, and the woodland grounds in winter to eschew the blustering winds"—all such as these were to be regarded as noxious weeds to be rooted out. They are spoken of as the " filth " of the body politic, and were to be treated as such.

There was no hesitation, therefore, in 1547 in passing "An Act for the Punishment of Vagabonds;" the chief provisions of which astounding piece of legislation were to the following effect: All the former Acts against Vagabonds and sturdy beggars being repealed, it is provided that every man or woman, not being prevented from working by old age, lameness or disease, who shall be found loitering or wandering and not seeking work, during three days, or who shall leave work when engaged, may be lawfully apprehended, and brought before two justices of the peace ; who, upon confession, or on the proof of two witnesses, "shall immediately cause the said loiterer to be marked with a hot iron in the breast, the mark of V, and adjudge the said person, living so idly, to his presentor, to be his slave."

The convicted delinquent was to become the slave of his "presentor," as he was called, for two years, who was to give him bread and water and refuse food to eat, and "to cause the said slave to work, by beating, chaining, or otherwise, in such work and labour, how vile soever it be, as he shall put him unto." If the slave should run away during the said two years, he was to be pursued, and any person detaining him was liable to a penalty of ten pounds. Convicted of running away, the justices could cause the runaway slave to be branded on the forehead or the ball of the cheek with the letter S, and then adjudged to his master as a slave for ever. The penalty for running away a second time was to be put to the death as a felon. The master to whom the slave was so adjudged might put a collar of iron about his neck, or fetters on his limbs. If no man could be found to take the culprit as his slave, he was to be sent to the place where he was born, and there kept in slavery to work on the public roads ; or alternatively he might be let or sold to any private person who was prepared to chain, starve, and beat him according to the tenour of this Act.

There were special provisions in the statute for committing clerics convicted of offences to limited periods of slavery ; while infant beggars might be bound to the service of any person willing to take them, to use their services till the males came to twenty-four years of age and the females to twenty ; and if they ran away, they were to be brought back and made to suffer the severer discipline of slavery.

Merely to recall an enactment of this character seems almost like an outrage upon modern thought and feeling. It reveals the extraordinary state of society that an English Parliament could calmly contemplate not merely the infliction of death as a meet punishment for the comparatively venial offence of vagrancy, but could specifically revive by name an institution which the nation was supposed to have outgrown. These things were being done, be it observed, at the time when the foundations of modern England were being laid ; and surely of all things abhorrent to the national sentiment, there is nothing so damnable as slavery. It is not surprising that this remarkable Act was repealed two years later, the Government (perhaps influenced not a little by the insurrectionary wave which passed over the country in 1549) acknowledging that the law could not be carried out because of "the extremities" of the penalties imposed.

In 1551 an Act was passed for the suppression of gigge-mills, a newly devised invention for "the perching and burling of cloth." The ostensible reason given forth for this enactment was that the new mechanical process was "spoiling the true drapery of this realm ;" but the underlying motive was a deadly fear of the jealousy of the operative class manifested towards machinery which interfered with their manual labour—a jealousy which led in some parts to the outbreak of violence, and might therefore revive the wave of insurrection. The country was truly in a parlous state.

XI

AFTER THE REFORMATION

The Reformation robs guild craftsmen of their pension funds—
Severe penalties against vagrancy still fail—growing prosperity
of the country—Yet body of unemployed remains large—The
exclusiveness of the trade guilds a deterrent to general
employment—" Pierce Pennilesse " on the rise of " base men " to
affluence—The struggle between preconceived notions and actual
experience—As to provision for impotent poor—Compulsory
almsgiving instituted (1552)—Appointment of Collectors of
Alms—Amending statutes (1555 and 1557)—Any refusing alms to
be committed to prison—New Act in 1573—Registration for
relief of all poor, aged, and impotent persons—Overseers of the
Poor to be elected—All not wholly disabled to be set on work—
New Act in 1576 empowers provision of material for pauper
labour—And Houses of Correction for the idle—These tentative
enactments—In which the justices and not the ratepayers'
representatives constitute the rating authority—Last twenty
years—A quotation from " Anatomie of Abuses " on the working
of the system of legalised benevolence.

THE closing of all the religious houses by Henry VIII.
brought down upon the country an avalanche of destitution
and vagabondage ; and as the years of that arbitrary
monarch grew to a close the evil of pauperism increased.

This evil has generally been recognised as an indirect
effect of the Reformation. In addition to the suppression
of the monasteries, whereby a great source of charitable
relief was cut off, there was the seizure of the guild funds
in towns and villages during the reign of Edward VI.,

whereby was destroyed at one blow the workman's hope of support in sickness and old age. A widespread controversy afterwards raged on " the true conditions of Christian charity." Academic discussions, however, do not fill empty stomachs.

The legislature then went back to the comparatively mild provisions of the Act of 1532; passing over the heavier inflictions contemplated by that of 1536. Of these statutes it has been ably observed by Sir G. Nicholls, the great historian of the English Poor Law, that " each gradation in the scale of punishment was tried, abandoned, re-established with added stringency, and again abandoned, with a lingering pertinacity which can only be accounted for by the struggle between experience and preconceived notions."

The parishes were called upon to relieve the sick and the aged; and the justices were to punish the able-bodied beggar according to the first statute of Henry VIII. The time was steadily, if slowly, approaching when compulsory provision for the poor would place this difficult question upon the basis of all subsequent legislation; yet for years after the Reformation vagabondage was the great evil of English society.

With the sudden repeal of the wicked and foolish Statute of Vagabondage it seems to have been felt that the whole economic position needed carefully reviewing —that something more effectual than severity was necessary to be applied to a large number of the population who were unable to work, or unwilling to work, or for whom no work was provided—a large body who from various causes found no place in the ranks of the industrious.

There was a large number of these who would not be content to starve whilst beggary or thievery offered a last resource.

The country, generally, was growing richer in the advance of profitable industry, and the population by the end of the sixteenth century was not far short of five millions.

In the towns the close organisation of the trade guilds excluded from competition with the recognised artisan all who had not been apprenticed and brought up to the craft or calling. The workmen in the towns formed, to all intents and purposes, an exclusive caste. Yet some of the more fortunate of the humbler classes were forcing their way to wealth ; resolute spirits who climbed to fortune by never-ceasing toil and thrift. Writes that lively satirist of the age, Thomas Nash, in his " Pierce Pennilesse "—when painting the situation in 1592—he is always eloquent on the subject of the

<blockquote>
" ungentle frown
When changing fortune casts us headlong down " :—
</blockquote>

" Having spent many years in studying how to live, and lived a long time without money, having tired my youth with folly, and surfeited my mind with vanity, I began at length to look back to repentance, and addressed my endeavours to prosperity ; but all in vain. I sat up late and rose early, contended with the cold and conversed with scarcity ; for all my labours turned to loss ; my vulgar muse was despised and neglected."

And yet " base men," as he calls them, could thrive.

" I call to mind," he continues, " a cobbler that was worth five hundred pounds ; an hostler that had built a goodly inn ; a carman in a leather pilch [a thick shaggy protection worn in much riding to ease the seat] that had whipped a thousand pounds out of his horses' tail."

So that the road to wealth was opening out to the meanest, if they could but find the entrance to it.

Still there was a vast amount of poverty in the country, of which the law was bound to take cognizance. In 1552 a tentative process, by which the principle of a public contribution for the relief of the poor, was optimistically approached by yet another new statute.

It was ordered that a book should be kept in each parish, in which should be entered the names of all householders, and also of the impotent poor. In Whitsun week two or more persons were to be appointed as Collectors of Alms; and on the Sunday following, when the people were at church, "the said Collectors shall gently ask and demand of every man and woman, what they of their charity will give weekly towards the relief of the poor." The money collected each week was to be distributed by the same Collectors, "after such sort that the more impotent may have the more help, and such as can get part of their living, have the less; and by the discretion of such Collector to be put in such labour as they are able to do."

If any person, being able to contribute, refused, he was to be gently exhorted by the parson and churchwardens; and if these exhortations failed, he was to be sent for by the bishop, to be induced and persuaded to so charitable a deed.

A statute of 1555, and another of 1557, continued to provide for the impotent poor by weekly collections; the principle being held by Parliament to be "good and beneficial for the commonwealth of this realm." The same principle was maintained by the statute of 1563, but something more stringent than the exhortations of churchwardens, parson, and bishop was to be applied. "If any person of his froward and wilful mind shall obstinately refuse to give weekly to the relief of the poor according to his ability," the bishop had power to bind him to appear at the next sessions, when the justices, if he continued obstinate, might determine what sum he should pay, and commit him to prison if he persisted in his refusal.

The statute was thus worded :—

"The Poor and impotent persons of every parish shall be relieved of that which every person will of their charity give weekly; and the same relief shall be gathered in every parish by Collectors assigned, and weekly distributed to the poor; for none of them shall openly go or sit begging. And if any parishioners shall obstinately refuse to pay reasonably toward the relief of the said poor, or shall discourage others; then the Justices of the Peace at the Quarter Sessions may tax him to a reasonable sum; which, if he refuses to pay, they may commit him to prison."

As an illustration of how the plan worked in actual practice it is recorded that the " Collectors assigned " to carry out the provisions of the Act in the parish of St. George's, Canterbury, were Christopher Lewys and Thomas Kyng, and that the amount of the year's collection was the miserable sum of injd.

In 1573 was passed " An Act for the punishment of vagabonds, and for the relief of the poor and impotent." It repealed all previous enactments by one sweeping law ; but though the old severity against rogues, vagabonds, and sturdy beggars underwent little mitigation, it emphatically declared that poor, aged, and impotent persons should be provided for.

It required the justices of the peace in their several divisions to make diligent inquiry for all such impotent poor, and to register them, as before, including those born within the division and those who had lived there by alms within the preceding years ; to assign them convenient places for their habitation, if the parish had not provided for them ; to assess the inhabitants of the division to a weekly charge, and to appoint Overseers of the Poor, who should have the power to set to work all such diseased or impotent persons who were not wholly disabled.

It will be observed that this Act approaches nearer the system of parochial administration which was subsequently developed; but as yet the justices, and not elective officials, were to make the assessment, which is an essential difference.

By an Act of 1576 a stock of wool and hemp was to be provided for setting the poor at work, and Houses of Correction were to be established.

For some twenty years the law remained in this state of transition, and then was passed the epoch-making statute 39 *Elizabeth* which (with that of 43 *Elizabeth*) formed the ground-work of the English Poor Laws till the comparatively modern date of 1834.

The voluntary system of legalized benevolence had signally failed, as most voluntary systems of this kind do fail; human nature is such that it generally requires compulsory powers which permit of no evasion to collect contributions levied alike upon the generous and the grudging.   But voluntaryism was worthy of a trial, and while it lasted offered a fine field for the exercise of that fine spirit of Christian charity which every one admires, if all of us do not practise.   Commenting upon the subject in 1583, Stubbes in his " Anatomie of Abuses," a vehement denunciation of the luxury of the times, says :—

"The sabbath day of some is well observed, namely in hearing the word of God read, preached, and interpreted ; in private and in public prayers; in singing of godly psalms; in celebrating the sacraments; and in collecting for the poor and indigent."

It has been seen that the voluntary system for the relief of the poor and the needy was associated from the very earliest times with the Church.   Consequently, when the system gave way to compulsory methods, the machinery of the Church was still utilized ; as through the church-wardens and overseers of the poor, always elected in vestry ; as in the practice of fixing legal notices on church doors ; and so on. And because in those days attendance at church was also compulsory upon all adults, it was inferred by legislators that no parishioner would escape the attention of the alms collectors and other Church officials. To this day legal notices of various kinds, and particularly those connected with rating, are regularly affixed to the doors of all churches and other places of worship—it still remaining a legal fiction that this is the most effective method of publication possible.

XII

"SPITALS"

Hospital, hospice, *hospitium*, a home of rest and entertainment—
Knights Hospitallers—St. John Ambulance Society—Monastic
Infirmaries—Monkish leeches—Sad effects of the Dissolution—
Five "royal" hospitals refounded as civic institutions—
"Spitals" and Spitalfields—The Spital Sermons—At St. Mary's
—Attended by royalty in state—At St Bride's—At Christ
Church—Attended by Governors of the Royal Hospitals—
Customs and civic ceremonials—St. Bartholomew's—A mediæval
institution for sick poor—Its quaint management—Reconstruc-
tion at Reformation—St Thomas's—The Savoy Hospital—Bridewell, a charity and penal establishment—Located in lawless
district of "Alsatia"—The flogging in Bridewell—An industrial
training-school for poor boys—Modern reconstruction—Why
"Bridewell" became a common name—Eighteenth-century
hospitals—Guy's Hospital—Medical foundations and charitable
institutions.

THE word "hospital" in the past has had a wide signification, being sometimes applied to an institution for the
reception of the poor and the aged, or to one for the
mentally defective, or again to an asylum for the crippled
and the permanently incapacitated, as well as to one for
the treatment of the sick.

Originally the term "hospital" was used generally in the
form of "hospice," to denote an inn or house of entertainment for pilgrims and wayfarers. The Knights
Hospitallers, for instance, were founded to provide

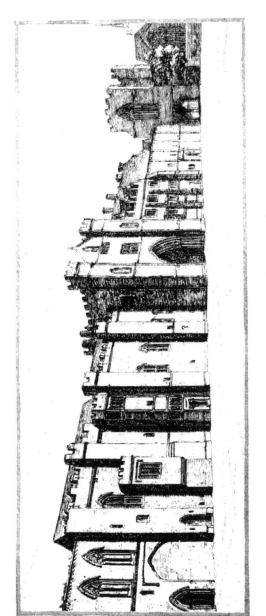

PRIORY OF KNIGHTS OF ST. JOHN IN 1580.

To face p. 13).

hospitium, or lodging and entertainment for pilgrims to the Holy Land. But in process of time the word "hospital" came to indicate a resort, shelter, or asylum for the sick and infirm only.

The Hospitallers were a charitable brotherhood who devoted themselves to tending the sick in hospital, and took their rise during the hardest fighting in the Crusades ; being known at various periods of their history as Hospitallers of St. John of Jerusalem, Knights of St. John, Knights of Rhodes, and Knights of Malta, changes more significant of their history as a military order than as a religious or benevolent organisation.

They vowed themselves to poverty, charity, and obedience ; to live a life of austerity, asking alms, of which two-thirds were to be given to the poor. But, like the Templars and other mediæval "religious" orders, if they began in poverty, they ended in luxury and corruption. The order was suppressed in England in 1559. St. John's Gate, Clerkenwell, is a relic of their ancient possessions ; and the name is perpetuated in the modern St. John Ambulance Association, established in 1877, by the new Order of St. John of Jerusalem, revived and reorganised on the Continent in 1852 for rendering energetic assistance to the wounded in war, and incorporated by Royal Charter in England in 1888. Its beneficent work is best known by its dissemination of instruction in "first aid," or preliminary treatment of the sick and injured pending the arrival of a medical man. It is interesting to note that the original fraternity, as a hospital order, admitted women to affiliation. They also made it a duty to bury the dead, criminals and suicides.

The hospitals of mediæval England were founded for a variety of benevolent objects ; the primary class, to which belonged such institutions as the Strangers' Hall at Winchester and the Pilgrim House, Battle, was for the reception of travellers, as poor wayfarers going to Rome or popular shrines ; another class was for women lying-in, for the sick, the feeble, and the destitute, St. John's at Canterbury being one of the most ancient, and that of St. Katherine's-by-the-Tower being established for women and children ; a number, to which reference will be made in a separate chapter, were founded for the reception of the insane, as Holy Trinity, Salisbury, though this institution, like many others of its kind, also took in the indigent sick and women in child-birth. Of the lazar-houses for lepers something has already been said. Another class, to which also a separate chapter will be devoted, were almshouses for the poor and the aged, or, as they were called, Bedehouses. But to every kind of "hospital" a chapel was invariably attached, and in pre-Reformation times the life of the inmates was essentially one of religious routine.

In olden times ignorant neglect of every hygienic law, a woful disregard of all sanitation, public and private, was responsible for the repeated visitations of plague and pestilence, which added to the misery of the people, and sometimes impoverished a whole town or countryside. In some quarters the air was scarcely ever free from infection.

Of public provision against these waves of plague and pestilence, which periodically swept away thousands of the population, there was practically none.

Wolsey, we read, when giving an audience to poor petitioners, invariably carried in his hand an orange in which a sponge of scent was inserted, a device which perhaps smothered a stench if it could not ward off infection. A favourite pomander was an orange stuck over with cloves. Of public efforts, the favourite device when the scourge commenced its ravages was to burn tar-barrels in the streets.

The genesis of the hospitals and homes for the relief of the indigent sick begins with the old monastic establishments of the land. It is much to be feared that the pre-Reformation institutions, monastic and non-monastic, were all very badly managed. At first there was little discrimination between one kind of afflicted person and another; the leper, the lunatic, and the cripple were often herded together.

Every day in a large monastery, soon after *mixtum*, or breakfast, the infirmarer went his round in the hospital.

The monks were the earliest leeches. In most religious houses of any considerable size was a bleeding-house called "Fleobo-maria," and the operation was known as "minution." The monks of the Middle Ages desired to be bled regularly on account of eating meat, each one submitting to about four bleedings a year. In one order the brethren were bled five times a year : in September, before Advent, before Lent, after Easter, and at Pentecost, each bleeding lasting three days. After the third day they came to Matins, and on the fourth received absolution.

Among the ancient documents relating to the priory of Lewes is a deed of 1307, from which it would appear that the patrons of such foundations held it as a valued privilege to be treated by the monkish leeches. In the said deed William de Echingham, in surrendering certain of his privileges for a large money consideration, sets forth the following as the first among them, if not the most important :—

"The Priory was bound to receive me, with my wife and all my family four times every year, for myself and my wife to be blooded (*flebolomisandos*) and to dwell there at the expense of the priory each time for three days and on the fourth day to the hearing and singing the mass," &c., &c.

All mediæval hospitals being religious foundations or in some way attached to religious houses, the suppression of the latter naturally proved most disastrous to them. The sick people were sent back to their own houses ; the brethren and sisters were dispersed. One house contained a hundred blind men who were all turned adrift ;. another contained a number of aged priests who were thrown upon the streets ; and for a time London was without a single institution for the relief of the suffering.

This could not continue, and in a short time (as will appear presently) St. Bartholomew's, St. Thomas's, the Bethlehem, and, under Queen Mary, the Savoy, were all re-founded as hospitals under new statutes.

As we have seen, the lazar-houses, for the reception of leprosy and contagious disease, were becoming obsolete at this period, even had they not been suppressed.

When the problem of the poor forced itself upon public notice for solution, after the Reformation and the Dissolution of the Monasteries, it was seen that the objects of public concern were principally of two sorts : the sick and the impotent who were unable to work ; the idle and sturdy who were unwilling to engage in any honest employment. It was to provide in some measure for both these in and about the metropolis that Edward VI. founded three hospitals—Christ's and St. Thomas's, for the relief of the impotent during infancy or sickness ; and Bridewell, for the punishment and employment of the vigorous and idle. (By a later enactment Houses of Correction, frequently called " Bridewells," were provided for every county.) St. Bartholomew's had just been inaugurated as a hospital for the sick, but was not fully endowed till 1552 ; and the Bethlehem hospital had been incorporated as a royal foundation for the reception of lunatics.

The "five royal hospitals" which were thus placed under "the pious care" of the Lord Mayor of London subsequently to the Reformation period are St. Bartholomew's, St. Thomas's, Bridewell, Bethlehem, and Christ's.

The name hospital, as applied to a place "for poore folkes diseased," was abbreviated to a Spital, or Spittle, and is seen in the London place-name Spital-fields, once a rural district in which was situated the Priory and Hospital of St. Mary, Bishopsgate Street.

"Spital Sermons" were originally preached at the hospital in a pulpit expressly erected for the purpose. Ben Jonson alludes to them in his "Underwoods."

This hospital had a large churchyard with a pulpit cross, from whence it was an ancient custom on Easter Monday, Tuesday, and Wednesday for sermons to be preached on the Resurrection, before the Lord Mayor, Aldermen, Sheriffs, and others, who sat in a gallery of two stories for that purpose; the Bishop of London and other prelates being above them. In 1594 the pulpit was taken down and a new one set up, and also a large house for the Governors and children of Christ's Hospital to sit in. In April, 1559, Queen Elizabeth came in great state from St. Mary Spital, attended by a thousand men in harness, with shirts of mail and croslets and morris pikes, and ten great pieces carried through London unto the court, with drums, flutes and trumpets sounding, and two morris dancers, and two white bears in a cart. On Easter Monday, 1617, King James I. having gone to Scotland, the Archbishop of Canterbury, the Lord Keeper Bacon, the Bishop of London, and certain other lords of the Court, and Privy Councillors attended the Spital Sermon with Sir John Lemman, Lord Mayor, and the Aldermen; and afterwards rode home and dined with the Lord Mayor at his house near Billingsgate.

The hospital itself was dissolved under Henry VIII.;

the pulpit was broken down during the troubles of Charles I.; and after the Restoration the sermons denominated "Spital Sermons" were preached at St. Bride's Church, Fleet Street, on the three usual days.

Subsequently the Spital Sermons were removed to Christ Church, Newgate Street, and attended by the Lord Mayor and Aldermen, and the Governors of Christ's, St. Bartholomew's, St. Thomas's, Bridewell, and Bethlehem Hospitals. It was the custom on Easter Monday for the boys of Christ's Hospital to walk in procession, accompanied by the masters and steward, to the Royal Exchange, from thence to the Mansion House, to join the Lord Mayor, Lady Mayoress, Sheriffs, Aldermen, Recorder, Chamberlain, Town Clerk, and other civic officers with their ladies. From thence the cavalcade proceeded to Christ Church, where the Spital Sermon was preached by one of the Bishops, and an anthem sung by the boys. On the Tuesday there was another procession of the schoolboys to the Mansion House, but accompanied by the matron and nurses instead of by the masters; on arrival each boy had the honour of being presented in turn to the Lord Mayor, who gave him a new sixpence, a glass of wine, and two buns. His Lordship then accompanied them to Christ Church to attend a similar service, the Spital Sermon on the Tuesday being usually preached by the Lord Mayor's Chaplain. This, briefly, is the history of the old City function known as the "Spital Sermons," which are now preached at Christ Church, Newgate Street.

No more notable example of a mediæval institution specially provided for the reception of the sick poor can be found than St. Bartholomew's Hospital, London. It was founded in the reign of Henry I., by a citizen named Rahere, who falling ill while on a pilgrimage to Rome, vowed that if he recovered he would show his gratitude to God by a charitable foundation for the sick poor. On his recovery and safe return he built the Augustinian Priory of St. Bartholomew at Smithfield, the church of which still stands in part, and beside it established his hospital. At first the hospital was a very small place, consisting of two large apartments, one for men and one for women, with the usual chapel attached for the daily singing of the Mass.

The hospital was a narrow, lofty apartment, dimly lit by narrow Norman windows, ill-ventilated, and heavy with the breath of the crowded patients. In the roof was a lantern, beneath which a fire burnt day and night to provide the necessary warmth, and perhaps also intended to counteract infection, the smoke from the brazier curling round and round the room, and never finding any sufficient outlet.

Beds for some sixty or seventy men were ranged round the walls, four patients in each bed, though in times of pressure this number was often exceeded. As the sufferers were brought in, they were laid in any vacant space without the least reference to their ailments, so that a fever case would be found in the same bed as one of palsy, and so on ; and if, as sometimes happened, one patient developed the plague, there was little hope of saving a single life among them.

The endowment of St. Bartholomew's Hospital must, at first, have been exceedingly small, as the master or hospitaller had to go every morning to the shambles at Newgate to buy the meat wherewith to feed the poor sufferers. In Becket's time a tithe of all goods coming into the palace of that princely ecclesiastic was sent to the hospital of St. Bartholomew.

The food was scanty, the remedies primitive, and the appliances crude ; but the tending of simple surgical

10

cases was not without skill, while the Sisters were really expert, as might be expected in a warlike age, in tying up a broken limb, or staunching a bleeding wound. And above all, even if there were little hope of recovery, it was better to die in hospital with all the consolations of religion at hand, than to expire, neglected and alone, in one's hovel of a home.

The Smithfield hospital was repaired and partly rebuilt by a bequest of the famous Sir Richard Whittington; and shortly afterwards, in the reign of Edward IV., its establishment was constituted of a master, eight brethren, priests, and four Sisters who served the sick. At the Dissolution the Priory and Hospital of Bartholomew fell with the rest, but five years later the hospital was re-founded, and endowed by the king and the City, as previously recorded.

At the inauguration of St. Bartholomew's in 1546, the Lord Mayor and principal citizens demonstrated "the great good of taking the poor from their miserable habitations," and thus induced the people to subscribe weekly to the support of the hospital till it was fully endowed in 1552. The number of the poor and sick to be maintained was limited to one hundred under the foundation of Henry VIII., but the numbers treated were increased from time to time.

After a beneficent existence of more than seven centuries, no hospital, it may be safely averred, holds a nobler record than St. Bartholomew's. Attached to it now are museums, libraries, and a magnificent School of Medicine, while its eight brethren have grown into a staff which includes thirty surgeons and physicians, with their attendant clerks and dressers ; and the four Sisters have increased fortyfold into a band of 160 trained nurses.

St. Thomas's Hospital, Southwark, was founded as an almshouse by the prior of Bermondsey in 1213 ; it surrendered to Henry VIII. in 1538.

In 1551 the City of London, having purchased of Edward VI. the manor of Southwark, including the hospital, repaired and enlarged it, and admitted into it 260 poor sick and helpless objects; upon which it was incorporated by the king in 1553, along with the other four "royal" hospitals.

Mention of the Savoy demands a few words on this hospital. Originally built as a palace by the all-powerful Simon de Montfort, in 1245, it was granted by Henry III. to Peter, Earl of Savoy, uncle to his queen, Eleanor of Provence, and from this obtained its name. In 1509, after being beautifully restored and rebuilt by Henry VII., it was opened as a hospital for the reception of a hundred poor people. The building was cruciform, and comprised the Hospital of St. John the Baptist in the Savoy and the Chapel of St. Mary in the Hospital, rejoicing in this double name and dedication.

Although the commissioners of Edward VI. reported that there was "no default and no disorder" to be found in its inmates, it was dissolved, and its revenues seized by royalty. Queen Mary re-founded and re-endowed the hospital, her maids of honour and the ladies of her Court "stored it anew with beds, bedding, and other furniture in very ample manner."

In Elizabeth's time the Savoy Hospital fared very badly, for although it escaped the royal claws, its revenues were embezzled by its unworthy master, who "sold away divers charities from it," ere he could be deprived of his office. (How many charities have suffered in like manner at the hands of those whose first duty it was to protect them?) The old building was demolished early in the nineteenth century to make the approaches to Waterloo Bridge.

Bridewell Hospital was endowed with the revenues of the Savoy, and fitted up by the City Companies in 1555.

Its history is interesting because it was always more or less of a penal establishment. At an early period it enfolded so many idle, abandoned, and "masterless people," that it proved a costly institution to the citizens.

It was situated in Whitefriars, close to that disreputable quarter which went by the name of "Alsatia"—a nickname derived from Alsace, the disturbed and unhappy frontier of contention between France and Germany— which, on account of James I. having foolishly preserved the mischievous right of sanctuary anciently belonging to the Carmelite monastery there, became a vile and dangerous slum, haunted by scoundrels and cheats, bullies and cut-throats, the common resort of skulking bankrupts and sullen homicides, broken lawyers, degraded clergymen, gaudy courtesans — in short, the vicious outcasts of London.

Bridewell, otherwise St. Bride's Well, was a prison as well a charity, and is perhaps better known as the former—"a house of correction for idle, vagrant, loose and disorderly persons, and night walkers, who are there set to hard labour, but receive clothes and diet." Hogarth shows us the prison side of Bridewell in "The Harlot's Progress"; it is depicted as a long, dilapidated, tiled shed, in which are seen a row of female prisoners beating hemp on wooden blocks, under the eye of a truculent-looking warder. The flogging at Bridewell, both of men and women, was administered on the naked back, before the court of governors, the president sitting with his hammer in hand; when his hammer fell, the punishment was deemed sufficient, and the culprit was taken from the post. The calls on the president to "knock" were always loud and incessant when a woman was being whipped; so that among the lower order it became a common form of reproach to cry after a woman, "Knock! Good Sir Robert! Oh! pray knock!" This

BRIDEWELL, 1822.

place of confinement, which was pulled down in 1863, was under the jurisdiction of the Governors of the Bridewell and Bethlehem Hospitals, and supported from the same funds.

It was also a hospital for indigent persons. Twenty "art-masters," generally decayed traders, were also lodged, and instructed about 140 apprentices. The boys learnt tailoring, weaving, flax-dressing, &c., and on leaving received the freedom of the City, and presents of £10 each. They wore a blue dress and white hats, and attended fires with an engine belonging to the hospital. The lads at last became so turbulent that in 1785 their special costume had to be abandoned. Yet it is recorded that some of the boys brought up in the institution rose to have seats on its board of governors.

The "Bridewell boys" had indeed made a bad reputation for themselves. Privileged to go to fires, they did more mischief by their audacity and perverseness than they did good by working their fire-engine. They infested the streets, behaving in so turbulent a manner as to terrorise the neighbourhood. In the November of 1755 a memorable report was presented at the court of governors, complaining of the behaviour of the boys at Bartholomew and Southwark Fairs; a number of them were severely punished, stripped of the hospital clothing, and discharged.

Afterwards, proper industrial training masters were engaged for the boys, and eventually their too notorious uniform was discarded for good.

The Lord Mayor and Aldermen now commit prisoners to Holloway Gaol; but for boys and girls found "under temptation to commit crime" they have reserved powers to send such youthful offenders to the substituted new schools—the one for boys being at Witley, in Surrey, where 240 of them are industrially trained; and the

House of Occupations, as the other is called, being in
St. George's Fields, where a similar number of girls
are trained for domestic service. The funds of this
"royal hospital" are still devoted to the maintenance of
destitute and neglected children.

It would seem that Bridewell Hospital was the first
Workhouse, the first House of Correction, and the first
Reformatory School established in England, a fact that
goes to explain why so many places of confinement in
the country have been called "Bridewells."

In the eighteenth century several hospitals for the
reception of the sick and the maimed, supported by
voluntary contributions, were opened in London. The
Westminster Hospital, the first of the character, was
founded in 1719. St. George's Hospital dates from 1733;
the London Hospital and the Middlesex Hospital from
1740; and in 1746 the Small Pox Hospital, an early
example of the specialised institution, was opened.

Guy's Hospital, Southwark, was founded 1722 by
Thomas Guy, a bookseller who amassed a fortune, his
principal gains having been from South Sea stock.
Gay's satire on the financial Bubble of 1720 may or may
not have applied in this case :—

> "How many saucy airs we meet,
> From Temple Bar to Aldgate Street !
> Proud rogues who shared the South Sea prey
> And sprung, like mushrooms, in a day."

Notwithstanding his wealth, Thomas Guy dined on his
counter, with a newspaper spread for a tablecloth. He was
a model of economy. He employed only one servant,
whom he agreed to marry. But a few days before the
ceremony, feeling sure of her prospective position, she
gave orders for some trifling repairs to be done in front
of the house. This was fatal to her chances of possessing

GUY'S HOSPITAL.

To face p. 150.

The history of the London Hospital begins with the meeting of seven stalwarts in the Feathers Inn, Cheapside, in 1740. There "a motion was made—whether with the sum of 100 guineas it would be proper to begin the said Charity. And unanimously agreed it was."

The history of the progress of these institutions is a humanitarian epic. A hundred years ago a patient was a "miserable object"; to-day he has all the resources of civilisation, all the skill of medical science, at his fullest command.

Most modern towns possess eleemosynary hospitals, even the smaller ones not accounting themselves fully equipped till they have established a cottage hospital or an infirmary, if only of the most modest dimensions. Medical foundations of older date, and often with an interesting history, are to be found in the towns and cities whose importance dates back into the centuries; as at Exeter, Hull, and Norwich. The oldest Birmingham hospital is responsible for its great triennial Musical Festival.

Charitable foundations of many kinds, and varying degrees of usefulness, are found everywhere up and down the country. The most interesting generally appertain to the older towns, such as Abingdon, Hythe, Ipswich, Winchester, Warwick, Southampton, Salisbury, and Sandwich; in some towns they may be described as both numerous and varied, as at Bath, Cambridge, Colchester, Croydon, Dover, and Falmouth.

Numbers of towns may be said to be rich in charities, as Manchester, Wakefield, Yarmouth, and York; and in not a few places the public benefactions are safeguarded by boards of trustees, as they are at Basingstoke, Burton, Canterbury, Congleton, Faversham, Grantham, Henley, Liverpool, and Okehampton. Leicester boasts "a Home for Penitent Females," and ancient Newark has been presented by Viscountess Ossington with a modern Coffee Palace, which cost not less than £25,000.

THE LONDON HOSPITAL IN 1753.

XIII

"BEDLAMS"

IN early times the lunatic was not kept in public custody; his own friends were expected to take charge of him. It was their duty to guard him from harm, and to see that he did no harm to others. Rigorous measures were often adopted with the intention of curing one "vexed with a demon" before resorting to the policy of confinement. The sufferer "possessed of devils" was taken to shrines and to holy wells in the hope that the fiends would be cast out. And not unfrequently, in the ignorance of the times, harsher measures were resorted to. The lot of any one mentally defective was a most unhappy one.

153

Sir Thomas More relates with much complacency how he ordered a lunatic beggar, whom he found howling in the street, to be soundly flogged at the whipping-post. On the title-page of Burton's "Anatomy of Melancholy" appear these eloquent lines :—

"But see the madman rage downright
With furious looks a ghastly sight !
Naked in chains bound doth he lie
And roars amain, he knows not why."

Another notable and semi-public institution rescued at the dissolution of the religious houses, and preserved to perpetual public utility, was the Star of Bethlehem Hospital, in Bishopsgate Without. Originally the "Spital" of St. Mary of Bethlehem, a priory of canons with brothers and sisters, founded in 1246, and first made a monastic hospital in 1330, it was given by Henry VIII. to the City of London, and by the efforts of Sir Thomas Gresham, founder of the Royal Exchange, was incorporated as a royal foundation for the reception of lunatics in 1547. The ancient priory hospital had been used for lunatics, amongst whom were certain out-pensioners, who, after being relieved, were sent away to beg, and became known as "Tom o' Bedlams"; and hence Shakespeare's reference in "King Lear" :—

"With a sigh, like Tom o' Bedlam."

And presently there is the terrible confession of the straits to which such helpless wanderers are put :—

"Mice and rats and such small deer
Have been Tom's food for seven long year."

The name Bethlehem, as attached to this institution, was contracted at an early date into "Bedlam," and this term came into general use to denote any madhouse

or lunatic asylum. Similarly the term Bedlamite was applied as a term of reproach, signifying not so much an inmate of Bedlam, as one who is to be considered a madman and a fool. Understood as a buffoon, it produced such a phrase as "a bedlam morris"; or sometimes, in the masculine, the term produced the nickname "Tom o' Bedlam," and in the feminine, "Bess o' Bedlam."

In many parts of England asylums for the reception of the mentally afflicted became commonly known as Bedlams. Till some thirty years ago there stood in the heart of Wednesbury two narrow thoroughfares or alleys of dilapidated tenements, known respectively as Bedlam and Beggars' Row; and although all record of their history had been lost, there can be little doubt they were the remnants of an ancient charity founded for the benefit of both the sane and the lunatic poor.

That the Bethlehem Hospital was used for the reception of distracted persons before 1547 is apparent from many references. Stow says the place had been set apart for this purpose at an early period—at a date long forgotten—because "a king of England not liking such a kind of people to remain so near his palace caused them to be removed further off" to this locality. As to the literary references of a date anterior to the incorporation of 1549, we have Skelton saying (1520) "Such a madde bedlame for to rewle this realme"; Tyndale, in 1528, uses the term "bedlam" in this sense; and Sir Thomas More (1533) writes: "More blasphemous and more bedelem-rype thys booke is." So that, irrespective of Shakespearean references in his Early English plays, there can be no doubt as to the character of the inmates of Bedlam prior to its reformed constitution.

Bethlehem Hospital formed, in its original institution,

a contracted and penurious charity; its governors discovered that the metropolis furnished them with more lunatics than they had calculated on; they consequently required from the friends of the patient a weekly contribution besides clothing. It is a melancholy fact to record in the history of human nature, that when one of their original regulations prescribed that persons who put in patients should provide their clothes, it was soon observed that the poor lunatics were frequently perishing through the omission of this slight duty from those former friends, so soon forgotten were they whom none had an interest to recollect. The hospital authorities, indeed, had to open a public subscription to provide a wardrobe.

Owing to its limited resources, the establishment was relieved by frequently discharging patients whose cure was extremely equivocal. Harmless lunatics were thrown upon the world, and went about as crazy beggars, chanting wild ditties, and wearing fantastic dress to attract the notice of the charitable, on whose alms they lived.

The partially cured "Tom Bedlo" affected clothing of a ridiculous cut and shape, extravagantly adorned with feathers and flying ribbons; he carried a long staff in his hand, and had an ox-horn slung at his side. Reference is made to this drinking-vessel in "King Lear":—

"Poor Tom! thy horn is dry."

Shakespeare also makes allusion to these poor creatures sticking sprigs of rosemary in their arms; this was done because rosemary was believed to be beneficial to the brain, and particularly for the memory—

"There's rosemary—that's for remembrance."

Of the habits of these itinerant lunatics the antiquary Aubrey has left us full information. When they were—

"licentiated to go a-begging they had on their left arm an *armilla*, or iron ring for the arm, about four inches long. They could not get it off; they wore about their necks a great horn of an ox in a string or bawdry, which when they came to a house, they did wind; and they put the drink given them into this horn, whereto they put a stopple."

As the wandering Bedlamites were practically vagrants, or at the least licensed beggars, and as their successful methods were easy of imitation, a race of vile mendicants arose, pretending to be Tom o' Bedlams, going about with the hospital's badges (in counterfeit) on the arm, arrayed in fantastic dress designed to excite pity, chanting mad songs, and in every way, by their studied extravagances, shamming the lunacy of the authorised hospital beggars.

These men were sturdy rogues of the most dangerous type; when their efforts to beg failed, they did not hesitate to commit depredations under cover of madness. They came to be known as "Abraham men"—to "sham Abraham" was to feign illness or distress in order to get off work—or sometimes they were called Jarkmen, from the word "jarck," an old cant term for a seal, because of the seal or licence which they carried as a safeguard. The word "Jarkman" soon came to be synonymous with vagabond, owing to the number of beggars who went about with spurious licences.

Dekker's "English Villainies" gives a lively description of the "progging Abram Cove." The impostor disguised himself in grotesque rags, knotted his hair, and practised other "disgusting contrivances" to excite pity, even having a mark burnt on his arm, which he showed as "the mark of Bedlam," thus counterfeiting the mark of the *armilla*. Sturdy mendicants of this character, when "shamming Abraham," went about the country frightening women and children and domestics ; sometimes they would come with "a hollow noise, whooping, leaping, gambolling, wildly dancing, with a fierce or a distressed look." They were known as "Poor Tom's flock of wild geese," or sometimes as "Tom of Bedlam's band of madcaps." Dekker has preserved for us their "maund," or form of begging :—

"'Good worship master, bestow your reward on a poor man that hath been in Bedlam without Bishopsgate, three years, four months, and nine days ; and bestow one piece of silver towards his fees, which he is indebted there—Three pounds, three shillings, three pence, three farthings'—or some such effect."

Or, it might be—

"Now, Dame, well and wisely, what will you give poor Tom ? One pound of your sheep's feathers to make Poor Tom a blanket ? Or one cutting of your sow's side, no bigger than my arm ? Or one piece of your salt meat to make Poor Tom a sharing horn ? Or one cross of your small silver towards a pair of shoes ? Well and wisely give Poor Tom an old sheet to keep him from the cold. Or an old doublet and jerkin of my masters. Well and wisely, God save the king and his council"

One formula, it will be seen, for the master, and an entirely different one for mistress of the house. Of such is the character of mendicity and imposture.

Numerous songs and ballads on the subject of madness belong to this period. They were certainly not composed by the madmen, many of them being degraded by the cant language of the gipsies with whom their habits of life associated them. That they sang them there seems little doubt. Dekker describes these luckless beings as sometimes merry, sometimes sullen ; they laughed at times, and at times wept ; they sometimes capered about singing, and at others moaned plaintively the sorrows of a much troubled mind. One verse of a " Mad Song" will suffice to illustrate the kind of composition associated with Tom-a-Bedlam :—

> " Of thirty bare years have I
> Twice twenty been enraged,
> And of forty been
> Three times fifteen
> In durance soundly caged
> In the lovely lofts of Bedlam,
> In stubble soft and dainty,
> Brave bracelets strong,
> Sweet whips ding dong,
> And a wholesome hunger plenty."

The Civil Wars no doubt cleared the country of many wanderers and vagabonds ; but till that period Bedlam beggars, genuine and spurious, were to be met with in plenty. After the seventeenth century they ceased to be recognised by the hospital.

The original foundation had provided accommodation for only six lunatics, but in 1644 the number was increased to forty-four, though applications for admission always exceeded the accommodation by many times that number.

The old Bethlehem Hospital for the insane, erected in Moorfields in 1676, was built in imitation of the Tuileries at Paris. It was a low, dismal-looking pile, with gloomy lines of strongly barred cells, and on each side of its heavy gates were wonderful effigies, chiselled by the elder Cibber, of raving and moping madness. Of these terrible presentments of " Melancholy" and " Raving Madness, or the " Brainless Brothers" as they were sometimes called (now preserved in the hall of the present hospital), an old topographer writes : "How those stone faces and eyes glared ! How sternly the razor must have swept over those bare heads! How listless and dead were those limbs, bound with inexorable fetters, while the iron of despair had pierced the hearts of the prisoned maniacs."

A French traveller who visited England during the time the hospital was being rebuilt in 1676, says in his memoirs: "This edifice cost £18,000 sterling, or near 240,000 francs of our money;" to which he adds the quaint remark, "All the madmen of London are not confined there."

Two wings appropriated to incurables were added to the main building in 1770, and the public were then admitted to the hospital as one of the regular sights of London. It may be imagined that the promiscuous crowd, who were admitted at a charge of a penny each, produced on the patients a degree of excitement which must have caused incalculable mischief. This state of things lasted till the removal from Moorfields to St. George's Fields in 1815, when the new Bethlehem Hospital was erected at a cost of £122,500, of which £72,819 consisted of parliamentary grants. Indigent lunatics have not ceased to be a costly charge to the State.

Even at this late date the patients' rooms were not properly warmed, nor was artificial light provided in them for the night time, nor were the windows glazed; and some of the inmates were still kept in chains.

Now, instead of chains and loathsome cells, everything about the institution is as humanitarian as the most progressive mind could wish. Nothing that can conduce to the well-being of the demented inmates, and tend to their possible recovery, is now overlooked or neglected.

Insanity is always on the increase, apparently progressing with the advance of civilisation; in 1751 the Hospital of St. Luke, opposite the Bethlehem Hospital, admitted patients to relieve the pressure on the latter.

Well into the nineteenth century lunatics were treated with great barbarity; men and women were herded together in one ward, and all violent or dangerous cases were manacled and chained to the walls like wild beasts. Regarded as mere nuisances, what mattered it if the mad were confined in solitude and kept in cold and darkness?

In the Museum of the College of Surgeons, London, is preserved a chain and belt of the kind formerly used for the purpose of securing lunatics. These contrivances were in frequent use up to the beginning of the nineteenth century, and must have added not a little to the sufferings endured by the insane in ages when unsoundness of mind was treated, even under medical authority, punitively and often torturingly.

A subsequent chapter will deal with the treatment of the pauper lunatic during the earlier years of the nineteenth century.

XIV

ALMSHOUSES

Pre-Reformation bedehouses — Bederolls — Chartered fairs for maintenance funds—Bedesmen—Ancient London almshouses —Whittington's benefactions—Westminster Almonry—Mediæval foundations—Private, manorial, and municipal almshouses — Wells and Higham Ferrars examples — Some architectural treasures—Post-Reformation foundations—Often built near the church—Bristol examples of the benevolence of merchant companies—England rich in such institutions—The growth of endowments.

OF existing almshouses dating back to pre-Reformation times a large number were attached to chantries, and the almsmen who tenanted them were poor men, not in holy orders, who lived on the endowment and received alms to pray for the souls of the founders. Such almsmen were commonly known as Bedesmen, and the tenement they occupied was called a Bedehouse, Beadhouse, or Bedhouse ; or sometimes it was known as a College.

Such dwellings for "poor religious persons" were usually erected near the church in which the founder was interred ; and there was always a Bederoll, or list of persons, generally members of the founder's family, to be prayed for. Very few of these foundations escaped spoliation in 1534, prayers for the dead being prohibited after the Reformation. The term Bede is derived from the Anglo-Saxon *bed, gebed,* "a prayer."

The fourteenth century was marked by the poverty into which many charitable institutions had fallen, probably the result of neglect and bad management. One or two of the more ancient institutions were privileged by Royal Charter to hold fairs for the purpose of raising funds towards their support and maintenance. St. Bartholomew's Hospital at Newbury in Berkshire, for instance, had the right to hold a fair every St. Bartholomew's Day, which was opened with a proclamation and the usual ceremonial by the proctor of the charity, the steward, and the bailiff. Tolls were collected from the stall-holders, which, with an impost of twopence levied on every publican in the town, produced a fund which was divided by the officials on the following day among the almsmen of this ancient charity, which dated back to the time of King John (1215).

In some places the recipients of such benefactions are still called Bedesmen, or Bedeswomen ; and in the remoter villages they are still clad in the antiquated garb of the foundation, the women sometimes appearing in early seventeenth-century costume, with quilted skirts and conical hats, like so many Mother Hubbards.

To trace the long and ever-widening stream of charity which has flowed through London alone would occupy many times the space this volume places at disposal. Its rich natives and commercial magnates have been ever mindful of its claims upon them. In 1332 William Elsinge founded a hospital for a hundred poor blind men ; in 1371 John Barnes gave a chest containing 1,000 marks to be lent by the City to young men beginning trade. One citizen gave money to relieve poor prisoners ; another left a sum to assist poor householders ; other successful merchants have made the city's water supply, the feeding of its poor, the easing of its overburdened ratepayers' pockets, and divers other philanthropies and benevolences the object of their solicitude. The famous Lord Mayor, Sir Richard Whittington, founded an almshouse for thirteen poor men, who were to have sixteenpence each per week, a sum equivalent to half as many shillings of present-day value, with clothing and apartments, on the condition of praying daily for the souls of the founder and his wife. This foundation, removed to a better site at Highgate, is still in existence. While a goodly number of these "religious" foundations disappeared at the Reformation, some were converted to other uses or survived in newer forms.

The Almonry at Westminster was originally an alms-house erected by Henry VII. and his mother, the Lady Margaret, to the glory of God, for twelve poor men and women; the building, however, was afterwards converted into lodgings for the choir-men of the Abbey.

Although Anthony Wood, the seventeenth antiquary, says that "almshouses were scarce before the Reformation; that over against Christ Church, Oxon, is one of the ancientest"; there were undoubtedly a number of good cottage specimens erected in the fifteenth century, and not a few interesting specimens of old almshouses are still to be found in many places throughout the length and breadth of the country; among them, for instance, those at Guildford, Chichester, Abingdon, East Grinstead, Ewelme, and Warwick. A complete list of ancient "hospitals," classified and arranged under counties, will be found in a volume of the "Antiquary's Books" Series, entitled "The Mediæval Hospitals of England" (London, Methuen, 1909).

However much the poor may have suffered immediately after the Dissolution, there can be no doubt, from the survival of so many seventeenth-century almshouses, that the lot of the needy old folk during the succeeding centuries was not quite a forlorn and neglected one.

In many parts of England noble and wealthy families have adopted as the most praiseworthy medium for perpetuating among their poorer neighbours a good name for works of Christian charity, the erection and endowment of almshouses; the powerful Wiltshire family of Hungerford afford an admirable illustration of this feeling at Corsham and at Heytesbury. The lords of manors sometimes felt it incumbent upon them to provide private almshouses for their decayed tenants and veteran retainers. The same feeling of responsibility for the welfare of the poor is indicated by the fact that even in mediæval times numbers of almshouses were under the control of the municipality; the burgesses of Northampton and Wallingford had public control of theirs, as had the commonalties of Huntingdon, Pevensey, Wilton, and other places, of theirs.

The city of Wells is rich in ancient charities, one of the most interesting being Bishop Bubwith's Almshouses, built in 1424, in the true mediæval style, and comprising a large hall open to the roof, with cubicles on each side for the inmates, and a chapel divided from the hall by an open screen at the east end. Unfortunately, the building was tampered with in 1850, but it is still a most interesting piece of architecture, the addition of a cinquecento sedilia to the south front, made by Bishop Still about 1607, giving a somewhat picturesque appearance to the whole.

A unique specimen of an ancient almshouse may be seen at Higham Ferrars, Northants. It dates back to mediæval times, and has a long hall such as it was customary in early English times for the whole family to sleep in. There is a long room, and at the east end, raised a foot, is a little chapel; on the south side is a long open stove; and originally the almsmen slept on the floor on reeds, each man wrapped in his blanket. It was founded by Archbishop Chichele, a native of this town, early in the fifteenth century, together with a school and college. The college was disestablished in the reign of Henry VIII.

Many old almshouses are architectural treasures, the Bablake Hospital at Coventry to wit. In the same vicinity the almshouses at Stratford-on-Avon present one of the most interesting street views in the country. Founded in the reign of Edward VI., at the same time as the Grammar School—to which the schoolboy Shakespeare took his "shining morning face"—for twelve poor men and twelve poor women, it received a further bequest in 1732, by which the former were to be provided with blue coats and the latter with blue gowns "every second year."

A good specimen of the "domestic Gothic" style is afforded by Abbot's Hospital, Guildford, the enduring memorial of George Abbot, the Puritan Archbishop of Canterbury, who, in 1619, founded this almshouse as a token of his affection for his native town. It is endowed for the maintenance of twelve brethren, ten sisters, and two nurses.

As late as 1517 a bequest was made to "the poor lazars" of Highgate to pray for the donor "by name in their bede-roll." This "spittle-house" became a common poor-house, after losing its character as a leper-house with religious associations, at the Reformation; the governor, however, commonly called the "guide," was a person of some medical education, apparently selected for this qualification.

The first almshouses founded after the Reformation are at Greenwich, established in 1576 by Lambarde, the historian of Kent, for twenty poor men and their

ABBOT'S HOSPITAL, GUILDFORD.

Photo by Chester Vaughan, Acton W.)

HOSPITAL OF THE BLACK FRIARS, IPSWICH (SIXTEENTH CENTURY).

wives, who are strictly required to use a form of morning and evening prayer composed by the founder, or the endowment becomes void.

Many almshouses may be found in close contiguity with the parish church, as at Aston Manor and Castle Rising. At Beaminster (the "Emminster" of Hardy's novels), a remote village in a corner of Dorset, a small block of almshouses lies almost hidden under the churchyard wall. They are built on the site of an old chantry house, which explains their proximity to the church. Endowed by Sir John Strode for six poor persons, they bear the inscription—

"God's House
Sit Honos Trino Deo
Anno Dom
1630."

Dedication inscriptions frequently afford interesting reading. On the Hall Almshouses at Bradford-on-Avon the Hall family motto is not inappropriately inscribed—

"Deo et Pauperibus."

("For God and the Poor.")

The almshouses at Milton, Dorset, which were founded in 1674, for six poor widows, were in 1780 swept away by Lord Milton because they were in too close proximity with the new residence he was then building. They were re-erected, however, with the rest of a demolished village, at a becoming distance from the mansion-house.

In looking for these charitable institutions it will be found that the ancient commercial centres, where merchants were prosperous and wealthy, were most prolific in them. Bristol boasts hospitals and asylums numbering about twenty, and supporting in the aggregate some two thousand poor persons; they offer shelter to poor citizens in general, and to superannuated persons, and make special provision for orphans and idiots. Chief among them are St. Peter's Hospital, Merchants' Hospital (for seamen and seamen's widows), and the Colston Almshouses, built in 1691.

Over the Merchant Venturers' Almshouses, Bristol (1698), an institution which maintains nineteen sailors and twelve widows, are these lines:—

> " Free from all the storms, the tempest, and the rage
> Of billows, we securely spend our age;
> Our weather-beaten vessels here repair—
> Have, from the generous Merchants and their care
> An harbouring here; we put no more to sea
> Until we launch into eternity;
> But lest our widows, whom we leave behind,
> Should want relief, they here a shelter find;
> Thus all our cares and sorrows cease,
> Whilst our kind founders turn our toils to ease,
> May they be with an endless Sabbath bless'd
> Who have afforded unto us this rest."

We have it on the authority of recorded history that at least two Saxon bishops were builders of houses for the poor, and there has been no cessation in the founding of almshouses to the present day; some by private benefactors, in commemoration of their own names and families, and not a few by the various trade interests for decayed members of their own calling. In and around London most of the City Companies have their own endowed almshouses, giving away upwards of £75,000 a year in charity and the support of such institutions. In mediæval times the almshouses of the craft guilds were to be found in many of the old trading towns.

No country in the world is so rich as England in

public charities—in comfortable almshouses, beneficent hospitals, and richly endowed schools. These provide, in as many cases as they can reach, for an amelioration of the condition of those born under the disabilities of poverty, or those who encounter losses and suffering through the accidents of life, it may be through imprudence or else some calamity no human foresight could guard against.

One of the earliest reliable inquiries into the subject, that of a parliamentary return under the Gilbert Act, showed that in 1780 the endowed charities of this country amounted to £528,710 a year. More than a century earlier—in 1665, to be precise—the bishops had furnished the Primate with certificates showing the various " Hospitals, Almshouses, Pluralists, Lectureships, Schoolmasters, and Physicians " in their respective dioceses.

A remarkable feature of many ancient benefactions is the enormous growth in the value of the original endowment, generally attributed to increased land values—to that " unearned increment" which results from the commercial activity of the community.

This has been an immense boon in many instances—Birmingham, to wit, now enjoys an income of £1,000 a week for the purposes of higher education from a Grammar School endowment which in 1552 produced £21 per annum.

But this enrichment of a charity has not always been to the public advantage, as was noted elsewhere (p. 73) with regard to doles. The Watts Charity at Rochester (mentioned on p. 91) affords an illustration of similar misapplication of opportunity in the management of a foundation. The " Poor Travellers," founded in 1597, was rebuilt in 1771, and renewed in 1865 from its own endowment fund. Yet this represents but a small portion of the resources of the charity, the revenues of which had grown to £3,500 in 1874, and double that amount in 1907. In 1855, by order of the Court of Chancery, a splendid set of almshouses was built on the Maidstone Road in good Elizabethan style, and embellished with two magnificent gateways costing £350 apiece. This elaborate outlay, made by the combined efforts of "Charity" and "Chancery," was for the accommodation of ten poor men and ten poor women, for whom a very ample and well-paid staff of attendants was also provided out of the funds—namely, a head nurse at £60, a porter at £50, and four nurses at £50 each, per annum.

XV

ELEEMOSYNARY EDUCATION

Monastic schools—Universities founded—Called "studies"—Contempt of learning—Rise of non-monastic schools—The poor scholar—The sizar—Education fostered by merchants—City of London school—The revival of learning—The Reformation—Loss of scholarships at Dissolution—The refounding of schools—Westminster School—Education and "breeding" in sixteenth century—History and anecdotes of Christ's Hospital—Its refounding for four hundred poor scholars—Enriched by legacies—Rules abrogated—The Blue Coat livery—The dietary—The "gag-eater"—The discipline—Charterhouse—A school and an almshouse—The Pensioners—"Colonel Newcome"—Charity schools—Scholars' grotesque garbs—Blue, grey, and green coats—Ragged schools—School anniversary celebrations at St. Paul's.—Misapplied funds—Masterships as sinecures—In eighteenth century—Inquiry by Select Committee (1816)—Reports abuse and malversation—A grave exposure—How admixture of classes was not tolerated—"No free boys of an inferior grade" allowed on the foundation.

THE history of the educational endowments of this country will be found to consist largely of records of shameless filching; of the wresting of schools established by charitable founders for teaching the children of the poor to the benefit of children beyond the needs of such eleemosynary assistance. The story of this ousting of the poor is interesting in many ways.

St. Augustine, to whom the first establishment of schools in this country has been traced, probably found not one solitary book in the land. Books had to be imported at great cost, so that only the opulent possessed them; the schools were consequently established in palaces, bishops' residences, and monasteries only.

Under the wing of almost every abbey and monastery there grew up a school for the education of the young; in the earliest times such existed at Glastonbury, St. Albans, Canterbury, Winchester, and Westminster, where the salary of a schoolmaster for teaching the boys grammar and religious subjects was paid by the almoner of the monastery.

Alfred the Great, in the ninth century, planted a school in every monastery. One result of this system was that the clerical youth of the country arrived at manhood as an educated class, and then occupied most of the public offices to the exclusion of the laity who had been allowed to grow up in ignorance, and were consequently unfitted for such public positions. Alfred becoming desirous that the laity as well as the clergy should be qualified, founded the two Universities for that specific purpose.

The upper ranks, however, held a supreme disdain for learning, and till the time of Edward the Confessor darkness prevailed. In the twelfth century learning increased, and schools spread from the monasteries and convents to the cities and towns. The Universities were then called "studies," but soon afterwards took the name of "Universities," from all kinds of learning being taught in them, and their doors being thrown open to foreigners as well as natives. The cathedral scholars, in the Middle Ages, were commonly taught by the bishop; a duty afterwards delegated to prebends. Between the Conquest and the death of King John there were 557 religious houses in England, each having a school attached. St. Martin's-le-Grand was early famous for its school.   Fitzstephens tells us that in the time of Henry II. London had also many non-monastic schools.

Besides relieving the sick and the destitute, the religious houses were in many instances educational institutions, although not always to the extent that is popularly supposed.   In many houses the school was allowed to fall into disuse as non-monastic schools came into existence.   Most of the brethren in a rich foundation were of gentle birth and good family, but poor boys were admitted who showed ability and an inclination to studious habits.   And if a poor boy were admitted to a monastery he was lucky if he were allowed to become one of its servants and to wear its livery.   His livelihood at least was assured; and if his abilities developed as they had promised he was possibly on the high-road to social eminence.

At Cambridge University one class of poor scholar was termed a sizar, because his assize or ration of food was given to him.   In former times each fellow had his sizar, who waited upon him at table, and was allowed, with certain other perquisites and privileges, the food that was left at each college meal.

Schools of ancient foundation which were independent of the religious orders, the cathedrals, or the collegiate churches, are now somewhat difficult to find.

Queen Elizabeth's School at Ipswich, though now housed in a fine modern building, erected (1851) in a style dictated by a remaining fragment of Wolsey's College, has records which go back to 1447, and was formerly conducted in the refectory of the Blackfriars' Convent.

About the time of the famous Sir Richard Whittington, who was Mayor of London in 1397, in 1406, and a third time in 1419, the cause of education began to receive the fostering attention of the mercantile class.

Although no secular school was actually founded by Whittington—he endowed a "religious college" which disappeared with the other chantries at the Dissolution, its site now being occupied by the school of the Mercers' Company; while the library he built for the Franciscan house afterwards became part of Christ's Hospital School—a succeeding Lord Mayor, Sir William Sevenoke, set up a school for boys in his native town, Sevenoaks; and a friend of his own, Sir John Neil, proposed to establish four new Grammar Schools in the City.

The City of London School was founded by Sir Richard's executor, John Carpenter. In fact, the mercantile intelligence of the great City of London was just becoming alive to the value of education to a trading community having vast interests in all parts of the world.

Although there had been a great increase of schools in the thirteenth century, many of them had decayed by the fifteenth century, languishing until the invention of printing brought a revival of learning; soon after which, as we read in the "Life of Colet," more schools were founded in the thirty years before the Reformation than in the three hundred preceding years:—

Stow says:—

"I myself have yeerely seen the scholars of divers of grammar schools repair unto the churchyard of St Bartholomew, in Smithfield, where, upon a banke boorded about under a tree some one scholler hath stepped up, and there hath opposed and answered, till he were by some better scholler overcome and put downe."

These public disputations ceased at the suppression of the priory.

Notwithstanding that we read of poor scholars at the Universities, education had long come to be regarded as a privilege of the rich and powerful. After the

Reformation Edward VI. appointed a commission (1549) "to take diverse orders for the maintenance and continuance of scollers"; for the impoverishers of the monastic foundations had too often swallowed up the poor scholars' exhibitions. Some were rescued, and there are existing to-day forty-four schools which claim to have been founded by, or under, Edward VI.

Eight London schools perished altogether at the Dissolution, and for a time the City was practically without schools. St. Paul's School, which had been founded by Dean Colet (1509), was never closed; St. Anthony's survived, and the Blue Coat School was established on the site of the Franciscan House. St. Thomas's School was taken in hand by the Mercers' Company, and the Merchant Taylors founded their school. In Southwark schools were founded at St. Olave's and St. Saviour's; and a few years later Charterhouse, of which more anon, was converted into an almshouse and school.

St. Paul's School, London, is peculiar in that it was not, like Westminster, Charterhouse, Eton, and Winchester, founded for poor scholars. It was established early in the sixteenth century for 153 sons of well-to-do citizens, each of whom, on entering, subscribed fourpence each towards defraying the expenses of the "pore scoler that swepith the schole."

Westminster School was refounded in Elizabeth's reign (1560) as "a publique schoole for Grammar, Rhetorick, Poetrie, and for the Latin and Greek Languages," designed for 120 boys, including forty "queens scholers" chosen from among the choristers, who were to be maintained and educated free of cost, and possess opportunities for being drafted off to Oxford and Cambridge in due course.

From this time schools began to be founded and

endowed in ever-increasing numbers, though it has to be confessed that lands and funds left for their support have in many instances been alienated, and schools founded for the poor have passed into the hands of the rich. In 1559 Queen Elizabeth taxed benefices one-thirteenth part for the education of students ; and many beneficed clergymen acted also as schoolmasters.

Aubrey informs us—

"there were very few free-schools in England before the Reformation. Youths were generally taught Latin in the monasteries, and young women had their education, not at Hackney, as now [1678] but at nunneries, where they learnt needlework, confectionary, surgery, physic, writing, drawing &c. . . . From the time of Erasmus [*temp.* Henry VIII.] till about twenty years last past, the learning was downright pedantry . . . The gentry and the citizen had little learning of any kind, and their way of breeding up their children was suitable to the rest. They were as severe to their children as their schoolmasters, and their schoolmasters as masters of the house of correction. Gentlemen of thirty and forty years old were to stand, like mutes and fools, bareheaded before their parents ; and the daughters—grown women—were to stand at the cupboard side during the whole time of the proud mother's visit, unless leave was desired, forsooth, that a cushion should be given them to kneel upon, brought by the serving-man, after they had done sufficient penance in standing. The boys had their foreheads turned up and stiffened with spittle."

If this were the etiquette of the family in the sixteenth century, it may be imagined with what tenderness the poor and dependent would be treated.

And if a stilted etiquette were the chief result of educating the quality, the greater the pity that the education originally intended for the poor should have been diverted to the privileged and well-to-do. This process of alienating educational endowments went on gradually and insidiously but without interruption from the period of the Reformation to the early nineteenth century.

Of an old foundation school no finer example exists

CHRIST'S HOSPITAL.

than Christ's Hospital, which till recently stood in Newgate Street. Originally a convent of the Grey (or Mendicant) Friars, which had been enriched with a valuable library, the gift of the immortal Whittington, already alluded to, it was presented by Henry VIII., at the Dissolution, to the City of London. The gift was confirmed by Edward VI., and well endowed, the child-king expressing his anxious desire to relieve the poor with which the capital was then swarming. Within six months of its incorporation as a Royal Hospital the old monastery had been patched up sufficiently to accommodate nearly four hundred poor scholars.

"In the year 1552," says Stow, "began the repairing of the Grey Friars' House, for the poor fatherless children ; and in the month of November, the children were taken into the same, to the number of almost four hundred On Christmas Day, in the afternoon, while the Lord Mayor and aldermen rode to Paules, the children of Christ's Hospital stood from St. Lawrence Lane end, in Cheape, towards Paules, all in one livery of russet cotton, three hundred and forty in number ; and in Easter next they were in blue at the Spittle, and so have continued ever since."

From the very foundation of this school legacies poured in upon it ; money and lands were left to benefit the charity ; some were gifts for the blind and aged, for apprenticing the boys, and for various other purposes not strictly applicable to the charity considered as a school. One bequest was to provide dinners of boiled legs of pork ; another to give roast beef and mutton in addition to the ordinary meat diet ; and a third was to provide certain boys with gloves on which was printed the legend, "Christ is risen." These were to be worn in the school processions at Easter ; and as might have been expected, this "charity" begot the uncharitable schoolboy rhyme —

"He is risen, He is risen,
All the Jews must go to prison!"

12

The old regulations of Christ's Hospital declared its intention to be for the maintenance and education of dependent children, but the rules were imperfectly carried out. In 1809 it was decreed—

"that no children of livery servants (except they be freemen of the City of London) and no children who have any adequate means of being educated and maintained, and no children who are lamed, crooked, or deformed, or suffering from any infectious or incurable disease should be admitted."

As to the clothing of Christ's scholars, everybody is familiar with the yellow-legged blue-coat boy. Leigh Hunt was a " blue," and thus pleasantly writes of his *alma mater* :—

"Our dress was of the coarsest and quaintest kind, but was respected out of doors, and is so. It consisted of a blue drugget gown, or body, with ample skirts to it ; a yellow vest underneath, in winter-time ; small-clothes of Russia duck ; worsted yellow stockings; a leathern girdle ; and a little black worsted cap, usually carried in the hand. I believe it was the ordinary dress of children in humble life, during the reign of the Tudors. We used to flatter ourselves that it was taken from the monks ; and there was a monstrous tradition that at one period it consisted of blue velvet with silver buttons."

The dietary of these blue-coated boys was certainly somewhat monastic. Till 1824 the breakfast was plain bread and beer, and the dinner three times a week consisted only of milk-porridge, rice-milk, and pea-soup. The old school rhyme, imperishable as the Iliad, runs :—

> " Sunday, all saints ;
> Monday, all souls ;
> Tuesday, all trenchers ;
> Wednesday, all bowls ;
> Thursday, tough Jack ;
> Friday, no better ;
> Saturday, pea-soup with thick bread and butter."

And, like the monks of old in their refectory, the boys ate their meat off wooden trenchers, and ladled their soup with wooden spoons from wooden bowls. The beer was brought up in leather jacks, and retailed in small piggins. Charles Lamb, who was educated here, does not speak highly of the feeding. The small-beer was of the smallest, and tasted of the leather in which it was served. The milk porridge was blue and tasteless, the pea-soup was coarse and choking. The mutton was invariably roasted to shreds, and the boiled beef was poisoned with marigolds. In connection with the last named a strange school custom prevailed. Any boy who dared to eat the fat of the beef was looked upon as a ghoul; he was fiercely denounced as "gag-eater," and shunned and loathed as a veritable monster. A strange self-denying ordinance for a hungry set of school-boys, surely.

Another "old blue," Samuel Taylor Coleridge, says in his "Table Talk," in 1832 :—

"The discipline of Christ's Hospital in my time was ultra-Spartan : all domestic ties were to be put aside. 'Boy,' I remember Boyer [the Beadle] saying to me once, when I was crying, the first day after my return after the holidays—'boy, the school is your father ; boy, the school is your mother ; boy, the school is your brother ; the school is your sister ; the school is your first cousin, and your second cousin, and all the rest of your relations. Let's have no more crying.' "

From 1552 to 1902, from the days of the Sixth Edward to the reign of Edward the Seventh, for a space of 350 years, this noble institution remained on its original site in Newgate Street. It was removed in 1902 to Horsham in Sussex.

Another very famous London school was Charterhouse, the name of which is a corruption of Chartreuse, the celebrated Carthusian monastery in France. At the Great Plague of 1349 the victims were so numerous that the grave-diggers could not cope with the work, and 50,000 bodies were huddled into trenches outside the walls of London on some waste-land subsequently consecrated, and called Pardon Churchyard. In 1370 Sir Walter Manny founded a Carthusian convent on the site. After the Dissolution the priory property passed into the hands of Thomas Sutton, who converted it into a richly endowed institution for forty-four boys and eighty decayed gentlemen; with a staff that included a master, a preacher, a schoolmaster, a physician, and a number of minor officers and servants. Each boy was to be educated, and each pensioner to receive food, clothing, lodging, and an allowance of about £26 a year.

The Poor Brothers annually celebrated the founder in a song with the quaint chorus :—

> " Then blessed be the memory
> Of good old Thomas Sutton,
> Who gave us lodging, learning,
> And he gave us beef and mutton."

The Charterhouse revenues escaped the envious eyes of James I., who desired to appropriate them to pay his army, and a great school arose as rich and catholic in its charity as Christ's Hospital, although, unfortunately, its character, too, became altered. About 1845 the numbers in the school varied from 150 to 180, of whom forty-four were foundationers or gown boys, who were fed, educated, and partly clothed by the institution. Each governor selected a boy in turn as a vacancy occurred, and the eligible age was from ten to fourteen. Most of these gown boys were either aristocratically connected or possessed interest with the upper class. The remainder of the boys, whose parents paid for them, lived in boarding-houses.

Similarly good Thomas Sutton's provision for poor

pensioners had been perverted, and at the date mentioned
this respectable brotherhood contained a goodly number
of Wellington's old Peninsular officers. The Poor
Brothers were eighty in number, received £36 a year,
rooms rent free, and were required to wear, when in
bounds, a long black cloak. By the regulations they
were to be in by eleven o'clock at night, and were fined a
shilling for every non-attendance at chapel. The chapel
bell rang at eight or nine at night, eighty strokes, but
when one of the brethren died intimation of the death
was given by one stroke less.

Thackeray has immortalised the school—he was educated there—in "The Newcomes." There is nothing in
fiction more pathetic than the novelist's description of
that grand character, that fine old English gentleman,
Colonel Newcome, ending his days as one of the Charterhouse pensioners. Thomas Newcome is shown in the
chapel, at the service, in the course of which occurs a
verse which is profoundly pathetic in its appropriateness—

"'I have been young and now am old ; yet have I not seen the
righteous forsaken, nor his seed begging bread.' . . . His dear
old head was bent down over his prayer-book. . . . He wore the
black gown of the pensioners of the Grey Friars. His order of the
Bath was on his breast. He stood there amongst the poor brethren,
uttering the responses to the psalm. The steps of this good man
had been ordered hither by heaven's decree to this almshouse."

Presently we get the solemn picture of the Colonel's
death. It was on a school half-holiday—

"At the usual evening hour, the chapel bell began to toll, and
Thomas Newcome's hands, outside the bed, feebly beat time ; and
just as the last bell struck, a peculiar sweet smile shone over his
face, and he lifted up his head a little, and quickly said 'Adsum,'
and fell back. It was the word we used at school when names were
called, and lo ! he, whose heart was that of a little child, had
answered to his name, and stood in the presence of the Master."

The human interest of our subject, it will be confessed, is by no means abated when the poor are but the comparatively poor.

Of real personages who have received their education at Charterhouse the list includes the names of Addison, Steele, John Wesley, Blackstone, Grote, Havelock, and John Leech. The school was moved, for sanitary reasons, to Godalming in 1872, and now accommodates a much larger number of boys.

Parochial charity schools, for the education of the children of the poor, were first instituted in and around London in 1688. These institutions will be found in a number of towns, founded at various dates subsequent and near to this.

A memorable law passed in 1697 ordained that every parish in the realm should provide a commodious school-house, and should pay a moderate stipend to a school-master. The effect was but slight, and that not immediate. In many towns educational foundations were lost through maladministration. In some cases the charities were merged in other funds ; thus at Rochester, where Sir John Hayward had bequeathed property for the perpetual support of three charity schools, which he had set up during his lifetime, the charity is " now incorporated " with St. Nicholas' National School. In 1602 Thomas Parke bequeathed property for the education of ten poor children in Wednesbury ; subsequently his son Richard confirmed the bequest and augmented it ; yet not a vestige of the benefaction can be traced now. And this is the case in many places.

The old free schools or charity schools dispensed little more than reading and writing ; and it was a well-conducted foundation which added to these primary subjects a sufficient knowledge of arithmetic to enable the learner to go behind a tradesman's counter and serve customers without the aid of a ready-reckoner. Not less reprehensible was the dressing of the scholars, both boys and girls, in a costume antiquated and grotesque enough to make them the butt of ridicule among their companions.

There was a "Grey-coat" School, similarly named from the colour of the clothing worn by the inmates, founded at Westminster in 1698, for the education of seventy poor boys and forty poor girls; and there was a "Green-coat" School at Camberwell, and another at Westminster for "poor fatherless children" adjoining the "abiding house for the poor," and "the Bridewell for the compulsory employment of the indolent."

There was also a "Green-coat" School at Buckingham, but the most common livery of the charity school was the "blue-coat," as exemplified at Chester, Kendal, Newbury, Reading, Warrington, and many other old towns; Newport, I.O.W., having a "Blue-coat" School for girls.

Two free schools at Coventry and Warwick respectively go by the curious name of Bablake Schools, a term derived from a piece of land in Coventry formerly so called, on which the school there is situated. The boys were clothed in blue and yellow, and as a similar uniform was adopted for the school in the neighbouring town, it may be the Warwick school borrowed this name. There was anciently a monastic institution of the name in Coventry standing on the site of the free school.

Bedford is eminent for its school endowments, applied chiefly to higher education ; and so are most of the older cathedral cities, as Durham, Oxford, and Salisbury ; while Carlisle and Gloucester worthily include ragged schools with theirs. Chelmsford has an industrial school for destitute boys, and Beccles an endowed "Writing and Account School."

There was at one time no more beautiful or touching

sight in London than the anniversary of the charity
schools, when some eight thousand children were
wont to assemble for divine service at St. Paul's
Cathedral. In endless ranks the children marched
through the city streets in all sorts of quaint cos-
tumes, marshalled or headed by pompous beadles;
the boys in knee-breeches of Hogarthian days, with
glittering pewter badges on their coats; the girls in blue
and orange, with quaint little mob-caps white as snow,
and long white gloves, covering the whole of their little
arms. At a given signal these little innocents would all
rise up in church, and in their fresh, happy childish
voices sing the Old Hundredth in a manner calculated
to bring tears to the eyes of even the comparatively
unemotional. On the scene inside St. Paul's, which has
been happily likened to a " nosegay of little rosy faces,"
a sweet little poem has been written by William Blake,
which begins :—

"'Twas on a Holy Thursday, their innocent faces clean,
  Came children walking two and two, in red and blue and
    green ;
  Grey-headed beadles walked before, with wands as white as
    snow,
  Till into the high dome of Paul's they like Thames' waters
    flow.

  Oh, what a multitude there seemed, those flowers of London
    town ;
  Seated in companies they were, with radiance all their own ;
  The hum of multitudes was there, but multitudes of lambs,
  Thousands of little boys and girls, raising their innocent
    hands.

  Now like a mighty wind they raise to heaven the voice of
    song,
  Or like harmonious thunderings the seats of heaven among ;
  Beneath them sit the aged men, wise guardians of the poor ;
  Then cherish pity, lest you drive an angel from your door."

One of the greatest benefits to the community, the education of the humblest classes, was the latest to arrive. The old foundation schools in too many instances were wholly diverted from their original purposes; founded for the benefit of the poor, they all too frequently became schools for the well-to-do. The masterships were used to provide sinecures for clergymen, who pretended to give instruction to the few pupils they were unable to refuse admission. The funds bequeathed for popular education were misapplied and misappropriated, if not wholly wasted. The children of the poor were defrauded to benefit their "betters," under cover of an iniquitous system of patronage and venality.

Fielding, in his "Joseph Andrews," touches upon the state of popular education in the middle of the eighteenth century :—

"Joey told Mr. Andrews that he had very early learnt to read and write, by the goodness of his father, who, though he had not interest enough to get him into a charity school, because a cousin of his father's landlord did not vote on the right side for a churchwarden in a borough town, yet had been himself at the expense of sixpence a week for his learning."

A Select Committee was appointed in 1816 to inquire into the education of the lower orders in the metropolis, with particular instructions to consider what was fit to be done with respect to the children of paupers found begging in the streets. The report was decidedly in favour of extending the blessing of education "to the poor of all descriptions," and strongly advised a further investigation into the charitable foundations for the education of the poor throughout the country. A Commission was soon afterwards appointed to inquire into the condition of all the endowed schools of the land; and a number of official reports on the subject have since appeared, nearly all of them complaining of serious abuse and malversation.

The evils exposed were many and notorious; but the most scandalous and widespread were that schools founded for poor children were educating an entirely different class; and that the accommodation intended for scholars with a residentiary qualification was being utilised for paying boarders from a distance. In many instances foundation scholars were reduced to the very lowest possible limit to make room for profitable "paying boarders" having no possible claim whatever upon the charity.

Of course many other faults and abuses came to light— as inefficiency in the teaching, absurd curricula, and mis- management of the funds; but everywhere the chief cause of complaint was that the children of the rich had ousted the children of the poor, sometimes the usurpers being actually induced to come from a distance by scholarships, fellowships, prizes of all sorts, and boarding- houses to live in, all provided at the expense of the charities.

As to this monstrous abuse, one reformer (evidently a man of sporting proclivities), speaking of the example of the Manchester Free School, said :—

"Supposing those rich parents had established a stud of racing horses, for which they built stabling, provided trainers, and sub- scribed money for plates to be competed for, and all this solely for horses bred and reared in that particular parish; how would they like for richer and more powerful men living at a distance, to offer tempting annual sums of money to these trainers to get their horses into the stables provided for those bred and reared in that parish alone, and to allow their horses to run or compete for the annual prizes belonging to the parish horses? Of course, this would not be permitted in such a case; but in that of boys, it is thought to be perfectly fair."

There was scarcely a grammar school in which boarders were not received. At Rock in Worcestershire all the scholars were boarders. Bewdley Free Grammar School, founded for thirty inhabitant children, had not one foundation scholar, though the master took thirty boarders. And when the inhabitants appealed to the Court of Chancery, they obtained very little comfort from that quarter, the only result being that the school was then shut up altogether (1835). Morpeth Grammar School was the subject of a lawsuit which lasted 150 years.

Barnet Free Grammar School, with twenty-four governors and two schoolmasters, in 1850 had seven free boys and twenty-three boarders. Grantham Free Grammar School, founded by Bishop Fox in 1528, and endowed by Edward VI. in 1553 for the free education of boys in or within one mile of Grantham, had an income from endowment of £800 a year, with eight exhibitions and four scholarships. While the report very modestly stated that "the free boys seldom go to college," an extensive advertisement issued by the five masters announced that "extensive playgrounds, both in grass and gravel, have been set apart for the masters' boarders." And, of course, the two classes of boys were never allowed to mix together in the playgrounds. Henley-on-Thames Royal Free Grammar School, founded in 1605, free to twenty-five scholars, with an income of £362, issued this advertisement :—"N.B.—The day scholars are *few and select*, as there is an endowed *lower school* in the town"—it being understood that the admixture of the classes was, of course, not to be tolerated. Lichfield Grammar School, founded by Edward VI., and to which were attached no less than nine exhibitions, had but twenty-eight scholars in 1851, when the headmaster's advertisement announced that "there are no *free boys of an inferior grade* upon this foundation."

It is unnecessary to go on enumerating further in-stances of this description—there are plenty of them to be found in the Educational Register of 1851. Suffice it to say these examples are fairly typical of the state of the English endowed schools in the initial half of the nineteenth century.

XVI

LICENSING BEGGARS AND BADGING PAUPERS

Overburdened parishes licensed their surplus poor to beg abroad,
  but limited them to one area—No parishioner to distribute
  alms outside his own parish—Stow, the historian, a licensed
  beggar—A licence equivalent to a "rate in aid"—Bedesmen
  called "Badgemen"—The badging of paupers in receipt of
  out-door relief—Penalty on recalcitrant paupers who tried to
  escape the "badge of poverty"—Paupers in iron collars.

As the sixteenth century wore on, after the disruption of
society by the dissolution of the monasteries, and its
logical sequel the Reformation in the Church, vagrancy
increased more alarmingly than ever. From this
diseased state of society arose many complications—for
instance, the difficulty of distinguishing between the
needy poor and the sturdy poor, and discerning the
exact point at which poverty merged into crime—and
many legislative ponderosities.

In the Tudor statute of the middle of the sixteenth
century which instituted weekly collections for the relief
of the poor, committing to the admonition of his bishop
any parishioner who refused such voluntary contribution,
there was a further provision of a rather novel nature.

It is therein directed that if any parish has more poor
than it is able to relieve, upon certifying the number
and names of the persons with which it is overburdened

to two justices of the peace, they may grant to as many
of such poor folk "a licence to go abroad to beg and
receive charitable alms out of the said parish"; in which
licence the names of the places to which such poor
folk may resort shall be named ; and if any of them
transgress the limits to them so appointed, or beg at
other places than are named in the licence, the party so
transgressing is to be taken for a valiant beggar and
punished according to the statute of Henry VIII. (1531),
and the licence taken from him.

By the Act of Henry VIII. justices, mayors, or sheriffs
might license all aged poor and impotent persons who
"lived by alms and charity," to beg within an appointed
area, registering their names on a roll, and delivering
to each licensee a letter containing his name, witnessing
that he is licensed to beg, and naming the limits of the
area to which he is licensed.   If the person begged
beyond those prescribed limits he was to be imprisoned
two days in the stocks, and fed on bread and water, and
then sent back to his own parish.   Nor was any charitable townsman permitted to distribute his alms outside
his own parish, on pain of forfeiture, for this would
encourage wandering on the part of the poor.

It is a matter of history that Stow, who spent his life
in the study of history and topography, and to whose
"Survey of London" we are so much indebted for
our knowledge of the ancient capital, was granted a
licence to beg in his old age.   At the age of eighty,
having fallen into poverty, he petitioned James I. "for a
recompense of his labour and travel of forty-five years
in setting forth the 'Chronicles of England,' and eight
years taken up on the 'Survey of the Cities of London
and Westminster,' towards his relief in his old age ;
having left his former means of living, and only
employing himself for the service and good of his

country." A generous monarch and grateful country granted his prayer by Letters Patent under the Great Seal, reciting that—

"Whereas our loving subject John Stow (a very aged and worthy member of our City of London) this five-and-forty years to his great charge, and with neglect of his ordinary means of maintenance (for the general good, as well of posterity as of the present age) compiled and published divers necessary books and chronicles; and therefore we, in recompense of these his painful labours, and for the encouragement of the like, have, in our Royal inclination, been pleased to grant our Letters Patent, under our Great Seal of England, thereby authorising him, the said John Stow, to collect among our loving subjects their voluntary contributions and kind gratuities."

These Letters were granted for one year, but produced so little that they were extended for another twelve-month, one entire parish of the City of London giving the munificent sum of one shilling and sixpence! Such was the reward of a man who spent his life in the production of monumental works of literature. The memorial bust of this amiable and devoted historian is to be found in the church of St. Andrew's Undershaft.

There was formerly a hospital of Our Lady and St. Catherine at Newington, which continued till the year 1551, when their proctor, William Cleybrooke, being dispossessed of his home, was graciously granted a licence to beg. And no doubt many others to whom the community owed an obligation were "rewarded" in this cheap and ready manner.

Sir Walter Scott is said to have known a "character" who was the last person in the south of Scotland to wear the livery of the licensed or privileged beggar, and who died just before the close of the eighteenth century. The dress is described as a long blue gown of worsted or frieze, with a belt about the waist. The badge worn on the breast was of white metal, some five inches in diameter, and bearing an embossed inscription. The Scottish " Gaberlunzie man" will be described in a subsequent chapter.

All licensed beggars were to wear openly both on the breast and on the back of their outermost garment some "notable badge or token" to be assigned by the parish authorities, with the assent of the justices (1555).

This permission to go abroad to beg has been looked upon as something equivalent to a modern "rate in aid" of an overburdened parish ; and with regard to the custom of badging the poor it may be observed that there was a contemporary statute of near date against excess and extravagance in apparel—if it was desirable to curb the aspirations of the rising middle class, who aped the dress and fashions of their social superiors (Shakespeare alludes in the last act of " Hamlet" to " the toe of the peasant," wearing fashionable peaked shoes, with extravagantly long points, coming so " near the heel of the courtier"), it could not possibly be out of place to insist that the dependent poor should be unmistakably labelled for the behoof of their neighbours. And not only were licensed beggars compelled to wear a badge, but some towns went farther and put them into distinctive liveries. It was in the reign of Edward VI. that beggars were first ordered to wear their badges openly "on the back and the breaste."

Almshouse men had previously been known as " badge-men," because they wore some special dress, or other badge, to indicate that they belonged to a particular foundation. Crabbe alludes to the term—

> " He quits the gay and rich, the young and free,
> Among the badge-men with a badge to be."

The same poet has also a reference to the "bedesman"—

> "Seated with a grey bedesman"

—a name by which the inhabitant of an almshouse was known in pre-Reformation days (as previously explained, p. 162); and in this particular case the pensioner who told off the number of his prayers by the counting of his beads was evidently uniformed in grey.

At a later period, after the introduction of the Elizabethan Poor Laws, we get another form of the parochial "badge of poverty"—indeed, it cannot claim to be abolished at the present day, in view of the uniform or liveries worn by workhouse inmates and charity children.

This practice of labelling the victims of poverty was extended in the reign of William III. to those who were in the receipt of outdoor parish relief. In 1698 it was ordered that every man "upon the collection of the parish"—and his wife and children, too, if living with him—should wear a badge upon the shoulder of the right sleeve of the uppermost garment; to wit, "a large Roman P. with the first letter of the name of the parish cut in red and blue cloth."

This mark was to be distinctly visible on every person in receipt of parish pay, the penalty for omitting to display the badge ranging from the reduction, suspension, or withdrawal of the weekly pay to committal to the House of Correction with hard labour and a flogging. In any breach of the ordinance the beadle acted the part of informer, reporting the contumacy to churchwardens and overseers.

In 1630 Thomas Harvey, of Withington in Staffordshire, bequeathed £160 to provide a fund for buying "medley cloth for ye poor of ye parish of Leigh, yearly, for ever"; and eleven years later a second benefaction provided twenty-four yards of the same cloth yearly to clothe six poor men and six poor women in alternate years.

13

The badge was sometimes worn on the arm ; it was often a monogram of the initial letter of the name of the parish and the letter P for pauper ; sometimes the letters were worked in cloth and sometimes the whole badge was of cast brass.

In Bilston parish accounts we may find among the "disburstments" in 1703, "For setting ye badge upon 8 persons, 1/4"; in 1719, "cloth for badges, 2/-"; in 1726, "brass letters for marks, 7/7"; and other payments for a similar purpose.

In the Overseers' Book of Burton-on-Trent occurs this reference to the subject :—

"6th. September 1702. Whereas several persons that receive alms out of the poor's levy of this liberty do often omit the wearing of the public badge of this town, or observe the same : It is there-fore ordered that when any such poore person or persons shall, or their children bee seen without such badge or to observe the same, that upon the view of either of the Overseers or reliable information thereof to them of the neglect of wearing or observing such badge, such poore person or persons shall for a fortnight thereafter lose his or their allowance out of the poore's levy, and the like penalty shall be continued so often as any such offence shall be committed, and not put in pay again till such badge is worn."

A resolution passed at Cheadle in 1761 runs :—

"That a list of such persons as have pay out of the parish be entered in a book, with their respective weekly or monthly allowances, and that badges be prepared with the letters C. P. and be fixed upon em, and that each person receiving pay shall have un fixed to their coat or gown on the outside of the arm."

That the stigma attaching to the wearing of the badge was keenly felt by the unfortunate paupers is manifest from some of the other official records of this parish :—

"6th. June 1703. It is resolved that Elizabeth Salisbury, Mary Budworth, Hannah Scott, and Ann Hinckley be taken out of the constant pay on their stubborn refusal to wear the badge publicly."

Many old parochial records show how peculiarly distasteful to the paupers was the wearing of their badge of degradation. By an Act of Parliament the wearing of it was eventually ordered to be discontinued (1810) ; and so passed one of the many indignities heaped upon the poor and unfortunate in an inconsiderate age.

In some places, indeed, the poor would appear to have been treated literally like dogs. Thus we read in Reeves's " History of West Bromwich " (p. 125) :—

"In Mr. Smith's days (he was governor of the Workhouse in 1730) the poor in the House wore an iron collar round their necks with their names and parish engraved thereon. It was after a few years discontinued, and again used in 1766 for a short period."

XVII

VAGABONDAGE: ITS POVERTY AND CRIME

Poverty a source of crime—The vagabond—The rogue—Impostors
and impostures—Nothing new—"Caveat for Cursetors" (1566)
—Celebration of rich man's funeral by the "Canting Crew"
(1521)—"Caveat against Cut-purses" (1614)—The tricks of
Bartholomew Fair—The training of a cut-purse—John Selman
and Mary Frith, experts—Their interesting careers—The
users of Cant and Flash languages—A curious catalogue of
offenders.

THERE is no more prolific source of petty crime than
driving, desperate poverty. It is impossible to consider
the history of vagabondage without dealing at the same
time with the rogue and the trickster, and all the host
of petty offenders who wander about the country,
homeless and shiftless, eking out a living somehow,
honestly it may be occasionally, and failing that,
dishonestly, without the least compunction.

How rampant was roguery in the Elizabethan age is
made manifest by the frequent references to the subject
by contemporary writers. In the expressive slang of the
period, the art of "taking in" the simple-minded was
called "coney-catching." The phrase is used by Shakespeare, but of all the Elizabethan dramatists, the dissolute
Robert Greene perhaps had the most intimate acquaintance with the vices and villainies of city life. In 1591
the reprobate "Robin" Greene wrote, in two parts, "The
Croundworke of Coney-catching," and the following year

THE
Groundworke of Conny-catching;

the manner of their Pedlers-French, and the meanes
to vnderstand the same, with the cunning slights
of the Coui___ it Cranke.

Therein are handled the practises of the *Visiter*, the fetches
of the Shifter and Ruslar, the deceits of their Dores, the deuises
of Priggers, the names of the base loytering Losels, and
the meanes of euery Blacke-Art mans shifts, with
the reproofe of all their diuellish
practises.

Scum-caug. *Tho: Hearne.*

Done by a Iustice of Peace of great authoritie, who hath
had the examining of diuers of them.

*July 28, 1726 Giue me by mr. Bartholomew Gent. Fem. of Vniv.
Colledge.*

Printed at London by Iohn Danter for William Barley, and are to
be sold at his shop at the vpper end of Gratious streete,
ouer against Leaden-hall. 1592.

SHARPS AND FLATS IN THE AGE OF ELIZABETH.

appeared " The Third and Last Part of Coney-catching
with the newly devised Knavish Arte of Fool-taking."
Then came " A Disputation betweene a Hee-coney-
catcher and a Shee-coney-catcher, whether a Thiefe or
a Whore is most hurtful in Cosonage to the common
wealth." The same year (1592) he wrote " The Defence
of Coney Catching by Cuthbert Coney-catcher," and the
following year "Questions concerning Conie-hood, and
the nature of the Conie." All these works deal with the
rogues, thieves, and sharpers with which London then
abounded.

The vagabond is one who wanders vaguely about
from place to place, always avoiding settled employment ; the rogue is one who also avoids work and
lives by trickery. For centuries the eye of the law
has regarded these two classes as identical, perhaps
because one merges so easily into the other, and
both are equally deserving of repression. Upon both
has fallen the incurable disease of laziness ; they have—

" Fever-lurk
Never work."

The methods of the profession have varied but little
with the lapse of the centuries. In the time of Elizabeth
it had already produced the sham sailor and the lame
or maimed beggar who pretended he had been broken in
the wars. In the time of Charles II. the cheating gambler
was known as a "ruffler," a "huff," or a "shabaroon."
The confidence trick, in which the confiding rustic
is beguiled by the honest stranger into trusting him,
was practised three centuries ago, even in the well-
known form of "ring dropping." The woman who
"drags the lay," as singing a hymn along the gutter
is called, often leading two or three borrowed children
by the hand to excite compassion, had her prototype

two hundred years ago, and was then known as a "clapperdudgeon." The man who pretends to be deaf and dumb went about then, and was known as a "dummerer." The burglar then flourished as the house-breaker; and it must be borne in mind that when people invariably kept all their money in their houses housebreaking was a far more serious crime, as robbery often meant the complete ruin of the victim. In those bygone times the pickpocket plied his trade, but was then the cut-purse. The footpad, though the genus is not yet extinct, found more opportunities to lurk for his victim in lonely places when roads were unlighted and totally unguarded, than in these days of a systematic policing; while the dashing highwayman, who more boldly waylaid the traveller upon the open high-road, though belonging to an era which has long since passed away, is still not unhonoured and unsung in the realms of romance.

The words "cut-purse" and "pickpocket" are of historical value. When purses were suspended from the girdle, thieves cut the string or thong by which they were attached; but when pockets were adopted, the method of filching of course changed to meet the new fashion of carrying money. But an all-round and never-failing dexterity was ever a necessary accomplishment of the thief who ventured to steal from the person; as Autolycus says in "The Winter's Tale"—

> "To have an open ear, a quick eye, and a nimble hand,
> Is necessary for a cut-purse."

The implements employed consisted of a knife with a razor-like edge and a "horn thumb," or case of horn fitted on to the thumb to receive the edge of the knife when the dexterous cut was made.

In 1566 was first printed that remarkable work on vagrants, entitled " Caveat for Cursetors," written by a Kentish gentleman named Thomas Harman. " Cursetor " is the fine-sounding name this historian of the vagrant fraternity (which he says " began within these thirty years, or little about ") uses to signify vagabonds. It is a name borrowed from their own language, which they term " Pedler's French, or Canting." To show the long continuance of the Canting fraternity, he describes the scenes at the burial of a " man of worship " in Kent, in the year 1521. " There was such a number of beggars, besides poor householders dwelling thereabouts, that scarcely they might lie or stand about the house." To provide for this vast host in the ancient custom a large barn was utilised, a fat ox was roasted and served out with an accompaniment of drink ; and a dole of twopence was given to every man. It was when feudal hospitality of this ancient character was fast passing away that the army of beggars and the whole of the Canting crew found themselves deprived of what they called their " bousing and belly cheer " ; and thereupon took to helping themselves. For, as the sententious Martin Tupper hath it—

> " Clamorous pauperism feasteth
> While honest labour, pining, hideth his sharp ribs."

This warning to Cursetors calls to mind Ben Jonson's " Caveat against Cut-purses," which appears in his play of " Bartholomew Fair," a comedy crowded with amusing characters typical of the lower orders in the days of James I. (1614). There is a gingerbread woman who is twitted with making her wares of " stale bread, rotten eggs, musty ginger, and dead honey " ; a tapster who adulterates a half-pound of tobacco with a quarter

of a pound of colt's-foot; and a rascally ballad-singer
who diverts the attention of a "silly squire" with his
singing, while a confederate tickles the ear of the
simpleton with a straw to make him withdraw his hand
from his pouch, in order to rob him instantly. To add
to the humour of the situation the ballad-singer, to whom
the stolen purse has been rapidly and secretly passed,
sells the squire a copy of the ballad, "A Caveat against
Cut-purses," of which the burden is—

> "You oft have been told,
> Both the young and the old,
> And bidden beware of the cut-purse so bold,
> Then if you take heed not, free me from the curse,
> Who both give you warning, for, and the cut-purse,
> Youth, youth, thou hadst better been starved by thy nurse,
> Than live to be hanged for cutting a purse."

The girdle purse, or *gipciere*, was in use till the Restoration, when the street thieves were equally dexterous
either as cut-purses or as pickpockets. Stow informs
us that in 1585 a person named Wotton, a broken-
down merchant, "kept an academy for the perfection
of pickpockets and cut-purses" at an alehouse on
Smart's Quay, near Billingsgate. "Two devices," continues Stow, "were hung up—one was a pocket, the
other was a purse. The pocket had in it certain
counters, and was hung about with hawk's bells, and
over the top did hang a little sacring bell. The
purse had silver in it, and he that could take out a
counter, without noise of any of the bells, was adjudged
a judicial *nypper*, according to their terms of art;
a *foyster* was a pick-pocket, a *nypper* was a pick-purse
or cut-purse."

A notorious cut-purse was John Selman, executed for
practising his light-fingered thievery at the Chapel Royal
on Christmas Day, 1611, during the attendance of

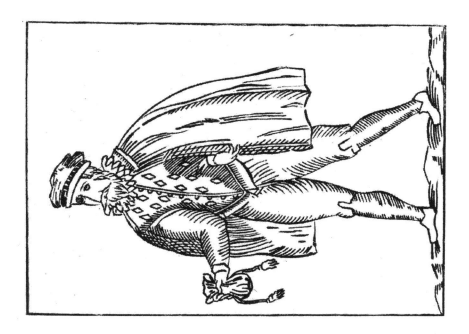

King James and his Court at service there. He was the prototype of the modern swell mobsman, wearing "a fair black cloak lined and faced with velvet"— practically the same thing which detectives know as the "cover," which present-day pickpockets use in their nefarious operations.

The most noted female practitioner, in what Dr. Johnson termed the "Biographia Flagitiosa," was Mary Frith, better known as Moll Cut-purse. According to her biography there is apparently nothing new under the sun ; for she usually worked in company with two other thieves, just as pickpockets do now. One, called the *bulk*, created an obstruction ; Mary, the *file*, cut the purse, and handed it to a third, called the *rub*, who carried it off. Moll always wore masculine attire, from the time she had been punished for this as an offence, when a young girl. For a wager she had ridden, booted and spurred, carrying a trumpet and a flag, through the streets of London ; and after doing penance at the door of St. Paul's Cathedral to atone for this offence, resolved never to resume woman's garb ; doublet and breeches being found so much more convenient to her way of life.

In the character of a highwayman she once robbed the Parliamentary general, Fairfax, of two hundred gold jacobuses on Hounslow Heath. Being a staunch Royalist, there seemed something quite appropriate in this. She had established herself opposite the Conduit, in Fleet Street, as a broker or negotiator between thieves and the public. When Charles I. passed her door one day, in 1639, she rushed out, caught his royal hand, and kissed it. In celebration of this delectable act of loyalty the law-contemning lady caused the Conduit to run with wine at her own proper charges and cost. After an adventurous career this remarkable character died of dropsy at the age of seventy, having composed her own epitaph in the form of an acrostic—

"M erry I lived, and many pranks I played
A nd, without sorrow, now in grave am laid ;
R est, and the sleep of death, doth now surcease
Y outh's active sins, and their old-aged increase.

F amous I was for all the thieving art,
R enouned for what old women ride in cart,
I n pocket and in placquet, I had part
T his life I lived in a man's disguise,
H e best laments me that with laughter cries."

At the close of the eighteenth century was published "A Dictionary of Cant and Flash Languages used by gipsies, beggars, swindlers, shoplifters, peterers, starrers, footpads, highwaymen, sharpers, and every class of offenders from lully prigger to high tober cloak." This curious brochure was compiled by an attorney, named Potter ; and of this class of offender he catalogues not less than sixty-one, from " Abram-man," one who went about fantastically dressed with ribbons and fox-tails to ape the begging Bedlamite, to " Upright-man," the chief of a begging crew ; and including " Clapperdudgeon," the beggar who went about in a patched cloak, accompanied by his " mort" and children ; " Cully," the wretch who preyed upon the earnings of a woman's prostitution ; and others equally interesting in their villainy. Of the foregoing list in the title it may be necessary to explain a few of the more obscure terms ; a " peterer" was a rogue who made a practice of stealing trunks and boxes from coaches and chaises ; a " starrer," one who broke windows to steal the goods in them ; a " lully prigger," one who stripped and robbed children of their clothes ;

and "high tober cloak," a well-dressed and well-mounted highwayman.

In the same Flash tongue, a "scellum" is a thief; a "dommerer," or "dummer," a beggar who pretends to be dumb; a "corinthian," a debauched reveller; a "flutter-grub," a field labourer; a "crank," an impostor; "a mort," a wife or mistress; and "nawth," the poor and destitute.

XVIII

THE GIPSIES

Arrive in England in fifteenth century—Origin and name—Act of
1530 banishes them—To depart the country under their governor,
Philippe Lazar (1545)—Yet found occupying a church-house
in 1560—Accounted felons 1597—Joined by English vagrants
and "loyterers" : hence their English names—Dekker's de-
scription of Egyptian "moon-men" villanies—How they forage
—Dress fantastically—Thieve and poach—And tell fortunes—
"Egyptian roges" described in Holinshed's Chronicles—
Pedlers' French—Romany language—Arnold's "Scholar Gipsy"
—North Britain gipsies—"Jonny Faa the Gypsie Laddie"—
Gipsy Hill tribe—Queen Esther of Yetholm—Child-stealing—
Maggie Tulliver's adventure—Divination—Allusions by Crabbe
and Gay—The gipsy blood.

IN the fifteenth century a new and undesirable element
made its appearance in the lower stratum of English
society, to swell the already overcrowded ranks of thriftless wanderers. These were bands of nomads, having no
regular means of subsistence, who came to be known
as Gipsies.

The name gipsy, being a corruption of "Egyptian,"
assumes that Egypt was the original home of this
strange people, as was widely believed when they made
their first appearance in Europe early in the fifteenth
century. This, however, was a mistake, of which their
language leaves no doubt, proclaiming as it does that
they are wanderers from a more distant East, an outcast
tribe from Hindostan.

The French made a similar error in calling them Bohemians, imagining they were the expelled Hussites of Bohemia. In different countries they obtained different names for themselves; as Gitanos in Spain, Zingari in Italy, and Pharaoh-nepak (or Pharaoh's people) in Hungary; although they called themselves Sintè, asserting that they came from Sind—that is, Ind or Hindostan. Notwithstanding their intercourse with other nations, their manners, customs, visage, and appearance have remained distinctive for centuries; and in this country their pretended knowledge of futurity has given them considerable power over the ignorant and superstitious.

By some, this ubiquitous people has been identified with the lost ten tribes of Israel, and much mystery attached to them accordingly. In his " Spanish Student " Longfellow informs us that the gipsies of Spain—

> ". . . came with Hercules from Palestine
> And hence are thieves and vagrants."

In 1530 an Act was made against their itinerancy, in which it was set forth that—

> " Many outlandish people, calling themselves Egyptians, using no craft or faict [practice] of merchandise, have come into this realm, and gone from shire to shire, and place to place, in great company; and used great subtle and crafty means to deceive the people; bearing them in hand that they by palmistry could tell men's and women's fortunes, and so, many times, by craft and subtility have deceived the people of their money, and also have committed many and heinous felonies and robberies."

This description of the familiar fortune-telling impostors would apply almost with equal aptness in recent times as in the reign of Henry VIII. They were to depart out of the country forthwith, said the law, upon pain of imprisonment and forfeiture of goods. Seven years later, Thomas Cromwell, the King's factotum, and "the hammer of the monks," whom he was at this time engaged in suppressing, and in other ways ruling England "under a terror," wrote to the president of the Welsh Marches, desiring him to cause the "Gipcyans" to depart beyond the sea, or in default of obedience to execute them without hesitation. The latter charges them with "falsehoods, felonies, and treasons." The term "treasons" here is scarcely significant of political sedition; it may be better understood if interpreted in association with a statute passed in 1531 for the punishment of beggars and vagabonds, which took cognisance of the growth of "a disturbed and restless disposition, the interruption of industry," and other symptoms of social—not political—disorders.

It appears from the State records that in 1545-6 at a Privy Council "a passporte was signed for the Egiptiones to passe with their Bagge and Baggage, under the conduct of Philippe Lazar their governour, according to my Lord Admyralles ordere to embarke at Londone." It would be interesting to know how many—or, rather, how few —were deported on this occasion.

A curious record exists in the Churchwardens' Accounts of the parish of Stratton in Cornwall. In mediæval times many parishes possessed a "church-house" which was used at different seasons throughout the year for the parochial celebration of the succeeding Church festivals, particularly for the various Church Ales (see Chapter V.). From the Stratton accounts it would appear that the church-house there was let at Fair times to the merchants attending with their wares for sale; and also, on various other occasions, to the gipsies.

Thus, occurs an item for the year 1552:—

" Received of the Egypcions for the church house, **xx** *d.*"

Twenty-seven years later is found an entry still more puzzling:—

"Received of the Jewes for the church house, ij *s* vj *d*."

The word "Jewes" is not erased, but the word "Jeptyons" is written over it. Did these poor wanderers call themselves Jews to escape persecution? Or did this scribe confuse these banished peoples? Anyway, in 1560 the "Jepsyons" again occupy the church-house for one night, and pay the sum of sixpence as rent. Perhaps the stern Tudor laws were not rigorously enforced in that remote corner of the country.

The oft-quoted statute of the thirty-ninth year of Elizabeth's reign included among proscribed "rogues and vagabonds" all persons "pretending themselves to be Egyptians." These "Egyptian" pariahs, or gipsies, were to be dealt with by the very summary process prescribed under the statute of Philip and Mary, which declared them to be felons outright, and liable to hanging.

There was also an earlier statute of Elizabeth which accounted "all pretended Egyptians" as felons:—

" Every person which shall be seen or found in any company or fellowship of vagabonds commonly called Egyptians, or counterfeiting, transforming, or disguising themselves by their apparel, speech, or other behaviour, like unto such vagabonds, and shall continue and remain in the same by the space of one month, every such person shall be deemed and judged a felon, and shall suffer the pains of death."

This special Act is instructive in two directions. First, it seems to indicate pretty clearly that our modern gipsies are of a mixed descent, representing natives of nomadic tendencies, equally with the original oriental immigrants to whom they joined themselves, and whose

wandering modes of life they adopted. Also it shows
the existence of a condition of English life which might
be considered somewhat rare and exceptional, did we
not remember the traditional popularity of the life led
beneath the greenwood tree by the Robin Hood
class in Plantagenet times. But no doubt the denizens
of the woods in Tudor times were of a distinctly
lower type, with nothing whatever of the heroical about
them. They were the sloughed cast-offs of civilised
society, who elected to go forth from its conventionalities
and restraints, to indulge themselves freely in the
extremest licences of vagabondage. The bolder and
more heroical spirits of Elizabeth's time who "spurned
the base mechanical arts" found outlets for more
honourable employment in life beyond the seas—the
wild and profligate, perhaps, in seeking adventures in
the Spanish Main. But the less adventurous, and
perhaps the more unimaginative, to whom regular labour
was equally irksome, instead of joining themselves to
sea-rovers went out of the towns and villages to the
wealds and heaths ; they discoloured their skins, gave an
oriental fashion to their ragged apparel, learnt the gipsy
dialect, and put on the gipsy nature of cheating and
pilfering. To some minds there is a charm about a free
and roving mode of life from which even the precarious-
ness of it cannot detract. The sunny side of it was
recognised by the dramatic poets; and in "The Beggar's
Bush" of Fletcher the whole aspect of vagrancy is
given a freshness which makes it look so like an
essential part of nature, that we do not wonder that
"pretended Egyptians" were numerous enough to have
a statute to themselves.

Almost from the moment of their arrival on these
shores these alien wanderers were joined by numbers
of English "loyterers" possessed of the same nomadic

tastes, and whose aversion from honest labour made them apt pupils of the "cozening art."

This assimilation may possibly explain how the gipsies became possessed of such common English surnames as Smith, Stanley, Taylor, Davies, Roberts, Finch, Jeffery, Cooper, Boswell, Mansfield, Lee, Herne, Lovatt, Lowell, Loveridge, and others of like familiar sound, which they have come to bear. Carew is said to be an Anglicized form of the Hindu name "Kuru." Some amount of originality, however, often distinguishes the baptismal names they affect, as Wisdom, Logan, Ambrose, Jasper, Leviathan, and Nethen, and a selection of some of the more obscure biblical names, as Tamar, Athaliah, and Sheba. The names Sinfi, Femi, and Liti are as pretty as they are original.

Whatever the gipsy characteristics may have been at their earliest landing on the shores of this country, it is quite clear that all the distinguishing features by which they are now known were already stamped upon them in the sixteenth century. Dekker, the Elizabethan dramatist, who has left us, in a pamphlet called "The Bellman of London," a lively description of the London vagabond, in a kindred work called "English Villanies," gives us an equally cynical and satirical account of the gipsies. He applies to them the usual and familiar epithets, "priggers," "cheaters," and "pilferers," and says they are known as "moon-men" :—

"Their name [he says] they borrow from the moon, because the moon is never in one shape two nights together, but wanders up and down Heaven like an antic, so these changeable stuff companions never tarry one day in a place but are the only base runagates upon earth. And as in the moon there is a man, that never stirs without a bush of thorns at his back, so these Moon-Men lie under bushes, and are indeed no better than hedge-creepers. They are a people more scattered than Jews, and more hated, beggarly in apparel, barbarous in condition, and beastly in behaviour, and bloody if they

14

meet advantage. A man, that sees them, would swear they had all the yellow jaundice; or that they were tawny Moors' bastards, for no red-oaker man carries a face of a more filthy complexion; yet are they not born so, neither hath the sun burnt them so, but they are painted so; yet they are not good painters neither, for they do not make faces, but mar faces. By a bye-name they are called Gypsies; they call themselves Egyptians; others in mockery call them Moon-Men. If they be Egyptian, sure I am they never descended from any of the tribes of those people that came out of the land of Egypt; Ptolemy, King of the Egyptians, I warrant, never called them his subjects, no nor Pharaoh before him. Look, what difference there is between a civil citizen of Dublin and a wild kerne, so much difference there is between a counterfeit Egyptian and a true English beggar. An English rogue is just of the same livery.

"They are commonly an army about fourscore strong, and they never march with all their bags and baggages together, but like boothalers [pillagers], they forage up and down countries, four, five, or six in a company. As the Switzer has his wench and his cock when he goes to the wars, so these vagabonds have their women, with a number of little children at their heeles, which young brood of beggars are sometimes carried—like so many green geese alive to a market in paires of paniers, or in dossers like fresh fish from Rye comes on horse-back—if they be but infants, but if they can straddle once, then as well she-rogues as he-rogues are horst, seven or eight upon one jade, strongly pineoned and strangely tied together.

" Let them be scattered worse than the quarters of a traytor are after he's hanged, drawne, and quartered, yet they have a trick, like water cut with a sword, to come together instantly and easily againe; and this is their policie, which way soever the foremost ranks lead, they stick up small boughs in several places to every village were they passe, which serve as ensigns to wait on the rest.

" Their apparell is odd and fantastick, though it be never so full of rents. The men wear scarves of calico, or any other loose stuff, hanging about their bodies, like Morice dancers, with bells and other toys to entice the country people to flock about them to wonder at their fooleries, or rather rank knaveries The women as ridiculously attire themselves, and wear rags and patched filthy mantles uppermost when the undergarments are handsome and in fashion.

" The battles these outlaws make are very bloody. Whosoever falls into their hands never escapes alive, and so cruel they are in these murthers that nothing can satisfy them but the very heart-blood of these whom they kill. And who are they, think you, that thus go to the pot?—alas ! innocent lambs, sheep, calves, pigs. Poultry-ware are more churlishly handled by them than poor prisoners are by keepers in the Counter in the Poultry. A goose coming amongst them learns to be wise, that he will never be goose any more. The bloody tragedies of all these are only acted by the women, who carrying long knives, or skernes, under their mantles, do thus play their parts. The stage is some large heath or furze-bush common, far from any houses, upon which, casting themselves into a ring, they enclose the murdered till the massacre be finished. If any passenger come by, and wondering to see such a conjuring circle kept by hell-hounds, and demand what spirits they raise there, one of the murderers steps to him, poisons him with sweet words, and shifts him off with this lie that one of the women are fallen in labour ; but if any mad Hamlet, hearing this, smells villany, and rush in by violence to see what the tawny divels are doing, then they excuse the fact, lay the blame on the actors, and perhaps (if they see no remedy) deliver them to an officer to be had to punishment ; but by the way a rescue is surely laid , and very valiantly, though very villainously, do they fetch them off and guard them.

"The cabins where these land-pirates lodge in the night are the outbarns of farmers and husbandmen in some poor village or other, who dare not deny them for fear they should ere morning have their thatched houses burning about their ears , and these barns are both their cookrooms, their supping-parlours, and their bed-chambers, for there they dress after a beastly manner what-soever they purchased [stole] after a thievish fashion. Sometimes they eat venison, and have greyhounds that kill it for them , but if they had not, they are hounds themselves and are damnable hunters after flesh.

" Upon days of pastime and liberty they spread themselves in small companies amongst the villages, and when young maids and bachelors—yea sometimes old doting fools that should be beaten [accustomed] to this world of villanies, and forewarn others—do flock about them, they then profess skill in palmistry, and forsooth can tell fortunes, which for the most part are infallibly true, by reason that they work upon rules which are grounded upon certainty ; for one of them will tell you that you shall shortly have some evil luck fall upon you, and within half an hour after you shall have your pocket picked, or your purse cut."

Thus did that competent authority, Thomas Dekker, express his opinion of gipsies.

Harrison, in his description of England prefixed to Holinshed's Chronicles (1587), describing the various sorts of cheats practised by the voluntary poor, after enumerating those who maimed or disfigured their bodies by sores, or counterfeited the guise of labourers or serving-men, or mariners seeking for ships which they had not lost, to extort charity, adds :—

"It is not yet full three score years since this trade began ; but how it hath prospered since that time it is easy to judge, for they are now supposed of one sex and another to amount unto above ten thousand persons, as I have heard reported. Moreover, in counterfeiting the *Egyptian Roges*, they have devised a language amongst themselves which they name Canting, but, by others 'pedlers' French,' a speech compact thirty years since of English, and a great number of odd words of their own devising, without all order or reason ; and yet such is it as none but themselves are able to understand. The first deviser thereof was hanged by the neck, a just reward no doubt for his deceits, and a common end to all of that profession."

Of their peculiar lingo much has been written, not a little of it mere guess-work. Thus "tinker" has been derived from "tinkler," and associated with "Zingaro." The Romany language—by the way, why "Romany," when the earliest appellation they applied to themselves seems to have been Sinde (? Indians) and not Romees or Romino people ?—has been allied to Sanscrit ; and again just as positively derived from Elizabethan slang.

In volume vii. of *Archæologia* will be found an article in which the writer professes to demonstrate the connection of "Zingari or Gipsy Language" with the "Hindostanic" tongue, and protests against confusing it with the cant and fabricated gibberish of beggars. There will also be found a short vocabulary, arranged on the comparative method. Other authorities declare that beggars and thieves are largely indebted to the gipsy language for much of their slang.

A rhyming slang has been put forward as one of the bases of Shelta (to which subject allusion will be made later), a secret language of antiquity, said to have been framed in remote times by Irish scholars and poets. The system of its derivation has even been formulated, the following being among the methods stated to have been employed : (1) Spelling the Irish word backwards ; (2) prefixing an arbitrary letter or letters ; (3) substituting another letter for the initial ; (4) the transposition of letters.

If the Romany speech and the English language have not a common source, one has evidently borrowed from the other ; but which is the original and which the derivative it would be difficult to determine. Here are just a few examples, where it almost appears that Romany words (which are given first) have been adopted into colloquial English (given second) : *Mami,* a grandmother —*mammy,* a mother ; *pal,* a brother—*pal,* a partner, or close companion ; *tauno,* little—*teeny,* very little ; *mang,* to beg—*maund,* to beg.

Of the Romany words which, since the popularising of the cult by George Borrow's writings, are to be met with occasionally in current literature, a brief selection may be useful.

A *Romany* is a gipsy, and a *Georgio,* a non-gipsy, or Gentile stranger ; a *chal* is a lad, and a *chi* a lass ; a *kinchin* is a child, and a *chickno* a youth ; a *rye* is a gentleman, and *chokengres,* police ; *chories* are thieves, and *chore* is to steal ; *lavo* is a word, and *lil* is a book or a paper ; *gyres* are horses, and *petul* a horseshoe ; *tacho* is true, and *dukkerin* is fortune-telling.

From the foregoing it may be seen that *Romano-lavo-lil* stands for a gipsy word-book ; *Lavengro* means word-master (*engro* being the Borrovian ending for master, or fellow) ; and *Petulengro,* as a surname, neatly fits the head of the Smith tribe.

Matthew Arnold's poem, "The Scholar Gipsy," tells "the oft-read tale again" of Glanvil, the latitudinarian philosopher of the Restoration period :—

> "The story of the Oxford scholar poor
> Of pregnant parts and quick inventive brain
> Who, tired of knocking at preferment's door,
> One summer morn forsook
> His friends, and went to learn the gipsy-lore."

Glanvil, writing in 1661, descants upon a lad who, forced by poverty to leave his studies, joined himself to a company of vagabond gipsies. Among these strange people he quickly got so much of their love and esteem as they discovered to him their mystery. After a while there chanced to ride by a couple of scholars, his old acquaintance at Oxford. They immediately spied out their former friend among the gipsies, and he gave them an account of the necessity which drove him to that kind of life. He told them the people he went with were not such impostors as they were taken for, but that they had—

"a traditional kind of learning among them, and could do wonders by the power of imagination, their fancy binding that of others —that himself had learned much of their art, and when he had compassed the whole secret he said, he intended to leave their company, and give the world an account of what he had learned."

Banishment by Act of Parliament in the reign of Henry VIII., and severe penal laws against them in the reigns of Philip and Mary and of Queen Elizabeth, do not seem to have had much effect in diminishing their numbers—living out in the open country, they were practically out of reach of the officers of the law. In Scotland, on the other hand, they seem to have enjoyed some indulgence. Readers of Scott's "Guy Mannering" will recall that striking character, the strange old gipsy

MARGARET FINCH, QUEEN OF THE NORWOOD GIPSIES.

To face p. 215.

woman, Meg Merrilies. In the North of Britain the gipsies were commonly known as " Faws." In 1754, John Fall was a well-known proscribed gipsy; and "Jonny Faa the Gypsie Laddie" was a popular Scottish song about that time.

On the outskirts of the metropolis a favourite gipsy haunt was the neighbourhood of Norwood, a situation convenient for London and Croydon. An aged sybil of some authority among them, named Sarah Skemp, died there in 1790. At Gipsy Hill, the history of which warrants its name, died in 1760, at the age of 109, another tribal queen and reader of the stars, Margaret Finch. Of her it has been observed by Mr. Larwood, in his "History of Signboards," that "when a girl of seventeen she may have been one of the dusky gang that pretty Mrs. Samuel Pepys and her companions went to consult in August, 1668." Dulwich Woods also, at the beginning of the last century, were the resort of a succession of dark-eyed Cassandras who beguiled credulous youth with their prophetic voices, till magisterial authority drove them away.

In 1865, when "Queen Esther," of Yetholm, in the Cheviots, claimed sovereignty over all the gipsy peoples of this realm—there seems to have been, at different times, a number of claimants to this honour—it was calculated that in the British Isles there were no less than a quarter of a million of them, of all castes, colours, and characters, of various occupations, degrees of education and position in life, from wealthy horse-dealers and petted prizefighters to ragged travelling tinkers and unashamed beggars. There is such a thing as gipsy pride of birth—

" What care we though we be so small—
The tent shall stand when the palace shall fall."

The least of the crimes popularly ascribed to these outlandish people is that of child-stealing; in the reign of William III. this was punished by branding the offender when caught with the letters R. M. T.; on the shoulders with R. (for rogue); on the right hand with M. (for man-slayer); and on the left hand with T. (thief).

Not the least delightful episode in George Eliot's immortal novel, "The Mill on the Floss," is little Maggie Tulliver's running away from the irksomeness of conventionalism to indulge her rebellious soul in the ideal delights which her childish imagination had painted of the "half-wild" life of free-roving gipsydom.

In this case the gipsies promptly restored the foolish child to her parents, doubtless because it was safer, and they felt sure of a reward. The kidnapped victim was supposed always to be disfigured—

> "lest the stolen brat be known,
> Defacing first, then claiming for his own."

The chief stock-in-trade of the gipsy is his professed power of divination; this petty rogue of a fortune-teller—

> "Will take upon him to divine men's fate
> Yet never knows himselfe shall dy a beggar,
> Or be hanged up for pilfering cloaths
> Hanged out to dry upon the hedges."

The poet Crabbe has painted a picture of the gipsies of an English fen :—

> "Where, lo! a hollow on the left appeared,
> And there a gipsy tribe their tent had reared"

—and in contemplating the various members of the tribe there encamped, he closes the uncomplimentary review

with " two brown boys "—" young ruffians " he styles
them ; and tries in prophetic gipsy-fashion—

> " To trace the progress of their future years ;
> Through what strange course of misery, vice, deceit,
> Must wildly wander, each unpractised cheat."

Gay, in his pastorals, makes the allusion:—

> " Last Friday's eve, when as the sun was set
> I, near yon stile, three sallow gipsies met ;
> Upon my hand they cast a poring look
> Bid me beware, and thrice their heads they shook ;
> They said that many crosses I must prove,
> Some in my worldly gain, but most in love."

That into a stock of oriental origin an amount of
English blood has been absorbed seems quite clear.
The English element is a result of a revolt against
the conventional ; it is what Mr. Hilaire Belloc has
called a reversion to the natural, to the primitive
instincts of our race. For, as he points out, the
Saxon and the Viking swarmed to England in search
of adventure as well as nutrition ; the Norman followed :
and we are at bottom a nomadic race. In Elizabeth's
days we swarmed over the seas. At home the same
spirit prompted a number to join themselves to the
tents of Kedar ; and ever since, with a characteristic
contempt for their stationary brethren, these have been
moving along the highways, never stopping in the cities,
travelling not as shiftless tramps, but always self-support-
ing, and as happy in their independence as the nomads
of the world's childhood.

As the heaths and roadside margins have gradually
disappeared, the ranks of the hedge-creepers have been
swelled by cadgers and mumpers taking to tent life,

and exchanging the shelter of the common lodging-house for the lee-side of the old hedge.

To-day but few Children of the Heath are of the pure Romany stock. The blood-gipsy is swarthy as a Moor, and carries well some picturesque touch of oriental colour in his dress. He is full of vitality, of amazing vigour, and by no means deficient in intelligence. His women-kind are often handsome, and of erect carriage, their bold, swarthy features set off by a crown of blue-black hair. The real gipsy, with his oriental features and primitive habits, in a proper setting of his natural everyday surroundings, " fills the picture."

XIX

THE ITINERANT TRADER

The trader who carries his stock with him—Autolycus—A pedlar's song—Pedlars' cries—Derivation of the term "pedlar"—Pedlar's fardel—Porter's knot—Pedlar's Acre, Lambeth—Tranters—Hawkers—First licensed (1789)—Tinkers' talk—A link with Druidical bronze-workers—Irish beggars—An ancient *lingua franca*—A canting song (1620)—Street traders—Street cries—Costermongers—Courts of Pie-powder—"The Needy Knife-grinder" parody—Catnach Press ballads—Scottish ballad of "The Gaberlunzie Man"—Its plot and authorship.

A LITTLE removed from the vagabond and the nomadic beggar, and even above the ballad-singer and the wastler or wandering musician, though ofttimes a companion on the road with this vagrant train, was the itinerant tradesman—the pedlar, the chapman, the tinker—who carried his stock-in-trade about with him, and paid no man rent, either for workshop or stallage.

The line between begging and street-trading is not infrequently very indistinct, the English beggar often hiding himself behind a licence to sell. And when a gentleman of the road, beggar or trader, leaves the king's highway and crosses a field to steal a turnip or snare a rabbit, he instantly becomes a criminal. How prone these gentry are to "miche" about—that is, to loiter with intent to thieve—was known to Shakespeare, who uses the word "micher" as a synonym for a low, skulking thief.　To "miche" or to "mouche" is still to pick up a living while tramping about.

Of this class is Autolycus, the roguish pedlar in "The Winter's Tale"; like his Greek prototype, Autolycos, he is the craftiest of thieves, born under Mercury, the thievish planet.　Even the clown fails not to recognise him as a sly pilferer, and despises him for "a prig that haunts wakes, fairs, and bear-baitings."　But then, how he is welcomed at every door!　"O master!" says one, "if you did but hear the pedlar at the door. . . . He sings several tunes faster than you'll count money; he utters them as he had eaten ballads, and all men's ears grew to his tunes."　"I love a ballad only too well," says another.　"He hath songs, for man or woman, of all sizes," is the reply.　And presently in comes Autolycus, singing gaily and selling his wares off just as fast and as easily as he sings:—

> "Lawn, as white as driven snow,
> Cyprus, black as e'er was crow;
> Gloves as sweet as damask roses;
> Masks, for faces and for noses:
> Bugle-bracelet, necklace-amber,
> Perfume for a lady's chamber;
> Golden quoifs, and stomachers,
> For my lads to give their dears;
> Pins and poking-sticks of steel;
> What maids lack from head to heel;
> Come, buy of me, come; come buy; come buy;
> Buy, lads, or else your lasses cry:
> Come buy.

> Will you buy any tape,
> Or lace for your cape,
> My dainty duck, my dear-a?
> Any silk, any thread,
> Any toys for your head,

Of the new'st and fin'st, fin'st wear-a ?
    Come to the pedlar ;
    Money's a meddler,
That doth utter all men's ware-a."

A composition arranged and published in 1667 as a glee for three voices has been attributed to Shakespeare, and is supposed to have been appropriate to put in the mouth of this character. Known as "The Pedlar's Song," it begins :—

"From the far Lavinian shore,
    I your markets come to store ;
    Muse not, though so far I dwell,
    And my wares come here to sell,
    Such is the sacred hunger for gold.
        Then come to my pack,
            While I do cry
        What dy'e lack ?
            What d'ye buy ?
    For here it is to be sold."

According to the "Fraternitye of Vacabondes" (1575), with which Shakespeare was doubtless acquainted, petty traders of this kind were called Irish-toyles. A character of this name is mentioned in one of Dekker's plays, entitled "English Villanies" (1620).

"An Irish-toyle," says the authority named, "is he that carrieth his ware in hys wallet, as laces, pins, poyntes, and such like. He useth to shew no wares untill he have his almes , and if the good man and wyfe be not in the way, he procureth of the children or servants a fleece of wool, or the worth of xij*d*. of some other thing, for a peniworth of his wares."

A chant belonging to a somewhat later period, by which the pedlar of needles was wont to advertise his wares, ran in this wise :—

> " Bodging needles,
> Codging needles,
> Darning needles,
> Muslin needles,
> All sorts of needles, oh ! "

To cry his pins he indulged in rhyme, as :—

> "Any row, a penny, oh ! "

Or later, when they became cheaper, it was :—

> " Twenty rows a penny,
> Isn't that a many ? "

The Pedlar is grouped with the Palmer, the Pardoner, and the Poticary, in John Heywood's merry interlude called " The Four P's," written about 1543. These are the only characters in the play, and are doubtless put forward by the dramatist as the embodiment of travelled knowledge combined with unscrupulous assertion. It is a droll farce which turns on a dispute as to which shall tell the grossest falsehood ; the motive is worked out with much skill, till the accidental assertion of the Palmer that he never saw a woman out of patience in his life, takes the rest off their guard, all of whom declare it to be the greatest lie they ever heard, and the settlement of the question is thus brought about amidst much mirth.

The pedlar, one who travels from place to place on foot selling small wares, was not so called because he tramped about on his feet (Latin, *pedes*, " feet "), as most people imagine ; but because he carried a *ped*, or hamper without a lid, in which he stored fish or other articles to hawk about the streets. The " pedlar and his pack " is a familiar association of terms ; and an ancient authority notes the difference between a porter and a pedlar to consist in this, " that the porter's pack reacheth over his head, and so answerable below; but the pedlar's is a small truss, bundle, or fardel, not exceeding the middle of his head." Every reader of Shakespeare knows the word "fardel"—

> "Who would fardels bear
> To groan and sweat under a weary life," &c.

The porter's knot consists of a strong fillet to encircle the head, attached to which is a strong and thick leather pad resting on the shoulders, upon which a heavy load can be borne, every part of the body being called upon by this method to support the burden. The porter's knot may still be seen in use along the quay-side in the Port of London.

In Swaffham Church there is a portrait of one John Chapman, a great benefactor of the parish, who is represented as a pedlar with his pack. According to a tradition in Lambeth a pedlar left a sum of money for the public benefit—there is a "Pedlar's Acre" in the parish—on condition that his picture, with a dog, should be preserved for ever in the glass of one of the church windows. Such a figure formerly existed in the south window of the middle aisle, and its removal in 1884 to another position caused much annoyance locally. On the "Pedlar's Acre" at one time stood a public-house with the sign of a pedlar and his dog; while on the tap-room window appeared the following lines :—

> "Happy the pedlar whose portrait we view,
> Since his dog was so faithful and fortunate too ;
> He at once made him wealthy and guarded his door,
> Secured him from robbers, relieved him when poor.
> Then drink to his memory, and wish fate may send
> Such a dog to protect you, enrich and befriend."

In Ducard's "History of the Parish of Lambeth" (p. 30)

a capital engraving of the Pedlar and his Dog is given; in Allen's "History of Lambeth" (p. 62) is a coloured picture of the stained-glass window.

In some parts of the country a pedlar is called a traunter or tranter. A hawker is an itinerant trader who either carries his wares himself, or employs a beast of burden to assist him in doing so.

In 1789 hawkers were first licensed, and charged a further duty upon every horse or other beast of burden used for carrying goods about. This was to keep these wanderers under control, but the Act did not extend to the selling of newspapers, fish, fruit, or victuals, nor to the real workers or makers of British goods selling the same, nor to any travelling tinker, cooper, glazier, plumber, or harness mender.

Of all the travelling tradesmen who, century after century, have trudged the highways and the byways of the country, in search of odd jobs, none can boast a more ancient lineage than the tinker, whose very name recalls the "ting ting" of his roadside activities as a mender of pots and pans and kettles. It has long been known that the travelling tinkers used a sort of secret jargon among themselves; does not Shakespeare make the roystering Prince Hal declare that he could drink with any tinker in his own language? and was not the immortal Bunyan, a wayfaring worker like his father before him, familiar with the "tinkers' talk"? On the other hand it is strange that George Borrow, who was always on the alert for any strange scraps of philological lore, and whose acquaintance with tinkers should certainly have given him good opportunities of hearing their lingo, makes no mention of it in his writings.

Recent investigations have tended to identify this tinkers' talk, otherwise "minklers' thari," or Shelta, as it is properly called, with the ancient Irish tongue. To add to the romance of the discovery it is recalled that the old Celtic bards (and possibly the Druids) had an artificial secret tongue peculiar to themselves. To account for this speech passing to the possession of the lowly tinkers, old Leland, the antiquary of early Tudor times, is thus quoted :—

"The bronze-workers of old time formed a very close corporation, having many secrets, and being in all probability allied to the learned class of bards. Hence they may have used the same secret language. And it is probable that the tinkers, or modern itinerant metal-workers, are the direct descendants of the artificers in bronze."

It is a matter of history that Charles II. issued a proclamation against Irish beggars, for the country at that time was inundated with wandering mendicants who hailed from the sister isle.

In remote times metal-working was often associated with occult practices, as in the forging of magic swords; and it is by no means impossible that among the Cant terms of the common lodging-house, the "flash tongue" of the modern tramp and the travelling tinker, may be found some interesting remnants of an ancient *lingua franca.*

Can any of these Cant terms be traced with the least degree of certainty to their real origin, either as corruptions of Irish, or as exhibiting vestiges of an Eastern tongue—*loge,* a watch; *deeker,* a spy; *larkin,* a girl; *strammul,* straw; *coored,* whipped; and *mang,* to boast?

Here is a curious old Canting song from Dekker's "Lanthorne and Candlelight" (1620), which conveys little or nothing to the ordinary mind :—

"The ruffin cly the nab of the harman-beck
If we mawned pannam, lap or ruff-peck
Or poplars of yarum; he cuts bing to the ruffmans
Or els he sweares by the lightmans

15

> To put our stamps in the harmans
> The ruffin cly the ghost of the harman-beck
> If we have a booth, we cly the jerke."

It becomes dimly intelligible when we know that "nab" means head; "harman-beck," the constable; "pannam," bread; "lap," porridge; "ruff-peck," bacon; "yarum," milk; "ruffmans," the woods; "lightmans," the day; "stamps," the legs; "harmans," the stocks; while "mawned" signifies begged; "bing," away.

The humblest class of merchant among town-dwellers includes the street traders, whose method of advertising is the cheap and ready one of bawling out, at the top of their voices, the nature and price of the wares they have to vend. The street cries of London in vogue a century or so ago are of themselves a subject of no little interest. They recall many forgotten details of household economies, and frequently illustrate old-time usages and methods of distribution. Some of the cries would no doubt perplex the present-day housewife, though at the time they were used, they all met a public want and stood for a real public convenience. Some of the criers commenced business before breakfast, and ere midday had come the street cries were legion. A number of them, of course, varied with the time of day as well as the season of the year, as, for instance, "Hot rolls" in the morning, "Strawberries, fine strawberries," and "New potatoes" in the summer-time.

Other seasonal cries were "Cherry ripe, O!" "Baking or boiling apples," "Green hastings" (these were early peas); "Lavender, sweet lavender, six bunches a penny"; or perhaps "Rabbits, wild rabbits"; and when there was a good catch of fish it might be "Mackerel, O!" or "Herrings, alive, all alive!" Some of the cries would sound strange to the ear now; as "Band-boxes," "Baskets," "Buy a broom," "Hair brooms," "Hot

spiced gingerbread," "Brick-dust," "Sand, O !"
"Bellows to mend," "Chairs to mend," "Bill of the
play"; more familiar, perhaps, were "Old clothes,"
"Cat's and dog's meat," and "Dust, O !" To these
daily cries the postman added the din of his bell.

The whole range of street cries has been picturesquely
treated in a work by Charles Hindley, published about a
quarter of a century ago. Among the female traders of
bygone days not the least persistent character was that of
the Orange Woman; she is figured to the life by Ben
Jonson, glorified in real life in the person of Nell Gwynne,
and although most commonly presenting herself as a
"bold wench" who also vended playbills at theatre doors,
was once exemplified at Lambeth in a street oddity known
as "Old Nanny."

It was an eighteenth-century character who earned for
himself the proud title, "King of Itinerant Tradesmen."
He was a vendor of gingerbread who for years was to be
seen on the fringe of all the street crowds of London, and
without whose lively presence such assemblages as the
Lord Mayor's Show would have been incomplete. He
was never known to the public otherwise than as Tiddy
Doll—a nickname acquired by his practice of singing at
the close of his address the fag-end of some popular
ballad which he could wind up with "Tiddy Dol-lol."
The music of his famous chorus is actually printed by
Hone in his "Everyday Book." In person Tiddy Doll
was tall, well made, and handsome; he affected the dress
of a man of rank, with a gold-laced suit of clothes, lace-
ruffled shirt, laced cap and feather, white silk stockings,
and, by way of concession to trade, a fine white apron.
He generally harangued his customers in this strain :
"Mary, Mary, where are you *now*, Mary ? I live, when
at home, at the second house in Little Ball-street, two
steps underground, with a wiscum, riscum, and a why-not.

Walk in, ladies and gentlemen, my shop is on the second-floor backwards, with a brass knocker at the door. Here is your nice gingerbread, your spice gingerbread ; it will melt in your mouth like a red-hot brickbat, and rumble in your inside like Punch and his wheel-barrow." And then he would set up his rollicking " Tiddy Dol-lol," and consequently was never without a good-humoured crowd among whom to vend his wares. In Hogarth's print of the execution of the " Idle Prentice" at Tyburn, Tiddy Doll is seen holding up a gingerbread cake in his left hand, and addressing the mob, in his usual attitude, with the " Mary, Mary" rigmarole.

In the same line of trade was the " Pig Pye Man," whose vaunted wares were quite innocent of pork, being nothing more than pie-crust baked in the shape of little pigs, having currant eyes—tempting trifles such as doubtless delighted the hearts of his juvenile customers. He occasionally varied his attractions by crying for sale—

> " Puffs and Pieses
> Of all sorts and sizes,"

but even then found a serious trade rival in the female vendor of " Pudding Pies," who is so humorously described in the Roxburghe Ballads.

A costermonger was originally one who sold costards or apples from a stall ; in Ben Jonson's play, " Bartholomew Fair," there is a " costard-monger" who bawls out, " Buy any pears ! fine, very fine pears !" Metaphorically the head is called a costard, because it is round like an apple.

A huxter, huckster, or hutler (to which word " hawker" is akin), was also a fruiterer, who pitched his load in a market and sold it there.

In the North Country, tinkers, ballad-singers, or itinerant beggars were known as randies or randy-beggars.

THE PIG-PYE MAN.

To face p. 228.

In all ancient manorial markets and fairs there was a rough-and-ready tribunal to try pedlars, hawkers, and others who committed offences during the time of selling in the public streets, and more particularly to compel them to fulfil the terms of their contracts. It was called a Court of Pie Powder, from the Norman-French *pied poudreux*, "dusty foot," because the offender was apprehended promptly, while the dust of the road was still upon his feet. (A vagabond is called in French *pied-poudreux*.) In "Hudibras" occurs the couplet rhyming the name of this market court as it was pronounced in the English vernacular :—

> "Have its proceedings disallowed or
> Allowed, at fancy of pie-powder."

The Pie Powder Court of St. Bartholomew's Fair, the most famous of its kind, was held in Cloth Fair to the last. The actors and other stage performers regularly took advantage of its procedure and its powers. In 1804 an action was brought by a Fire-eater against a spectator who had half suffocated him by pushing a bundle of lighted matches under his nose. The defendant was fined a guinea, and ordered to be turned out of the Fair by the constable. In the accompanying illustration, the Court is shown adjudicating upon a dispute between rival members of neighbouring theatrical booths.

Southey, in his youth being of broad Jacobin sympathies, sedulously inculcated in his earlier effusions that there was a natural and eternal warfare between the poor and the rich. For example :—

> "Cold was the night-wind; drifting fast the snows fell;
> Wide were the downs, and shelterless and naked;
> When a poor wanderer struggled on her journey,
> Weary and way-sore."

It is this style that George Canning parodies in his well-known dialogue between the " Friend of Humanity" and the " Needy Knife-grinder," the former thus affecting profound sympathy with the lowly wayfaring tradesman :—

> "Tell me, Knife-grinder, how came you to grind knives?
> Did some rich man tyrannically use you?
> Was it the squire, or parson of the parish,
>   Or the attorney?
>
> Was it the squire, for killing of his game? or
> Covetous parson, for his tithes distraining?
> Or roguish lawyer, made you lose your little
>   All in a lawsuit?"

Asked to tell his pitiful story, the Knife-grinder replies :—

> "Story! God bless you! I have none to tell, sir;
> Only last night a-drinking at the Chequers,
> This poor old hat and breeches, as you see, were
>   Torn in a scuffle.
>
> Constables came up for to take me into
> Custody; they took me before the justice;
> Justice Oldmixon put me in the parish-
>   Stocks for a vagrant."

This ridicule of philanthropic sentiments and republican enthusiasm is no doubt very clever. But, all the same, there was undeniably a callous heartlessness about old-time politics.

The unfettered life of an itinerant trader, untrammelled by conventionality and bound by no rules of trade, naturally developed amongst those who followed it, any latent eccentricity of character. As a result, the period when it was recognised as a more legitimate form of

trading to earn a living in the streets than it is now, was
far more prolific than the present day in the production
of those queer characters and human oddities which add
so much to the interest, variety, and quaintness of life out
of doors.

In 1802 there died, at Charles Street, Hatton Garden,
an eccentric female known, when she appeared as a
teacher of languages, as Chevalier John Theodora de
Verdion, but more commonly as Dr. Verdion, she having
at one time obtained a livelihood as a quack doctor. She
always appeared in male attire, was a regular frequenter
of Furnival's Inn Coffee House, and for many years her
eccentric figure was one of the most familiar in the streets
of London, where she might be seen, going from door to
door, hawking old books and dealing in medals. She
died, in her fifty-ninth year, of cancer in the breast, and
her mode of life was thus summed up in her epitaph :—

> " Stop, Gentle Reader, and behold
> A Beau in Boots, searching for Gold !
> A Walking Bookseller, an Epicure,
> A Teaching Doctor, and a Connoisseur ! "

Among the old-time cadgers and itinerants were to be
reckoned ballad-singers and the hawkers of broadsheets.
In the nineteenth century most of the wares vended by
these street traders emanated from the Seven Dials Press,
in the dismal metropolitan parish of St. Giles. The older
printed sheets were wretched impressions of blotchy
lamp-black and oil on execrable tea-paper ; but in 1815
James Catnach started an office which beat all his rivals
and precursors out of the field by issuing broadsheets
and ballads on good white paper produced with real
printers' ink.

He also revolutionized the trade by publishing collections of songs by the yard, and giving for one penny—

formerly the price of a single ballad—strings of poetry. Street-singers then punctuated their musical efforts with the cry, "Songs, three yards a penny! Songs, beautiful songs!" The sheets, often embellished with rude and quaint woodcuts, mainly comprised songs and ballads, and the "last dying speeches" of criminals; but fertility of resource extended the business of the famous Catnach Press in many ways—in carols, drolleries, bacchanalian ditties, the original effusions of beggar-bards, morbid legends, historic scandals, or whatever was likely to appeal to a vulgar and depraved taste. As examples, may be named "A Letter Written by Jesus Christ," "The Wanton Wife of Bath," "The Woful Lamentation of Mrs. Jane Shore," and "The Dorsetshire Garland, or Beggar's Wedding." The events of the day, too, were turned to profitable account by the issue of broadsheets containing the "Trial of Queen Caroline," "The Cato Street Conspiracy," and the murder of Weare by Thurtell. On the last-named occasion, when the excitement about the execution was likely to die out, Catnach brought out a second penny broadside headed in large type "WE ARE alive again." The public, reading the two words as "WEARE," resented the trick, and called it a "catch-penny," an opprobrious term which stuck to the Seven Dials issues ever afterwards, though they continued to sell just as well.

Catnach received large sums in coppers, which he used to take to the Bank of England in a hackney coach; when his neighbours in Seven Dials refused to take them, for fear of catching a fever, which was said to have spread through their contact with low cadgers and hawkers, he boiled them *en masse* with a decoction of potash and vinegar, which made them bright and restored them to popularity. St. Giles's parish, it may be noted, bears the reputation of having started the Great Plague of London in 1665.

DR. DE VERDION, THE FEMALE WALKING BOOKSELLER.

The Seven Dials Press never lost its prestige; its founder amassed a fortune from it, and left it as a valuable property to his family and successors.

Racier than any English contemporary picture of the travelling beggar, pedlar, or tinker, is that contained in the ballad of "The Gaberlunzie Man" (which is the Scottish name for this class of homeless wanderer), generally attributed to James V. :—

> "The panky auld carl came o'er the lea
> Wi' mony gud e'ens and days to me,
> Saying, 'Gudewife, for your courtesie,
>   Will ye lodge a silly poor man?'
> The night was cauld, the carl was wat,
> And down ayont the ingle he sat
> My dochter's shouthers he 'gan to clap,
>   And cadgily ranted and sang."

The insinuating vagabond was soon on good terms with the daughter:—

> "He grew canty, and she grew fain;
>   But little did her old ninny ken
> What thir slee twa togidder were sayen,
>   Whan wooing they were sae thrang.
>
> 'And O!' quo he, 'and ye were as black
> As ever the crown o' your daddy's hat
> 'Tis I wad lay thee be me back
>   And awa wi' thee I'd gang.'
>
> 'And O!' quo she, 'and I were as white
> As e'er the snaw lay on the dike
> I'd cleid me braw and lady-like
>   And awa wi' thee I'd gang.'"

The ballad tells how the "twa made a plot" to rise before cockcrow, shoot the lock, and run away together, ere any one else in the house was stirring—a plan they

successfully carried out. The "auld mither," rising in
due time, went first thing to the bed where the beggar
had lain, only to find him away and the "strae cauld."
Thinking he had robbed the house, eager search was
made in coffer and kist, but nothing being missing there,
the gudewife blessed her luck that she had entertained
an honest man. But presently, when she went to the
bed where the daughter lay and found " the sheets were
cauld," and that she was away too, all was instantly
lamentation and confusion, and the distressed mother
was—

> "Out o' her wit;
> She could na gang, nor yet could she sit,
> But aye she cursed and she banned "

Meanwhile the winsome Gaberlunzie Man, at a safe
distance, was initiating his bride into the mysteries of
life on the road :—

> "'My dear,' quod he, 'ye're yet owre young
> An' hae na learned the beggar's tongue
> To fallow me frae town to town
> And carry the Gaberlunzie on.' "

Of the habits and modes of life of travelling tinkers
and beggars nothing could be more instructive than this
ballad ; and the last verse clearly indicates that to this
resourceful fraternity of cadgers and impostors trading
or begging came indifferently :—

> "'Wi' kank and keel I'll win your bread
> And spinnels and whorls for them who need,
> Whilk is a gentle trade indeed
> To carry the Gaberlunzie on.

> ' I'll bow my leg and crook my knee
> An' draw a black clout owre my e'e,
> A cripple or blind they will ca' me,
> While we will sing and be merrie.' "

The Gaberlunzie of fiction who will occur to the minds of most readers is that shrewd and humorous character, Edie Ochiltree, a "blue gown" or licensed beggar described by Scott in *The Antiquary*.

The term Gaberlunzie is said to be derived from the French *gaban*, "a cloak with tight sleeves and a hood" (as in "gabardine," the name for the Jewish cassock), and *lunzie*, the diminutive of *laine* ("wool"), the whole signifying a coarse woollen gown, which was the livery of the King of Scotland's bedesmen, who were licensed beggars. These privileged mendicants, to whom the king himself distributed certain alms, were also known as "blue gowns," from the colour of their cloaks. They wore a pewter badge, which carried them unchallenged throughout the whole realm of Scotland, and their number was equal to that of the king's years, an extra one being added each returning birthday, though no new member has been added since 1833.

CHAPTER XX

BEGGAR-CRAFT

Lazarus and Dives—The patron saint of beggars—"Bedworth beggars"—The beggar's clack-dish—Beggar or footpad ?—The "Palliard," or born beggar—The "Patrico," or beggars' hedge-priest—Beggar marriages—The "Kinchin-mort" and "Kinchin-co"—Proctors—"Stalling to the rogue"—Beggars' Oak—Beggar barns—The notorious "Beggars' Bush"—The Rookery—The poor Irish of St. Giles's—Rats' Castle—Old Simon, a notable beggar—Cadgers' Hall—Low life in London—"Jolly beggars" of St. Giles's—The attraction of doles—A beggars' petition—"Noble poverty" at Winchester—Bath and Buxton forbidden to beggars—Carew, "the King of the Beggars"—His origin—And marvellous impostures—"The Accomplished Vagabond"—Various begging impostors—"Poor-Joe-All-Alone"—Miserly beggars—Inquiries of a Parliamentary Committee (1815)—The "lays" of the modern beggar.

THE typical beggar of Scripture is Lazarus, who (according to St. Luke's Gospel) was laid, full of sores which the dogs came and licked, at the gate of the rich man Dives, desiring to be fed with the crumbs which fell from the rich man's table. The enviable rich man is always named Dives; one of our early printed books, issued by Richard Pynson in 1493, is entitled "Dyves et Pauper."

As St. Giles is accounted the patron saint of cripples, St. Lazarus is sometimes looked upon as a patron of beggars. Or sometimes it is St. Martin, of whom the

236

legend tells that when a beggar requested alms of him, he having no money drew his sword (at that time he was a soldier) and cutting his cloak into two pieces, gave half to the beggar, and wrapped himself in the other half.

The lore of the Begging cult is interesting, if not extensive. Some places seem to have been infested by beggars more than the ordinary, and local proverbs have even grown up therefrom. In Leicestershire, destitute wayfarers were commonly known, for some reason now forgotten, by the common designation of "Bedworth beggars." Grose, the antiquary, throws no further light on the matter than remarking that Bedworth was probably some poor hamlet. Elsewhere it will be noted that some localities were studiously avoided by the begging fraternity (p. 272).

In former times beggars carried a dish, or rather a box, with a movable lid, and called a clack-dish, because of the noise made by clacking the lid upon it for the purpose of attracting notice, and bringing people to their doors to bestow their alms upon them. This receptacle was sometimes called a clap-dish, as in the proverbial simile —"His tongue moves like a beggar's clap-dish." It has been defined as "a wooden dish wherein they gather the toll of wheat and other corn in markets."

The border-line between the sturdy beggar and the footpad, between the tramp of the road and the highway robber, was sometimes obliterated ; when a tempting opportunity offered, the former often enough sunk himself in the latter.

> "'Sirrah!' says one, "Stand and your purse deliver!
> I am a taker—you must be a giver.'
> Unto a wood hard by, they hale him in
> And rifle him unto his very skin."

The words "pedlar" and "footpad" apparently have

something in common, for in the language of the fraternity the highway is called the "pad." And, by the way, any vagabond who speaks the Canting language, or Pedlar's French, is known among them as a Canter.

The born beggar was known as a Palliard, and was one who, says that notable authority of 1575, "The Fraternitye of Vacabondes," "goeth in a patched cloke, and his doxy goeth in like apparel." A writer of the early eighteenth century says that Palliard is—

"a cant name for a wretched set of men and women, whose whole delight is to live by begging, thieving, &c., or any thing but honest industry, and who to move compassion in the spectators, the women go about with one, two, or more small children, in a dirty, ragged condition, who are continually crying or making wry faces, as though starved with hunger, and the women make a lamentable cry, or doleful tale, of being a distressed widow, and almost starved, &c., at the same time her male companion lies begging in the fields, streets, &c., with cleymes of artificial sores, made with spearwort or arsenick, which draws them into blisters, or by unslacked lime and soap, tempered with the rust of old iron, which being spread upon leather, and bound very hard to the leg, presently so frets the skin, that the flesh appears raw, and shocking to the sight ; the impostor at the same time making a hideous noise, and pretending great pain, deceives the compassionate, charitable, and well-disposed passengers, whom, when opportunity presents, he can recover his limbs to rob, and even murder, if resisted."

High in the fraternity stood the Patrico, the orator or hedge-priest of the beggars. According to the authority of 1575, "a patriarke-co doth make marriages, and that is untill death depart the married folke, which is after this sort ; when they come to a dead horse or any dead catell, then they shake hands, and so depart every one of them a severall way." In fact, the two contracting parties were but "leased" to each other till the death—not of either of them, but of some convenient beast of the field—parted them. Such was married life among the old-time beggars.

It is no figure of speech to say that the licentious poverty of the able-bodied mendicant was positively "enjoyed."

Dekker (1608) uses two other Cant terms which are significant and illuminative :—

" Kinching-morts," he says, are " girles of a yeare or two old, which the morts [their mothers] carry at their backes in their slates ; if they have no children of their owne they will steale them from others, and by some meane disfigure them, that by their parents they shall never be knowne."

" Kinchin-co," again, was the name applied to a youth not yet thoroughly instructed in the art of vagabond knavery, a sort of undergraduate in the college of crime.

One of Dekker's tracts is entitled "Lanthorne and Candlelight"—which was the cry of the London bellman at night-time—and the subtitle of it is "the Belman's second Nights-walk, in which he brings to light a brood of more strange villanies than ever were till this yeare discovered." The lawless condition of low quarters of the city at that period, as Shakespeare also well knew, was a constant menace to society.

Proctors, it will be recalled, were those who in previous centuries collected alms on behalf of lepers who were unable to do so for themselves. According to the rules of this fraternity "a proctour is he that wil tary long and bring a lye, when his maister sendeth him on his errand."

The " ordination " ceremony of admitting a member to the society of these Canting rogues, was known among themselves as " stalling to the rogue."

In Needwood Forest, Staffordshire, is a huge and picturesque old tree the lower branches of which spread out horizontally over a remarkably large area, offering an amount of umbrageous shelter beyond the ordinary.

This giant of the forest is called the Beggars' Oak, and the legend runs that from time immemorial beggars and homeless wanderers have had the right of sheltering beneath its cover, without being regarded as trespassers.

Villages in some parts of the country formerly possessed buildings known as "beggar barns." These barns usually belonged to the farm which was situated nearest the church, and wayfaring beggars were always given gratis a night's lodging and a meal in them. It was a popular belief that such homeless wanderers had a legal right to sleep in the church porch, and it was purely a sense of public decency which substituted the beggars' barn.

In the towns, in some low quarter or other, were to be found cheap lodging-houses; and in some of the larger cities a rookery of an inn to which the fraternity flocked in numbers. In London a notorious resort of the kind in the sixteenth and seventeenth centuries was "The Beggars' Bush," not far from St. Giles's Church. Here, at a later period, when "Stunning Joe Banks" was castellan, it was—

> " Hail Cadgers, who in rags array'd
> Disport and play fantastic pranks,
> Each Wednesday night in full parade
> Within the domicile of Banks."

At the weekly orgies held here a "lady" usually presided; and it was the time-honoured practice to pass round at intervals the platter, in which to collect the largess necessary for keeping up the revelry, in the shape of drinking, dancing, and singing, if nothing worse. To this establishment there was a cellar, a lower story, where the guests slept, packed closely together in bins, or box-beds. It was truly an infamous den.

The sign, " Beggars' Bush," accrued to the house as naturally descriptive of the rendezvous of beggars, a bush

being an ancient and very common tavern sign. A proverb of the time, "To go by beggars' bush," was interpreted as "to go on the road to ruin"; a phrase of
somewhat similar signification was, "We are brought to
beggar staffe." After the reign of Charles II. this notorious inn changed its sign from "The Beggars' Bush" to
"The Hare and Hounds."

St. Giles's parish, with its close nests of dark courts
and narrow alleys, long ago achieved an evil reputation
for filth and squalor, its chief slumland, once known
as the "Rookery," being formerly the home of "pedlars,
fish-women, news-criers, and corn-cutters," and a
miscellaneous population, half beggars, half criminals,
all much given to riotousness and debauchery. It
produced quite a number of "Jack Ketches," and, to
balance matters, a goodly proportion of malefactors as
well, to grace the Tyburn tree, in accord with the old
saying—

> "St. Giles's breed
> Better hang than seed."

Till the influx of swarms of Irish mendicants, St. Giles's
parish had not a greater proportion of poor than other
London parishes of similar extent and population; these
new-comers in the time of Queen Elizabeth settled in
this quarter, took up the poorer sorts of trades and
occupations, with the result that tenements were divided
and subdivided, let and sublet, till whole families,
sunk in the lowest depths of poverty, were crowded
together, occupying hundreds of houses from garret to
cellar, causing the subterranean dwellings of St. Giles's
to become a by-word.

In one well-known lodging-house, known as "Rats'
Castle," there lived about the middle of the eighteenth
century an eccentric individual known as Old Simon.

16

With his dog he lodged under the staircase of that dilapidated, ramshackle old house in Dyott Street; and this is the description of him contained in J. T. Smith's "Book for a Rainy Day" :—

"He wore several hats, and suffered his beard to grow, which was of a dirty yellow-white. Upon his fingers were numerous brass rings. He had several waist-coats, and as many coats, increasing in size, so that he was enabled by the extent of the uppermost garment to cover the greater part of the bundles, containing rags of various colours, and distinct parcels with which he was girded about, consisting of books, canisters containing bread, cheese, and other articles of food ; matches, a tinder-box, and meat for his dog ; cuttings of curious events from old newspapers, scraps from Foxe's 'Book of Martyrs,' and three or four dogs'-eared and grease-thumbed numbers of the *Gentleman's Magazine*. From these and such-like productions he gained a great part of the information with which he sometimes entertained those persons who stopped to look at him."

This remarkable mendicant (perhaps the original of the "Simple Simon" of our nursery rhymes) stood for many years at the gate of St. Giles's Church, and a portrait of him is to be found in Mr. J. T. Smith's well-known book, "Sketches from the London Streets."

In the neighbourhood of Fleet Street, as early as the time of James I., Shire Lane was known as Rogues' Lane, nearly every house in it being an infamous resort of some kind. One thieves' house known as "The Retreat" led by a back way into Crown Court; other dens had passages in the Strand. Nos. 9, 10, and 11 were known as "Cadgers' Hall," which was much frequented by beggars even in somewhat recent times ; every morning bushels of bread, thrown aside by the professional mendicants, were regularly found outside these houses by the police.

In a curious old pamphlet, dedicated by its author to Hogarth, entitled " Low Life ; or one-half the World knows not how the other half Live," first published in 1759, we get a unique picture of the manners of the rougher elements of society at that period. In a long catalogue of the commoner rogueries of London contained in it, arranged by the author for each hour of the twenty-four in a midsummer day, we have this set down among the doings of the early risers at 5 a.m. : "Beggars going to parish nurses to borrow poor helpless infants at fourpence a day, to persuade credulous charitable people they are their own, and have been some time sick and fatherless."

A description of "The Great Metropolis" in a popular magazine of 1836 contains the following :—

"Nothing short of absolute starvation can depress the spirits of the lower classes in the metropolis, or render them discontented with their situation in life   Even the beggars in the streets, though obliged to make demure faces, and to appear as if in the very depths of despondency when pursuing their calling, have their hours of unrestrained jollity.   They are in the habit of meeting in forties and fifties in particular houses, appropriated in different parts of the town for their reception, and spending whole nights in all manner of revellings.   I have been told by those who have put on ragged clothes for the purpose of enabling them to visit such places and see low life, without being suspected of being other than one of the parties themselves, that the scenes to be witnessed on such occasions are indescribably rich.   There is one of these houses—it is the most celebrated one in London—in St. Giles's.   There beggars of all descriptions congregate, and make up amply for the privations of the day in the shape of 'long faces,' mournful accents, &c., by the unrestrained enjoyments to which they give themselves up. The moment they enter the precincts of the place, their assumed character is laid aside, and they appear in their real one.   There miracles of every kind are performed.   Those who but a few hours before seemed at the very gates of death from apparent destitution, are all at once restored to the full enjoyment of life.   In one corner of the place you will see thirty or forty crutches, which were in requisition the whole of the day—and will be so to-morrow again —but which are quite useless now.   They who could not move without them, and scarcely with them, a short time before, are now among the most nimble in the company. Perhaps, they are dancing in the middle of the floor; for one leading feature in the amusements of these 'jolly beggars' is that of having their nightly dance. You see a glass of gin in every one's hand, except in the hands of those who are busy in broiling Yarmouth bloaters on the fire. There you see dozens of persons with eyes clear and keen as those of eagles, who were quite blind all the day. Those whom you saw in the streets in the morning, looking so ill, that you thought they would be in their coffins before the evening, are now, to use their own elegant phraseology, 'all alive and kicking.' Every symptom of sickness has disappeared."

Towns with an excess of doles and other demoralizing charities naturally attracted the begging brotherhood very powerfully; and as showing them to act in combination as an organised fraternity when necessary, it may be mentioned that in 1688 the beggars of Winchester petitioned the queen of James II. to the effect that the Corporation of that city having misspent, embezzled, and appropriated to their own use the charity estates, the reversion of the fines imposed on the city fathers for this offence should fall to them. The petition, however, cannot be regarded as quite genuine; it was in all probability a veiled political movement, for shortly afterwards a new charter was granted to Winchester. In 1699 a "Charitable Society of Natives" was established.

Few cities, indeed, can show such an array of ancient charitable institutions as Winchester. One of them still makes a free distribution of beer. The Hospital of the Holy Cross was founded by Bishop Henry de Blois in 1132; early in the fifteenth century Cardinal Beaufort engrafted on this charity the "Almshouse of Noble Poverty." This it is which provides a "wayfarer's dole" of a small horn of ale and a little roll.

Places of resort patronized by the wealthy also brought crowds of mendicants together. The fashionable city

of Bath, for instance, in obtaining powers to establish
a hospital and infirmary, in 1739, had to make special
provision for dealing summarily with the rabble of
beggars who habitually plied their trade along the streets
of that resort in swarms, to the annoyance of invalid
visitors, and the subversion of the town's good government. In the reign of Edward VI. it had been strictly
forbidden all infirm persons to visit Bath and Buxton for
the purposes of exciting pity and obtaining charity; for
at that early period these places had already acquired
fame as health resorts through their healing waters.

Through the wide range of English biography there
is no stranger career to be read than that of Bamfylde
Moore Carew, " King of the Beggars," born at Bickley,
near Tiverton, in 1693. This worthy was the son of the
Rector of Bickley, and a scion of the aristocratic family at
the head of which were the Earls of Totnes. The bells
rang merrily for his christening, and the boy's sponsors
were Major Moore and Mr. Hugh Bamfylde, both
gentlemen of high position.

While at school at Tiverton, where he was the ring-
leader in everything that was mischievous, he got into a
scrape through hunting a stag across some farm lands,
whereupon he ran away and joined himself to a camp
of gipsies. After a year and a half Carew returned
home, but soon rejoined his gipsy companions. From
this point his career is one long series of swindles and
impostures, all ingeniously carried out. He had im-
pressed the gipsies from the outset as an adept in
deception and subterfuge. He had a keen sense of
humour, and folks used to say some of his tricks were as
good as a play.

In 1713, when all idea of home life had been finally
abandoned by him, the country was disturbed by
Jacobite plots, and Carew, never slow to turn popular

sentiment to account, pretended to dabble in politics when he could make anything out of them. He often obtained parish aid as a shipwrecked seaman, or as an unhappy traveller who had been taken prisoner by Barbary pirates, and escaped with nothing but his life. In seaport towns, after a shipwreck, he never failed to turn up as a distressed mariner. At other times he was a rat-catcher, or a vendor of a marvellous secret cure for madness in dogs and cattle. One useful trick he possessed—throughout his life he had the wonderful power of attracting dogs and instantly making friends with them.

Sometimes he accoutred himself in an old blanket, and went about as a Bedlam beggar—"a poor Turlygood," as Shakespeare has it, who—

> "With roaring voice
> Strike in their numb'd and mortified bare arms
> Pins, wooden pricks, nails, sprigs of rosemary;
> And with this horrible object, from low farms,
> Poor pelting villages, sheep-cotes, and mills,
> Sometimes with lunatic bans, sometimes with prayers,
> Enforce their charity."

Impelled by his restless nature, he made a journey to Newfoundland, where he stopped but a short time, and on his return pretended to be the mate of a vessel, eloped with the handsome daughter of a respectable apothecary in Newcastle, and eventually married her. He continued his course of vagabond roguery for some time, when the death occurred of Clause Patch, the king or chief of the gipsies, whereupon Carew was elected to fill his place. At the time he married he had been playing at respectability for a brief spell, and when his wife discovered that he was connected in some mysterious way with the gipsies she was much distressed, though afterwards she seems to have condoned everything. What could be done with a husband who declared he would rather be King of the Beggars than King of England?

The doggrel anthem sung at his gipsy coronation was:

"Be it peace, or be it war,
  Here at liberty we are;
  Hang all harmenbecks, we cry,
  We the Cuffin Queres defy."

A "Cuffin Quere" is a justice of the peace, and the boast was rather unlucky, for he soon after fell into the hands of the law.

Convicted as a common vagrant, he was sentenced to be transported to Maryland. There he attempted to escape from the plantations, but was captured and made to wear a heavy iron collar. Escaping a second time, he fell into the hands of some friendly Indians, who relieved him of his collar. Leaving his new friends, he made his way to Pennsylvania, where he posed as a Quaker, pursuing his nefarious practices everywhere with undiminished zest.

Turning his back on America, he embarked for England, and escaped imprisonment on board a man-of-war by pricking his hands and face and rubbing into the punctures gunpowder|and bay salt to similate small-pox.

On one occasion, begging in the town of Maiden Bradley as a shipwrecked sailor, he was accosted by another beggar in the Cant language of mumpers. They joined forces, cadged together, and then caroused together. It was decided they should visit the adjacent manor-house, and beg in the character of two cast-away mariners. They succeeded in wheedling a cut leg of mutton, a wheaten loaf, and a shilling from the housekeeper. The food was promptly exchanged for liquor at the Green Man Inn, after which the two fell to disputing, and parted, each going his own way. The *dénouement* is startling. The second beggar was Lord Weymouth, master of the house at which they had begged. This time the arch-impostor himself had been deceived ! Lord Weymouth enjoyed the discomfiture of the Beggar King immensely, having planned the whole escapade with great deliberation.

On his arrival in England he had sought out and found his wife and daughter, and resumed his wandering life ; he is said to have joined the Pretender in Scotland in 1745, and accompanied him to Carlisle and Derby. Though he feigned lameness on this occasion, he kept up with the army on his crutches. With his usual shrewdness he saw, almost before any one else, that the expedition was doomed to failure, so at Derby he dropped his crutches, made the best of his way south-wards, and changed his note from "God Bless Bonny Prince Charlie" to "God Bless Good King George."

Towards the close of his adventurous life the arch-impostor performed another redoubtable feat in the art of deception. Squire Morrice of Launceston having made Carew's close acquaintance almost for the purpose, made a wager that he would never be duped by him. For a time Squire was successful in warding off all attempts. One day, however, returning from the hunt, he came across a poor old woman lying in the road desperately ill. Mr. Morrice promptly rendered all the aid in his power, gave the sufferer a substantial solatium, —and lost his bet !

The record of his frauds and deceptions was still further lengthened ; and when his relative, Sir Thomas Carew, of Hackern, offered to provide for the prodigal, if he would relinquish his wandering life and wild ways, he firmly refused.

It is believed that Carew settled down at last, after winning some prizes in a lottery, but nothing certain is

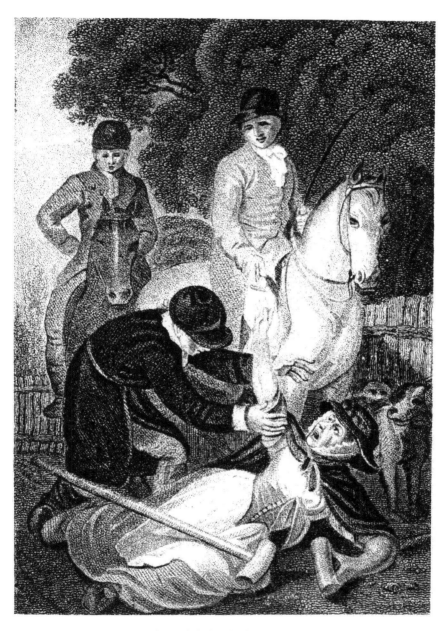

CAREW, DISGUISED AS AN OLD WOMAN, DECEIVES SQUIRE MORRICE.

To face p. 248.

known of his end, not even the date of his death, which has been given as early as 1758, and as late as 1770. Several biographies of this remarkable character have been written; the first appeared in 1745 as "The Life and Adventures of B. M. Carew, the Noted Devonshire Stroller and Dog-stealer"; another of the same date was entitled "The Accomplished Vagabond or Compleat Mumper exemplify'd in the bold and artful enterprises and merry pranks of Bamfylde Carew." Pedlars hawked the story of his adventures throughout the country, in the form of chap-books, for very many years after he had disappeared from this wicked world.

Of begging impostors there have been multitudes of examples These strange specimens of humanity contrive, while living amid rags, dirt, and wretchedness, to amass considerable sums of money. For obvious reasons they conceal their pelf during life, and it is only when the breath has left their miserable bodies that their imposture is discovered. Usually the hoarded coins are bestowed in holes and nooks, stuffed into straw beds, or sewn up in rags; although in a few cases the rich beggar has been known to venture his money in a bank or some carefully selected investment.

Among the many recorded examples of rich beggars have been an eccentric of the eighteenth century, known as Poor-Joe-All-Alone, who wore a very long beard, never lay in a bed for fifty years, and by will bequeathed £3,000 for the benefit of certain widows and orphans; Francis Beet, whose bed and rickety furniture yielded a hoard of £800; Alice Bond, who was found to have £300 in the Funds, in addition to the golden guineas and silver coins, amounting to £73, which were hidden about her room; Mary Wilkinson, a beggar and bone-grubber, in whose ragged clothing no less than £300 was found to be concealed; Esther Davies, who died in

London at the advanced age of 103, and whose long tenure of the double chances of a street beggar and a parish pauper enabled her to amass £160 ; Margaret Coles, another centenarian, who died amidst horrible filth and squalor in St. Giles's parish, and in whose hovel was found £30 in gold and £10 in copper ; and Daniel Eagle, who begged for thirty years in London, living in a room which was never cleaned for the whole of that time, and which no one but himself ever entered, and in which coin to the value of £25 was found. And the list of such miserly beggars might be almost indefinitely extended.

For eccentricity on the part of the rich beggar nothing could be more remarkable than the career of William Stevenson, who died at Kilmarnock in 1817.

Says Chambers :—

"Although bred a mason, the greater part of his life was spent as a beggar. About the year 1787, he and his wife separated, making this strange agreement—that whichever of them was the first to propose a reunion should forfeit £100 to the other. According to the statements in the Scotch newspapers there is no evidence that they ever saw each other again. In 1815, when about 85 years old, Stevenson was seized with an incurable disease, and was confined to his bed. A few days before his death, feeling his end to be near, he sent for a baker, and ordered twelve dozen burial-cakes, a large quantity of sugared biscuit, and a good supply of wine and spirits. He next sent for a joiner, and instructed him to make a good, sound, dry, roomy, 'comfortable' coffin. Next he summoned a grave-digger, whom he requested to select a favourable spot in the church-yard of Riccarton, and there dig a roomy and comfortable grave. This done, he ordered an old woman who attended him to go to a nook, and bring out £9, to pay all these preliminary expenses; assuring her that she was remembered in his will. Shortly after this he died. A neighbour came in to search for his wealth, which had been shrouded in much mystery. In one bag was found large silver pieces, such as dollars and half-dollars, crowns and half-crowns ; in a heap of musty rags was found a collection of guineas and seven-shilling pieces ; and in a box were found bonds of various amounts, including one for £300—giving altogether a sum of about £900. A will was also found, bequeathing £20 to the old woman, and most of the remainder to distant relations, setting aside sufficient to give a feast to all the beggars who chose to come and see his body 'lie in state.' The influx was immense; and after the funeral, all retired to a barn which had been fitted up for the occasion; and there they indulged in revelries but little in accordance with the solemn season of death."

A Committee of the House of Commons in 1815 reported that the sturdy beggar of that period was a capitalist and an epicure; ate fowls and beef-steaks for supper, and despised broken food; and even had money in the Funds. The evidence contained some famous stories of impostors; there was the lame impostor who tied up his leg in a wooden frame; a blind one who wrote letters in the evening for his unlettered brethren; a widow who sat for ten years with twins who never grew bigger; a wife who obtained clothes and money from eleven lying-in societies in the same year. But the Committee had also some glimpses of real wretchedness amidst these amusing tales of beggar-craft. They heard of a court of twenty-four houses in the neighbourhood of Portman Square where more than seven hundred Irish lived in abject poverty and utter misery; they were told that the court was totally neglected by the parish, was never cleansed, and that people were afraid to enter it through the dread of infection. They were informed of a yard in Whitechapel where two thousand people occupied forty houses in a similar state of wretchedness. Much more evidence of a similar nature reached the Committee; but all this evil was exhibited only to be immediately forgotten.

The active forms of present-day begging are as inventive and as deceptive as ever they were. During periods of trade depression, or in severe winters, the spurious out-of-works invariably make their appearance. These generally work in small gangs, and get themselves up in the rig most calculated to excite pity ; a common fake in imitation of bricklayers, navvies, and other out-door workers is baked clay on their ankle-jacks. They do the " chanting lay,"—that is, street singing—and, of course, always hail from a place as distant as possible. In London and the South they are "all the way from Manchester, and got no work to do."

Another dodge is known as the "shallow lay." In working the "shaller" lay the professional beggar makes capital of his rags and his disgusting condition of semi-nudity. He will expose naked knees and a shirtless breast, and if the weather is wintry or inclement he will pounce his flesh with a blue powder, so that it may have the appearance of being pinched with cold.

The part of the country in which the modern professional beggar is said to reap his richest harvest is in the working-class district of South Wales. And the season which yields him his best returns is, doubtless, the genial Christmastide, especially if the weather happen to be severe, for it is then the maxims of political economy generally give way to the promptings of illogical sentiment.

CHAPTER XXI

LITERATURE OF THE BEGGING CULT

Zenelophon of Shakespeare—Cophetua and the Beggar Maid—
"The Beggar's Daughter of Bednall-Green," a romance of
De Montfort's time—Martin Luther's "Book of Vagabonds
and Beggars"—The Beggar's Garland, a chap-book—"The
Beggars' Bush," by Fletcher—Gay's allusion to the Rufflers
of Lincoln's Inn Fields—"The Merry Beggars"—Burns's
Cantata, "The Jolly Beggars"—The gamut of human miseries
—In Moss's poem, "The Beggar's Petition."

THE beggar of classical story is Penelophon, or, as she is
called by Shakespeare, Zenelophon, the beggar-maid
who married a king. Cophetua, an imaginary king of
Africa, of immense wealth, disdained all woman-kind.
One day, from his window, he saw a beautiful barefooted
beggar-girl, and fell instantly in love with her.

> "So sweet a face, such angel grace,
>   In all that land had never been ;
> Cophetua sware a royal oath—
>   This beggar-maid shall be my queen"

Here Tennyson stops, but the old romance tells us
they married, lived together long and happily, and at
their death were universally lamented.

Few ballads of romance are more charming than that
of "The Beggar's Daughter of Bednall-Green." The theme
is not altogether dissimilar to that of Cophetua. Internal

evidence warrants its ascription to the time of Queen Elizabeth—the atmosphere, the setting of the picture, is Tudor rather than Plantagenet—although, as the *dénouement* discloses, it purports to deal with an historic incident of some three centuries earlier.

> "It was a blind beggar had long lost his sight;
> He had a faire daughter of bewty most bright;
> And many a gallant brave suitor had shee,
> For none was soe comely as pretty Bessee.
>
> And though shee was of favor most faire,
> Yett seeing shee was but a poor beggar's heyre,
> Of ancient housekeepers despised was shee
> Whose sonnes came as suitors to pretty Bessee."

So in great sorrow she went forth from Bethnal Green to seek her fortune elsewhere ; and presently coming to Romford took service at the "Queene's Armes," where this well-favoured damsel speedily made new friends and attracted hosts of fresh admirers. Four of her most persistent suitors were a knight, a gentleman of fortune, a London merchant, and the son of the innkeeper.

> "Then Bessy shee sighed, and thus shee did say,
> My father and mother I meane to obey ;
> First gett their good-will, and be faithfull to mee,
> And you shall enjoy your pretty Bessee."

She was asked where her father dwelt.

> "My father, shee said, is soone to be seene,
> The seely blind beggar of Bednall-Greene,
> That daily sits begging for charitie,
> He is the good father of pretty Bessee."

On hearing this they all slunk off, except the gallant knight, who "weighed not true love by the weight of the purse," though his kinsmen looked not so indulgently on the proposed alliance with a beggar-maid, and railed loudly against it.

> "Then spake the blind beggar, Although I bee poore
> Yett rayle not against my child at my owne doore ;
> Though shee be not deckt in velvett and pearle
> Yett will I drop angells with you for my girle."

And sure enough for each angel cast on the floor by the knight the beggar cast two, till he had dowered his Bessy with three thousand pounds, to which he added a hundred pounds to buy her wedding gown.

> "And all those that were her suiters before,
> Their fleshe for very anger they tore.
> Thus was the fair Bessy matched to the knight,
> And then made a ladye, in others' despite.
> A fairer ladye never was seene
> Than the blind beggar's daughter of Bednall-Greene."

The second half of the ballad is occupied by an account of the sumptuous wedding feast, held " within a gorgeous palace most brave," at which were present " nobles and gentles of every degree." The " jolly blind beggar " had not presumed " these states to disgrace " by his presence, till it was expressly desired by these gracious aristocrats.

> " But wee thinke thy father's baseness, quoth they,
> Might by thy bewty be cleane put awaye.
>
> They had noe sooner these pleasant words spoke
> But in comes the beggar cladd in a silk cloke.
> A faire velvett cap and a fether had hee,
> And now a musician forsooth hee wold bee.
>
> He had a daintye lute under his arme,
> He touched the strings which made such a charme,
> Saies, Please you to heare any musicke of mee,
> Ile sing you a song of pretty Bessee."

More than twenty more stanzas are occupied in reveal-
ing the story of his life, the recital of which explains to
his guests that he is Henry, eldest son of the noble
Simon de Montfort, slain at the battle of Evesham,
where he himself was left on the field for dead. But
he was only blinded, and a certain baron's daughter,
searching among the slain for her father's body, rescued
him. In secret the young lady nursed him back to
health, married him, and became the mother of the
fair heroine of the story.

> "And now, lest oure foes our lives shold betraye,
>   We clothed ourselves in beggars' arraye,
>   Her jewelles she solde, and hither came wee,
>   All our comfort and care was our pretty Bessee."

Thus at a wedding feast, and in the best troubadour
style of romance, is explained how the garb and
semblance of a beggar was assumed for the grim
purpose of escaping the vigilance of King Henry's spies.

> "Full forty winters thus have I beene
>   A seely [i.e., simple] blind beggar of Bednall-Greene."

The honourable company having been satisfied that
both father and daughter were "of noble degree," the
happiness of the bridegroom was supposed to be quite
complete.

> "In joy and felicitie long lived hee
>   All with his fayre ladye, the pretty Bessee."

In 1528 Martin Luther edited "The Book of Vagabonds and Beggars; with a Vocabulary of their Language," a curious work giving the ancient customs of the
mendicant fraternity; this curious work was translated
into the English tongue some sixty years ago.

The honest beggar may be a rarity, but when found it is only fitting that his virtues should be sung. There is extant a quaint old chap-book entitled "The Beggar's Garland," which tells in humorous verse how an honest beggar once outwitted a covetous knight. The latter had been left guardian to an orphan boy with an inheritance of ten thousand pounds, but he hired a beggar to take the child away and kill it. The beggar, however, became the boy's protector against his scheming guardian, while the beggar's wife stole the knight's daughter; they reared the two children, and the ballad ends with a particularly lively description of the wedding gaieties of the young pair. The story is a "virtue rewarded" version of the "Babes in the Wood."

"The Beggars' Bush," a curious Elizabethan play by Fletcher, the scene of which is romantically located in the Low Countries, shows the sixteenth-century dramatist a wonderful adept at Tyburn gibberish, and a learned "Corinthian" indeed; for most of the characters talk in the fancy language of beggar-craft. Near the opening of the play, for instance, occurs this passage :—

"Jarkman or patrico, cranke or clapperdudgeon,
Frater or abram-man—I speak to all
That stand in fair election for the title
Of King of Beggars.

.   .   .   .   .

Call in your crutches, wooden legs, false bellies,
Forc'd eyes and teeth, with your dead arms, not leave you
A dirty clout to beg with on your heads,
Or an old rag with butter, frankincence,
Brimstone and resin, birdlime, blood, and cream,
To make you an old sore, not so much soap
As you may foam with i' the falling sickness" . . .

And so on ; the whole drama being a revelation of the

17

iniquitous tricks, wiles, and dodges of the roguish begging fraternity.

Here is a beggars' "song" from the same play :—

> " Cast our caps and cares away,
>   This is beggars' holyday,
>   At the crowning of our king
>   Thus we ever dance and sing.
>   In the world look out and see
>   Where's so happy a prince as he?
>   Where the nation lives so free
>   And so merry as do we?
>   Be it peace or be it war,
>   Here at liberty we are ;
>   And enjoy our ease and rest ;
>   To the field we are not press'd ;
>   Nor are called into the town
>   To be troubled with the gown.
>   Hang all officers, we cry,
>   And the magistrates, too, by.
>   When the subsidy's increased
>   We are not a penny sess'd ;
>   Nor will any go to law
>   With the beggar for a straw.
>   All which happiness, he brags,
>   He doth owe unto his rags."

The old-time beggars had their own songs, those dating back to Elizabethan days being fanciful, and characteristic of the habits and sentiments of the fraternity.

For an exposure of the dodges and rogueries of mendicants, there is nothing more piquant than the ballad of " The Cunning Northern Beggar " :—

> " I am a lusty beggar
>   And live by others giving;
>   I scorn to work,
>   But by the highway lurk,
>   And beg to get my living."

The literature of the seventeenth century makes occa-

THE CUNNING NORTHERN BEGGAR.

(Roxburgh Ballad.)

A DEBTORS' PRISON (SEVENTEENTH CENTURY).

(See p. 349.)

To face p. 258.

sional references to the fact of Lincoln's Inn Fields being infested at that period with "Mumpers" and "Rufflers" —troops of idle vagrants, the name "Rufflers" being used for the vagabonds who assumed the character of maimed soldiers, broken in the Great Civil War, to beg of the people of quality who passed by. It was the favourite haunt of cripples with crutches who lived by mendicancy, which they carried on in the most barefaced, if not intimidating, manner. Readers of the *Spectator* will hardly need to be reminded of "Scarecrow," the beggar of that locality, who, having disabled himself in his right leg, asks alms all day in order to get a warm supper at night.

The poet Gay in his "Trivia" speaks of the Fields being the headquarters of beggars by day and robbers by night :—

> "Where Lincoln's Inn's wide space is railed around,
> Cross not with venturous step ; there oft is found
> The lurking thief, who, while the daylight shone,
> Made the walls echo with his begging tone,
> The crutch which late compassion moved, shall wound
> Thy bleeding head, and fell thee to the ground"

There was first printed in 1763 the ballad called "The Jovial Beggar," or sometimes "The Merry Beggars" :—

> " From hunger and cold who lives more free,
> Or who more richly clad than we ?
> Our bellies are full, our flesh is warm,
> And against pride our rags are a charm.
> Enough is our feast, and for to-morrow
> Let rich men care, we feel no sorrow.
>> No sorrow, no sorrow, no sorrow, no sorrow,
>> Let rich men care, we feel no sorrow.
>
> Each city, each town, and every village
> Affords us either an alms or pillage ;

And if the weather be cold and raw
Then in a barn we tumble in straw.
If warm and fair, by yea-cock and nay-cock
The fields will afford us a hedge or a hay-cock.
A hay-cock, a hay-cock," &c., &c.

Burns's cantata, "The Jolly Beggars," was founded on
an actual scene he one night witnessed in the humble
hostelry of Mrs. Gibson, more familiarly named Poosie
Nansie, at Mauchlin.   In Chambers's "Life and Works
of Robert Burns" (1856 edition) is given a song which
was printed in *The Vocal Miscellany* of 1734 :—

First Beggar. "I once was a poet in London,
            I keep my heart still full of glee,
        There's no man can say that I'm undone,
            For begging's no new Trade to me," &c , &c.

But Burns gives a lilt to the subject with :—

    " Here's to budgets, bags and wallets
        Here's to all the wandering train.
    Here's our ragged brats and callets.
        One and all cry out—Amen !"

As some are born great, some achieve greatness, and
some have greatness thrust upon them, so some men are
born poor and some become so either by fault or by
misfortune.   As human sympathy is generally stirred to
its greatest depths by those in the last-named category,
the causes of impoverishment and social degradation are
set forth with heartrending sequence in Thomas Moss's
pathetic poem, "The Beggar's Petition."
    The opening stanza is well known :—

    " Pity the sorrows of a poor old man !
        Whose trembling limbs have borne him to your door,
    Whose days are dwindled to the shortest span ;
        Oh ! give relief, and Heaven will bless your store."

After a number of finely expressed sentiments in this
strain we learn :—

> " A little farm was my paternal lot,
>   Then, like the lark, I sprightly hailed the morn ;
> But ah, oppression forced me from my cot,
>   My cattle died, and blighted was my corn.
>
> My daughter—once the comfort of my age !
>   Lured by a villain from her native home,
> Is cast, abandoned, on the world's wide stage
>   And doomed in scanty poverty to roam."

And so the unfortunate beggar runs through the gamut
of human miseries and misfortunes.

CHAPTER XXII

THE WHIPPING OF VAGRANTS

Rogues branded "R"—"Benefit of clergy" explained—Care of
infirm poor—Sturdy beggars whipped—Placed in stocks—Kept
in Houses of Correction—Instructions to judges at assizes—
"Rogue" defined—"To rogue about"—Queen Elizabeth's
coach encompassed with swarms of rogues—Tricksters, actors,
tinkers, and many others included in the category—Rogues not
to be harboured—Yet they mostly escaped the law—Resorts
of beggars in Hanoverian times—Whitechapel and Stepney—
Origin of "slums"—Records of whippings—In Surrey, Dorsetshire, Huntingdon, &c., inflicted on women and children—The
"whipsman"—Harsh and deterrent administration—Hull and
Halifax notorious—"The Beggar's Litany."

THE old punishment of flogging at the cart's tail, to
which vagrants were liable, was intended to ensure
greater publicity for the administration of the penalty,
and so to act as a deterrent.

By the Elizabethan Act of 1597 dangerous rogues were
to be branded on the left shoulder with the letter R.

With regard to this barbarous punishment it may be
noted that offenders condemned to branding who were
not in holy orders, and who claimed "benefit of clergy,"
were burnt with a hot iron in the brawn of the thumb
of the left hand to distinguish them from clerics. From
the time of Henry VII. to the abolition of the penalty
in 1778 this punishment was inflicted in open court,
generally in the presence of the judge, all the necessary

implements—the iron brand, the chafing-dish, and the iron gripper for keeping the hand steady—being always in readiness.

"Benefit of clergy," it may be explained, was a privilege enjoyed by churchmen in former times, whereby they, as a distinct order, escaped the jurisdiction of the secular courts. In ancient times when a clerk in holy orders was accused of crime the ordinary stepped forth and claimed him for the "Court Christian," in which the bishop or his deputy sat as judge. Before this judge and a jury of twelve clerks the prisoner declared his innocence on oath, sometimes strengthening his defence by the aid of twelve compurgators, or "witnesses"; and seldom did he fail to get off. At first this privilege had been confined to such as wore the clerical dress and tonsure, but even after Elizabeth's reign—when the clergy of the Reformed Church had ceased to affect the tonsure—the legal fiction long remained that none but clerics could read. While this sham held good every ruffian charged with crime and at a loss for a defence "prayed his clergy." When put to the proof he pretended to read—really he repeated it from memory, having been specially coached in it by a friendly adviser—a brief passage of Scripture. The beginning of the fifty-first Psalm was always selected, and as it saved thousands of felons from the hangman it came to be vulgarly known as the "neck-verse."

> "At this assizes fear not to appear;
> The judge will read thy neck-verse for thee here."

This omnipotent portion of Scripture consisted only of three easily learnt and appropriate words in the Vulgate —*Miserere mei Deus* ("Have mercy on me, O God"). By this device the poor and ignorant contrived to usurp one of the privileges of the learned and well-to-do.

And now to resume our main subject. Under the early Tudor laws destitution was treated as a crime, and wandering poverty was to be stocked and scourged out of existence. By the more enlightened laws passed in the closing years of Elizabeth's reign the impotent poor were to be nurtured and the sturdy mendicant punished.

The famous Act 39 *Elizabeth*, which made so wise and merciful a provision for the helpless portion of the community, was accompanied by "An Act for the punishment of rogues, vagabonds, and sturdy beggars." This Act repealed all previous statutes to the like effect. It prescribed, as of old, whipping, the stocks, branding, and the passing from parish to parish, but it empowered the justices assembled at Quarter Sessions to erect Houses of Correction within their respective counties or cities, and to provide funds for the maintenance of the same.

The Houses of Correction were for the employment of vagrants till they could be placed in some service ; or, if infirm of body, in some almshouse. In 1576 they were known as Abiding Houses.

Though the legislature had taken a more enlightened view of its duty towards the poor, the local authorities were found everywhere far readier to apply the penal clauses of the one Act than to tax themselves for the remedial measures designed under the other for the relief of the poor.

Justices and overseers often confounded the class that was to be relieved with the class that was to be punished. Consequent upon these two Acts instructions were issued by the judges at the assizes for carrying out their provisions. They were minute, and their precise directions were no doubt useful, if only interpreted rightly. But the definition of a "rogue," however intelligible to some, seems to have been liable to the harshest misconstruction. The articles thus began:—

"A rogue that saith he was born in such a town, in such a county, he ought to be sent thither."

The ninth article ran thus :—

"No man is to be put out of the town where he dwelleth, nor to be sent to the place of birth or last dwelling, but a rogue."

The third article enjoined :—

"If the husband and wife have house, and either of them rogue about, they must be sent to the town where the house is; and so of inmates."

To "rogue about" was to be living from hand to mouth, even if that living was derived from occasional labour—to be without regular service under a master—to be without a settled abode and a permanent occupation. The old definition of a rogue described him as "an idle sturdy beggar that wanders up and down from place to place without a licence." Another statutory definition of the class is—

"Persons whole and mighty in body, but having neither land nor master, not able to give an account of how they get their living."

Shakespeare's Autolycus, as we have seen, is a typical specimen of the clever species of the genus. And when a certain chronicler describes how, one evening, near Islington "a great parcel of rogues" encompassed Queen Elizabeth's coach, as she was riding abroad to take the air, "which seemed to put her in some disturbance," we must not conclude that they were thieves who contemplated an attack upon her royal person, they were merely a mob of professional beggars, "masterless men," "valiant and sturdy rogues," who followed no regular employment, and often swarmed about in gangs. The rogue, as distinguished from the mere vagabond and beggar, was comprised in the busy-idle classes which are minutely recited in the statute :—

"All persons calling themselves scholars, going about begging; all seafaring men pretending losses of their ships and goods at sea ; all idle persons going about either begging, or using any subtle craft or unlawful games and plays, or feigning to have knowledge in physiognomy, palmistry, or other crafty sciences, or pretending that they can tell destinies, fortunes, or such other fantastical imaginations ; all fencers, bearwards, common players, and minstrels ; all jugglers."

To the jongleurs and the scholars of an earlier era were now added the fortune-tellers and the play-actors. But even poor itinerant tradesmen came under the same category and were equally consigned to the constable by this sweeping statute; namely, all "tinkers, pedlars, and petty chapmen."

As the population outgrew the powers of the Government, the punishments for offenders became more and more severe ; whippings were more commonly inflicted, and instead of plain standing in the pillory, ears were nailed to the post, and even sliced off. Within city walls the population was at first kept well under control, the inhabitants of each ward being known to the alderman and his officers who, under a system of supervision which was almost personal, refused to harbour a rogue.

Smithfield in ancient times was the scene of honourable jousts and tournaments; Bartholomew Fair was held there for centuries, as well as markets for cattle and other commodities. After it had ceased to be a place of recreative exercise for the gentry it became the resort of bullies and bravoes, and obtained the name of Ruffians' Hall, otherwise the rendezvous of hectoring "swashbucklers"—literally swaggering fellows who intimidated by the clattering noise they made by swashing their swords and bucklers together.

A capital type of this sort of fellow is the hero of Gay's famous work, "The Beggar's Opera," Captain Macheath, the highwayman, a fine, rollicking, bold-faced ruffian who is "game" to the very last.

Wars and civil wars left crowds of idle soldiers who had no taste for settled work and became vagrants. These flocked to the towns, which became so densely populated that the ancient system of watch and ward broke down. When the Government could neither compel order nor prevent crime the punishments became positively savage. Apart from crime, vagrancy was an actual scourge, upon which neither laws nor proclamations made the slightest impression. Stocks, pillory, bread and water, whipping, every form of punishment with which these offenders were "roundly paid," produced but little visible effect, because for one who was punished a dozen escaped.

London especially swarmed with beggars, pretended cripples, idle and dissolute persons of every kind, hundreds of whom lived huddled together about Houndsditch and the Barbican, outside the walls. From time to time raids were made upon the denizens of these localities, but they merely dispersed to collect again. By the time of the Hanoverian succession other crowded districts, as Whitechapel and Stepney, had grown up outside the city walls, and beyond the reach of all local jurisdiction; districts populated by the working classes, but too often impregnated with criminals; where the people were uncouth, unruly, and grossly ignorant; a danger to society and a menace to the State. The only remedy provided for all these evils was repression—merciless floggings, foul and filthy prisons, and even hangings for the most trivial offences. The habitual vice was drink, which killed the sense of shame and stifled the voice of conscience. The degradation of the lowest classes during the initial half of the eighteenth century was appalling.

Vagrants regularly congregated at night in the purlieus of Westminster Abbey, where a night's lodging was to be obtained at the very smallest outlay; hence the neighbourhood acquired the name of the "back slums," the word "slum" (connected with *slumber*) meaning a place to sleep in.

"You shall comprehend all vagrom men" was the instruction every local Dogberry and Verges got from every local Justice Shallow. Let us see how the instruction was carried out.

An entry in the parish registers of Godalming, under date April 26, 1658, is to the following effect :—

"Here was taken a vagrant, one Mary Parker, widow with a child, and she was whipped according to law, about the age of thirty years, proper of personage ; and she was to go to the place of her birth that is in Gravesend in Kent, and she is limited to iiij days, and to be carried from tithing to Tything, till she comes to the end of the said journey."

A copy of the statute 39 *Elizabeth* for the suppression of rogues, vagabonds, and sturdy beggars, under which the persons punishable included scholars, wayfaring men, fencers, &c., who were to be whipped and sent out of the parish, is to be found carefully written at the end of the parish register in the church of St. Mary, Cerne Abbas. Also, to show the careful and conscientious manner in which the law had been carried out, is appended the following memorandum :—

" 1661—a registered book for all such rogues and vagabonds as have been punished according to law at Cerne Abbas in Dorsetshire; Oct. 11.—James Balden and E Balden, his wife, Thomas Balden, Robert Balden, and E. Balden their sons, and Joseph Dallinger, rogues and vagabonds and sturdy beggars, weare punished according to law at Cerne Abbas, and sent with testimoniale from Constable to Constable to Powell in Cornwall, the place of their ordinary abode, there to work at hard labour as good subjects ought to do."

The constable's accounts for the parish of Great Staughton, Huntingdonshire, contain some curious items:—

			£	s	d
1690. Pd. in charges, taking up a distracted woman, watching her and whipping her the next day ...			o	8	6
1710. Spent on Nurse London for searching the woman to see if she was with child before she was whipped...			o	2	o
Pd Tho. Hawkins for whipping 2 people yt had the small-pox ...			o	o	8

Numbers of cases are recorded at Wadhurst, Sussex; the register for the year 1663 contains these instances among others:—

11 June, Anne Diplock was whipped for a rogue.
10 Dec. John Palmer and Alice his wife were whipped for rogues.
23 Dec Thomasina Hemming, John Ballard, Margery Oiles, Robert Spray, and John Sargent whipped.

So universal was the practice of whipping vagrants and other like offenders that John Taylor, " the Water Poet," writing in 1630, says :—

> "In London, and within a mile, I ween,
> There are jails and prisons full eighteen,
> And sixty whipping-posts, and stocks, and cages"

At Newtimber, in September, 1615, it is recorded in the parish registers that—

" Robert Kinge, being about fifteene years of age, borne, as he confesseth, at Kynbury, in the Countie of Berkshire, was taken to the parish of Newtimber, vagrant, and there whipped according to the lawe, for his conduct to the parish of Kynbury aforesaid, being the place of his abode."

At Kingston-on-Thames, September 8, 1752, there were hanged no less than six persons, and at the same time "seventeen taken for rogues and vagabonds" were "whypped about the market-place and brent in the ears."

Here is a characteristic method of procedure, contained in the terms of a resolution, passed at Burton-on-Trent in 1749 :—

"Whereas great numbers of vagrants and sturdy beggars have for some time past frequented this town, and for preventing the same for the future, it is ordered that Robert Hinds be allowed 25/- quarterly for the care and pains in looking after and driving out of the town all vagrants and beggars by night and day."

On July 5, 1698, "a beggar woman of Slapton was whipt" at Mentmore, Oxfordshire ; on February 26th of the same year "Alice and Elizabeth Pickering, wandering children, were whipped according to Law and sent with a Pass to Shrewsbury, the place where they were born."

By the vagrant laws in force till 1744 it was enacted that persons found begging—

"were, by the appointment of the head-borough, or tithing-man, assisted by the advice of the minister of the parish, to be openly whipped till they were bloody, and then sent from parish to parish, until they came to the parish where they were born."

A CULPRIT BEING WHIPPED AT THE CART'S TAIL.

To face p. 271.

For the infliction of the flogging, the statute of 22 *Henry VIII.* had ordered the vagrant to be tied to a cart "naked" in the market-place; by the Act of Elizabeth's reign this was mitigated so far as the culprit was to be stripped only "from the middle upwards"; but, as before, the whipping, though not necessarily at the cart's tail, was not to cease till the body was bloody.

This degrading punishment was publicly inflicted on females without regard to their tender or their advanced age. At Burnham in Buckinghamshire the list of flogged preserved in the parish books includes "Anne Smith, a vagrant beggar about fifteen years old"; "Mary Webb, a child about thirteen years old, a wandering beggar"; and "Isabel Harris, a widd. about sixty years of age, and her daughter Elizabeth, with one child."

It may or may not be accounted a redeeming feature in the conduct of the Burnham parish officers that they sometimes recommended the poor women they had whipped to the tender mercies of the other parishes through which they afterwards passed the sufferers to their destination. But the nature of the recommendation recalls the witty Sydney Smith's celebrated formula—"A. never sees B. in distress, but he wishes C. to go and relieve him."

At Worcester and many other places men, women, and children were often whipped together promiscuously, even to the close of the eighteenth century, when the whipping of female vagrants was prohibited (1791); the usual fee paid to the "whipsman" was fourpence for each culprit receiving his official attentions. The stocks were often constructed to serve as whipping-post as well, so that duplicated penalties could be enforced with promptitude and dispatch. These matters were so frequently dealt with that they had to be conducted on strictly business lines.

The policy of a harsh deterrent administration of the
Poor Laws found favour in many places from the first.
As in the present day some workhouses in which the
discipline is rigidly severe are always avoided by the
tramp, so in the old days of stocks and whipping-posts
there were some towns the vagrant studiously avoided.
Among these, in the north, the towns of Halifax and
Hull were notably harsh in their punishment of delin-
quents ; whence arose the alliterative line known as the
" Beggars' Litany "—

" From Hell, Hull, and Halifax, Good Lord deliver us."

It is old gossip Fuller who designates this the Vagrants'
Litany, and then goes on to say : " Of these three fright-
ful things unto them, it is to be feared they least fear the
first, conceiving it to be the farthest from them.   Hull is
terrible to them as a town of good government where
beggars meet with punitive charity ; and it is to be
feared are oftener corrected than amended.   Halifax is
formidable for the law thereof," and so on.

This proverb is constantly quoted by old writers.
Taylor, the " Water Poet," rhymes thus about it :—

> " There is a proverbe, and a prayer withall,
> That we may not to three strange places fall ;
> From Hull, from Halifax, from Hell, 'tis thus,
> From all these three, Good Lord, deliver us.
>
> .　　　.　　　.　　　.　　　.
>
> The town's nam'd Kingston, Hul's the furious river,
> And from Hull's dangers, I say, Lord deliver.
> At Halifax the law so sharpe doth deale,
> That whosoe more than 13-pence doth steale,
> They have a jyn that wondrous quick and well
> Sends thieves all head-lesse into heav'n or hell "

Some localities have been so terrorised by tramp invasions that special measures have had to be devised against them—as the invention of the America "tramp cage."

In the *Wolverhampton Chronicle*, of the year 1819, it was stated that a notice-board erected at the entrance to the ancient town of Petersfield had the remarkable notice painted upon it—

"All persons found within this borough will be apprehended as Vagrants."

To this day the isolated effort of local authorities has signally failed to cope with what is a national evil. There are still thousands, if not tens of thousands, of vagrants in and out of the poorhouses, often in prison for petty offences, carrying infection from place to place, and committing depredations at night in the stockyards or outhouses of unprotected localities.

18

XXIII

THE FIRST GENERAL POOR LAW

Country swarming with vagrants—Disbanded soldiers—Discharged
sailors—Landless field labourers—First Poor Law, 1597—
Indigent to be registered and lodged—Overseers appointed—
Houses of Correction for the idle—Complementary Law of 1601
—An elective rating authority—Overseers to levy rates—To set
up Poor-houses—And set poor to work—"Grievous Groans for
the Poor" (1622)—Method of levying rates—Overseers—Their
number—Paid for attending monthly meetings.

How the country swarmed with beggars in Elizabethan
times is often indicated by the numerous entries made in
the parish registers of the time; those of Leeds, for
instance, for the year 1572 and onwards, record the
burials of persons described as such in entry after entry.
The excess of vagrancy at this period unmistakably
indicates a diseased condition of the national life.

The frequent expeditions of Elizabeth's reign threw
upon the world a number of disbanded soldiers and
sailors; and these, augmenting the ranks of the day-
labourers who could find no work, added materially to
the numbers of an ever-increasing and dangerous class
of vagabonds.

It was a transitional period between the military service
of feudalism and the creation of the standing army of
modern times; when troops were raised for a special
warfare—as the expedition to Cadiz—and at the con-

clusion of their engagement turned adrift, some of them with pockets filled with plunder, but not a few of them broken and penniless.   If they returned to their parishes they were told by the statute 39 *Elizabeth* " to betake themselves to some lawful course of life, on pain of being reputed felons."   The statute sets forth that lewd and licentious persons—

" have, of late, wandered up and down in all parts of the realm, under the name of soldiers and marines, abusing the title of that honourable profession to countenance their wicked behaviour, and do continually assemble themselves, weaponed, in the highways and elsewhere, in troops, to the great terror and astonishment of Her Majesty's true subjects."

There had been a ten years' war with Spain at the time of passing this Act, and we need feel no surprise that habitual thieves and beggars counterfeited disbanded troops.   For the genuine broken-down soldier the measure was indeed a hard one.   Its severity in all cases was admitted four years later when the complementary statute was passed requiring the parishes to provide a weekly sum, determined by the justices, towards the relief of the sick, hurt, maimed, and wounded soldiers and marines, having been in the Queen's service. If, after receiving such parochial allowance, they were found begging, they were to forfeit all claim, and to be deemed rogues and vagabonds.

As to the day-labourers wandering about the country unemployed, these included not only the labourers turned adrift on account of the thousands of acres taken out of tillage for conversion to pasture, but thousands more who could no longer earn a living because the great landowners had enclosed the common-lands upon which the peasant had hitherto turned out his cow, his pigs, and his poultry (see pp. 111 and 118).

Here, briefly, we may review the successive steps taken in the sixteenth century by which it was hoped to solve the difficulty of the poor without calling upon the community to tax itself directly for this purpose. First, the poor were restricted from begging, except within a certain specified district. Next, each parish was required to support its own poor, by means of charitable alms collected on Sundays, and stimulated by the appeals of the parson. Then was besought the charity of the people to provide houses and "material for setting the poor on work," a duty to which the clergy were expected to exhort them. The form of the Sunday collections was next altered ; each person was expected to set down in writing the amount he was willing to give weekly towards the poor, for the ensuing year. If the parishioner obstinately refused thus to pledge himself, he was to be exhorted by the bishop to do his duty by his poorer neighbours ; if still refractory, he was reported by the bishop to the justices ; and if he refused to yield to their persuasions, they were empowered to assess him to an amount reasonably within his means.

In 1575 it was ordered that Houses of Correction should be provided ; for the rule and good government of which censors and wardens were to be appointed by the justices ; and collectors were to gather the money for supporting these institutions.

By these successive stages the way was gradually prepared for the Act of 1597, which made a universal assessment of property, and the payment of poor-rates compulsory.

In 1597 Parliament gave its serious attention to the problem, and passed a new law dealing with rogues and vagabonds who were still to be punished with the stocks and otherwise, but at the same time the really helplessly indigent were to be registered, and convenient places established for their habitation, and overseers were appointed to find work for those who were not absolutely incapacitated.   Two years later Houses of Correction, in which the work was exacted, were built.

A House of Correction was an establishment in which, *after conviction*, were punished various "idle and disorderly persons," chiefly beggars, rogues, vagabonds, trespassers, servants running away, and fugitive parents of bastard children.

Every parish was charged with the support of its own poor, classified as the " Idle," who were to be compelled to work, and the " Impotent," who were to be relieved. Certain persons were made liable to support their own relatives.

A supplementary Act of 1601 placed the relief of the poor on a systematic basis by the appointment of overseers in each parish to levy rates with which to provide work for those who could not or did not procure it for themselves, and to establish Poor-houses for the reception of the infirm and unable.   The rating authority was now an elective one ; the overseers chosen in vestry were representatives of the parishioners, whereas the justices were neither elective nor representative.

There was no excess of zeal to put the Act in force. Dekker in 1622 published a pamphlet entitled, "Grievous Groans for the Poor," which clearly discloses the fact that the Poor Law was not in full operation twenty years after its enactment ; for the pamphleteer is moved to state that—

" though the number of the poor do daily increase, all things yet worketh for the worst in their behalf ; for there hath been no collection for them, no, not these seven years, in many parishes of this land, especially in the country towns ; but many of these parishes turneth forth their poor, yea, and their lusty labourers that will not work, or for any misdemeanour want work, to beg, filch, and steal for their maintenance, so that the country is pitifully pestered with them."

Undoubtedly the culminating Act of Elizabeth's reign (1601) did accomplish much towards clearing the country of beggars; Houses of Correction in every county locked up the idle, while in every parish the helpless were supported by the levying of a compulsory poor-rate. The principles of this new Poor Law were felt to be on right lines; it was made permanent at the Restoration, and remained in force till 1835.

When the Poor Relief Act of 1601 was passed there were, whatever the causes may have been, and at a time, too, when the population was comparatively so much smaller, no less than 10,000 beggars in the country. The Act was intended as a temporary measure, and was passed for a limited period; but was renewed at the beginning of the reigns of James I. and Charles I. It had in view the prevention and regulation of begging, but its main provision ran in these terms :—

"And also for setting to work all such persons, married or un-married (as) having no means to maintain them, use no ordinary or daily trade of life to get their living by ; and also to raise weekly or otherwise (by taxation of every inhabitant, parson, vicar, and other and of every occupier of lands, houses, tithes impropriate, propriations of tithes, coal mines, or saleable underwoods in the said parish in such competent sum and sums of money as they shall think fit) a convenient stock of flax, hemp, wool, thread, iron, and other ware and stuff to set the poor on work."

These two enactments are epoch marking. The statute of 1597 may be regarded as the first general Poor Law, and that of 1601 its complement. As before, vagabonds and sturdy beggars were to be whipped and passed from parish to parish ; but the assessment for the building of workhouses and the relief of the really destitute, which had hitherto been in the hands of the justices, was now transferred to parochial officers—the Overseers of the Poor.

A workhouse was a building provided by the parish for the reception and *employment of the poor*, sometimes in profitable labour, but frequently in such useless tasks as beating hemp.

The overseers were to be four, three, or two in number, "according to the greatness of the parish," substantial householders, nominated with the church-wardens at Easter vestry meeting. "And the said churchwardens and overseers shall meet together at least once every month in the church upon the Sunday in the afternoon after divine service, to consider of some good course to be taken," said the Act. Substantial men though they might be, it is on record that some of them charged the ratepayers for each monthly attendance the sum of one shilling, and a goodly allowance of ale.

The overseers were empowered, with the consent of two justices, to raise, weekly or otherwise, the levies, aforementioned, for the relief of the impotent, setting the able-bodied to work, and for putting poor children apprentices. In later times the pauper children were to be educated as well.

As the overseers not infrequently neglected the poor, or relieved only their own friends, it was ordained in 1691 that they should produce their lists of poor at vestry meeting. But as the justices could order any names to be added, this power was much abused till its withdrawal in the reign of George I.

XXIV

THE WORKHOUSE

Poor-house or Work-house?—"Abiding Houses," "Maisons de Dieu," &c.—Houses of Industry—Evolution of the workhouse—Hired cottages—Proposed "Hundred Houses"—United parishes—Permissive Unions (1782)—Industrial prisons—The strong-room and the lock-up—Bridewells—Havens of Rest—Sites on common-land — Permissive Workhouse Act (1723) — Iron-working as profitable employment — Workhouses as manu-factories of paupers.

THE bulwark set up as the defence against an excessive call for poor-rates was the workhouse. It had been customary prior to the establishment of these institutions to relieve the able-bodied poor at their own houses.

Sir F. M. Eden states that when first erected, these parochial establishments had an instant and striking effect in reducing the number of poor. The repugnance of the poor to the workhouses was so great that it was proposed, by way of weakening that aversion, to call them by some softer and less offensive name.

Workhouses were at first generally unhealthy; not being properly planned and constructed for the herding of a number of people together, some of them became positive pest-houses.

The Poor-house was miscalled the Work-house almost from the first, as soon as this parish institution became the acknowledged refuge of the idle, the dissolute, and the depraved. An Act of 1624 was passed for erecting "Hospitals and Working Houses for the Poor."

By enactments of the middle of Elizabeth's reign, poor, aged, and impotent persons were to be provided for in convenient "abiding-places" in which they could be settled. The amending Act made it easier for benevolently disposed persons to make the necessary gifts and bequests for providing and maintaining these abiding-places, styled variously Alms Hospitals, Houses of Correction, Abiding Houses, or Maisons de Dieu. They were to be founded, incorporated, and have perpetual succession for ever.

These institutions were to be under the control and management of overseers of the poor appointed for one year.

Any poor person installed in an "abiding-place" and refusing to work, or quitting it without permission, was to be counted a rogue and a vagabond and punished as such.

The workhouse, according to original intention, was provided for the impotent poor only. But the whole Poor Law system, like most other human institutions, was easily susceptible of abuse, especially under the narrow administration of the parochial area, and fell away rapidly from its original lines.

The Elizabethan code had directed that "the workless be set on work," and the parish had to organise employment for them. For two centuries this impossible task was attempted, populous places occasionally obtaining local Acts authorising the erection of special institutions —Houses of Industry they were usually called.

At Rochester Sir J. Hayward's almshouse for the accommodation of six poor women has always been known as "The House of Industry"; it is purely a charitable institution, and since 1823 its funds have provided for twice the original number of inmates.

Huddersfield, Shrewsbury, and other old towns still have their Houses of Industry, and Sunderland has its School of Industry. They were intended to be human hives, not havens of rest.

Houses of Industry were not almshouses, nor were they ordinary workhouses supported by poor-rates. They were institutions founded upon benevolent principles to provide workpeople out of work with means of earning an honest living, partly supported by voluntary contributions and partly by the sale of the goods which the workers produced. They were, in fact, public workshops where domestic trades were carried on, the committees controlling the institutions relieving the workers from all anxiety respecting the disposal of the product of their labours. Hours of work were fixed, meals provided, but out of working hours the workers returned to their homes, or, in case they had none, were provided with sleeping accommodation. This was not a general condition, however. The workers had to be natives of the town where such institutions existed, had to be of good moral character, and in all cases were heads of families. Single men were not admitted. These were the usual conditions, but they varied in different parts of the country. They were, in fact, founded to neutralize the terrible distress arising from periodic trade depressions, without encroaching upon the poor-rates.

The inscription over the old workhouse door at Maidstone which was demolished in 1907, ran :—

" Ut pauperes meliori vitæ regimini subjiciat ;
Ut industriam potius quam segnitiem promoveat ;
Ut ab impensâ vix tolerabili (iis tamen
Sublevandis impari) parochiam exoneret ;
Hoc, quod spectas, ædificium
Ex singulari suâ munificentiâ posuit.
THOS. BLISS, arm.
1720."

A rendering of this is :—

"To make the poor subject to a better rule of life ;
To promote industry in preference to sloth ;
To disburden the parish from an expense scarcely bearable
(inadequate however for those worthy to be relieved) ;
This building, which thou beholdest, he out of his own bounty
erected.
THOS. BLISS, Esq.,
1720."

Beneath, a smaller slab has this inscription :—

"If any would not work,
Neither should he eat."
2 THESS. III. chap., 10 verse.

The donor was Member of Parliament for the borough. This "workhouse" was sold in 1838, and then used as schoolrooms for the Bluecoat Boys and Girls' National School.

Like everything characteristically English, the work-house is an institution of slow growth and gradual evolution. Our authority, Sir F. M. Eden, states that the first workhouse in England was erected in 1723. But parish records in many parts of the country make allusion to the workhouse at an earlier date. Thus the registers of Aston-juxta-Birmingham mention, under date 1700, meetings about "settling ye work-house," and Bilston Workhouse is believed to have been erected in the same year.

The explanation is, simply, that at first cottages were hired for the use of the poor, and that special buildings for the herding of paupers under one roof came as a later development. These were almshouses, often unsuitable and very unhealthy, maintained at the public cost for the lodging and support of the indigent and such able-bodied as were out of employment.

Had their earliest and primary use been purely the provision of a home for the infirm poor, the name Poor-house, as being more descriptive, would have been more generally used.   But it is the appellation of Work-house which has persistently clung to these institutions, clear evidence that they were mainly called into existence as places in which paupers could be set to work, receiving in return for their labour, food, shelter, and clothing, known as "indoor relief."   An Act which came later denied relief to all who "refused the house"—the favourite "test" of Boards of Guardians to this day.

It was proposed in 1763 to establish among the less populous parishes, Hundred Houses, each to comprise an infirmary for the sick and disabled poor, and a place for the profitable employment of the other paupers.

The several parishes in the city of Bristol were formed into one united parish for the purpose of establishing a common workhouse in 1697.   This example was quickly followed by other ancient and populous places like Worcester, Hull, Exeter, Plymouth, and Norwich. Under a special Act of George I. Bristol erected its first workhouse building; but in 1722 a general permission was given for parishes to unite in providing a suitable house either by hire or purchase, for the keeping and main-taining of the poor.   Then in 1782 "permissive Unions" were recognised under an Act promoted by Mr. Gilbert, M.P. for Lichfield.

At first the workhouse was little better than an industrial prison.   The poor being regarded as pests, it was deemed best to dispose of them either in prison or in a workhouse; or, in those cases where so dis-agreeable a subject could be summarily dealt with, in a "Bridewell," which partook of the nature of both.   It seemed difficult at first to regard a workhouse as aught else than a place of confinement in which vagrants and sturdy beggars could be compelled to work. And generally they were nurseries of ignorance, idleness, and vice.

The earliest buildings erected for workhouses were arranged, not exactly in wards, but always "in two divisions, one for males and one for females." With some of them—and is not this fact indicative of the old spirit which invariably associated the poor with the criminal ?—a prison was conjoined. Bilston workhouse had a " strong-room " attached to it, and the iron-studded door of the lock-up in Wednesbury parish workhouse is still to be seen.

Offenders against the workhouse regulations at Birmingham were punished by being "confined to the dungeon by logger on the leg, or subjected to distinction of dress, or abatement of diet, or loss of encouragement money."

In the old workhouse at Newcastle-under-Lyme, erected in the eighteenth century, the accommodation for prisoners consisted of the felons' rooms, four very small apartments, without glass-windows or fireplaces, and used for temporary confinement only ; and a debtor's prison, consisting of two rooms of a more comfortable description, likewise attached to the workhouse, with the master as gaoler.

Old Tothill Fields Prison, adjoining "the Abiding House for the Poor," was originally designed as a Bridewell, or House of Correction, and a place of " penitentiary amendment " for vagrants, valiant rogues, and sturdy beggars, the inscription on stone over the door being :—

" Here are several sorts of Work for the Poor of this Parish of St. Margaret, Westminster, as also for the County, according to Law, and for such as will beg and live Idle in this City & Liberty of Westminster, Anno 1655."

Unhappily, in those early experimental days the conception of a poor-house as other than a penal establishment was of extremely rare occurrence. Still, to a few minds the idea of such an institution as a haven of refuge had already presented itself.

The accomplished Bishop Ken, who died in 1711, had formed a project for setting up in Wells a workhouse for the poor, in which they could be given employment at better wages than those offered by the tradesmen of the town.

A pious benefactor bequeathed a sum of money in 1734 for the benefit of "the riotous poor in the Workhouse." Although the adjective used may have been very fairly descriptive in some instances, it is believed the testator intended his benefaction for the "righteous" poor.

The first difficulty in erecting a workhouse, the provision of a site, was overcome when common or waste land, or charity land, could be utilized. The provision of a workhouse was often opposed and delayed to the utmost, even when common-land was available in any quantity.

With regard to the provision of suitable premises for carrying out the law, it was enacted that the churchwardens and overseers, by leave of the lord of the manor, might build on the waste or common-land, with part of the monies levied, "houses of dwelling for the poor, which cottages shall not be used for any other habitation, but only for the impotent and poor of the parish." At a later period, in the reign of George I., it was made lawful to hire houses, and to contract with any person for the keeping and employing of the poor, and to take the profit of their work.

Uttoxeter's first workhouse dated from 1703, and lasted till 1789, when the common on the High Wood was inclosed by Act of Parliament, part of the land being sold for the purpose of aiding the poor-rate of the parish and erecting a new workhouse. The inclosure was carried out by a body of trustees, and on the erection of the workhouse a stone tablet was inserted bearing this inscription :—

"This Workhouse was rebuilt by the trustees for enclosing the common within the constablewick of Uttoxeter, 1789."

Here is a resolution passed at a West Bromwich vestry illustrative of the working of the Permissive Workhouse Act of 1723 :—

"And for the defraying and payment of the charges of the said Workhouse it is alsoe agreed that the same shall be paid by the usuall four-penny levey of the Poore Rate such leveys to be collected in manner hereafter named. That is, one levey in this present year; and to continue the collection of two leveys yearly afterwards, more than the charges of the maintenance of the poor, until the expenses above said be fully satisfied and paid."

Like many other places, West Bromwich followed the plan of "profitable employment," and the material kept in stock there was iron, in the shape of nail-rods, the able-bodied paupers being set to work at nail-making.

It scarcely needs adding to this typical case that the provision of a workhouse had been delayed from time to time as long as possible ; and even after the passing of this heroic resolution there was a public meeting of ratepayers to protest against and oppose the erection of a parish workhouse. The original building used for housing the poor of this parish was a nail warehouse, in which both men and women were employed at nail-making, a domiciliary and ill-paid form of industry long familiar to the poorest class of iron-workers in the region now known as the Black Country. From con-

crete examples like this may be best gathered the
reluctant spirit in which the Poor Laws have always
been interpreted, and the parsimonious methods in
which, from the first, they were almost invariably
carried out.

Though the Act of 1601 has never been directly
repealed, it has been so modified by subsequent enactments that recently (1909), when a man at West Ham
demanded to be set to work for wages, the magistrates
declared they had no power to compel guardians of the
poor to find employment for paupers.

Making reference to the subject of the crowded workhouses, which year by year were becoming fuller of the
worthless and the thriftless, the *Examiner* in 1711
said :—

"This island can afford enough to support the dignity of the
Crown, the honour of the nobility, and the dignity of the magistracy, and yet leave enough to engage in industry which best
deserves encouragement, but not to the extent of sending every
living soul into the workhouse."

For although at first successful in reducing the cost of
relief, by 1722 it was found that these institutions were
not permanently effective, but had rather developed into
manufactories of paupers, and were steadily increasing
the burden of the poor-rates.

XXV

BUMBLEDOM

Vestry *v* Corporation—Parish business conducted at church—
Workhouse rules (1742) — The workhouse master — The
beadle—In literature and art—" The Election of a Beadle "
—Mr Bumble—The naming of parish foundlings—Crabbe,
" the poet of the poor "—His description of the workhouse—
And its inmates—Dr Langhorne's " Appeal to the Magistrates
on behalf of the Rural Poor "—His indictment of the parish
officials—Aversion to the " House " characteristic of the poor.

WORKHOUSE management offers another interesting field
for research. There were doubtless a few Arcadian spots
where life in the workhouse was patriarchal in form and
pleasant in character. But in many of the small and
slackly-supervised workhouses the master and the matron
were the veriest autocrats.

To provide the first workhouse for Walsall some
houses were purchased by the Corporation in 1717,
but ten years later a vestry meeting held at the church
resolved to erect a new workhouse, although it does not
seem to have been actually built till 1723.

Dissensions afterwards arose (1769) between the civic
authorities and the vestry as to the possession and control of the workhouse buildings ; the record of the litigation between them has not been preserved, but it is not
likely the Corporation could override the parish authorities in a matter relating to Poor Law administration.

As in many small parishes, the poor of Cheadle were at first housed in separate cottages, where they managed their own household affairs with little interference or control beyond the occasional superintendence of the vicar, churchwardens, or overseers. The only absolute rules and regulations to which they had to submit were compulsory attendance at church and the leading of sober lives, so that they fell not under the correction of the executive functionaries, the Church beadle and the parish constable. Being a small community, this primitive arrangement continued from the beginning of the century till 1761, when attention was called to the dilapidated condition of the buildings, and a proposal was then made for " an overseer of the workhouse " to be appointed at a " fixt salary or allowance "; but it was not till 1774 that the ratepayers summoned up courage enough to build a specially planned workhouse, which was erected on a site belonging to a local charity. To fortify themselves to the undertaking of this enterprise the parishioners passed the necessary resolutions at a vestry meeting, held after evening prayer the first Sunday in September, 1773. It was thus a dominant State Church took firm hold of local government.

The first workhouse in the county-town of Stafford was provided in 1735 by converting two old cottages standing in the churchyard. A more regularised institution was established a few years later, the ordinances for conducting which, passed at a vestry meeting in October, 1742, are so informative as to methods of management then practised, they are worth quoting :—

"(1) That no person shall presume to go out of the house without leave and whoever shall attempt so to do shall be punished at the discretion of the master.

"(2) That no person shall presume to smoke tobacco in the house and that none be allowed in the accompts.

"(3) Whereas some persons of turbulent tempers curse and swear and are very clamorous not only in the daytime, but even at night, when they are in bed, to the great disturbance of other persons and particularly of the sick, it is ordered that such persons so offending shall be debarred their meals and otherwise be severely punished at the discretion of the master or the vestry.

"(4) That care be taken that there be no waste fires made, but such as are absolutely necessary for sick people or lying-in women, and such as shall be necessary for dressing of Victualls and Washing and ironing of Linnen, except in the winter when the master is to judge what allowance of coals is necessary, and that Twelve Tun of coals be allowed for the whole year.

"(5) That the master do take care that none of the poor be suffered to sit up after nine in summer and eight in winter except the nurses attending the sick, and that the fires and candles be out, and all the servants and all the family in Bed by nine

"(6) That when any person dyes in the house, the nurse shall immediately go for a Coffin (which shall not exceed the price of Six Shillings for a grown-up person, and Three Shillings for children) and the deceased person shall be washed and laid in the coffin, &c., &c.

"(7) That the Cloathes of persons dying in the house (being first washed or cleaned) be brought into the Store-room, and such of them as are not much worn shall be lodged there till wanted ; but such as are very old either be mended up or cut to pieces to mend others , and the nurse who attended the party while sick shall deliver up all the other goods and money of the deceased to the master, or be severely punished if she purloin the same.

"(8) That whatever persons in the house appointed to any Labour or Service in the family, shall neglect their duty in the respective Labour or Service required of them, such persons so offending shall be sent to the House of Correction or otherwise punished as the nature of the offence shall deserve.

"(9) That for the encouragement of all such poor as shall discharge that they are appointed to do with care and diligence, it is ordered that every nurse attending the sick or infirm shall receive as a reward threepence per week.

"(10) Every person who is hired out to work and maintain himself the whole day shall have the half of his daily wages for himself.

"(11) Others who are subsisted in the house to have twopence allowed out of every shilling they gain. And that they who assist in the kitchen or the wash-house shall be paid one penny, twopence, or threepence a week, according to the nature of the business and as their service shall deserve.

"(12) That all poor who are in health go to church or to some other place of religious worship every Sunday morning and afternoon ; but if any of them instead of serving God shall be found begging or loitering away their time, or shall take the opportunity to get drunk or not to return in good time, they shall be expelled the house, or otherwise be severely punished."

There were a number of other regulations, but the most noticeable feature in the foregoing is the leaning towards religious equality displayed in the phrase, "some other place of religious worship," in the last one quoted. It breathes a spirit of toleration rarely met with in these old parish records.

The position of workhouse master was not infrequently filled by one who had to be provided with a berth, and had sufficient friends to secure for him this piece of preferment. In 1781 Richard Lambert was appointed to be governor of Walsall workhouse at a salary of £25, and the resolution passed upon this occasion is curious enough to be quoted. It ran :—

"That the said Richard Lambert keep good order and rule in the said house ; that he and the whole family go to rest and rise at necessary and reasonable hours ; that the said house and premises at all times be kept clean, sweet, and decent ; also to cause the seats and pews in the said church to be swept and cleaned every Saturday by the poor in the said house, without any expense to the inhabitants ; that he keep the poor in the said house to work (such as are not capable to go to out-work) in such employment as he shall think necessary and most convenient," &c , &c.

There were a number of other similar provisions for the good governance of the workhouse, but enough have been given to indicate the lines upon which the institution was worked. It will be observed that in those days of vestry government the workhouse was regarded as

an adjunct to the Church.   A resolution passed at a
Burton-on-Trent vestry in 1699 ordered "that the
Churchwardens and Overseers of the poor do stay att
the church upon every second Sunday in every month
after evening prayer to consider further or fitting means
for the better relief of ye poor."   In the following year
(1700) it was ordered " that the poore people who receive
reliefe from the parish do constantly come to church and
sitt on those seats (provided for them in ye south oyle)
or be putt out of ye poore's booke."

But the official most in evidence in the old days of
vestry government was the parish beadle. As his name
implied, he was the functionary who " bade" others
obey the law ; as a rule he was a pompous jack-in-office,
decked out in gorgeous raiment that marked only too
well the contrast between him and the hordes of beggars
and wretched paupers with whom he, as chief executive
officer, had to deal.

The art and literature of the country have made us
very familiar with this picturesque functionary ; sometimes he appeared as the bell-man or town-crier, and
sometimes as wielder of the whip which inflicted magisterial punishments.   Hood's allegorical drawing of him
in " The Progress of Cant" depicts him as accompanied
by the worrying dog of officialism, and carrying about
for constant reference and support a portentous copy of
the Vagrant Act.

Of sleek appearance, and an imposing mien such as
befitted his cocked hat and long robe, he carried as the
symbol of his authority a formidable staff with a shining
brass knob at top ; aiming in all things official at making
himself a terror to the poor.   In some parts of the
country he was known as the Ban-beggar—a name aptly
corrupted in other places into Bang-beggar.

Hogarth in his series of cartoons on the subject shows

his " Idle Apprentice " in one of them, getting a severe castigation at the hands of the beadle. The artist shows us the dissolute youth gambling on a tombstone during the hours of divine service; he is evidently trying to cheat his vile companions at the Old English game of Hustle Cap by concealing some of the halfpence under the brim of his hat. More illuminating, perhaps, is Dickens' sketch, "The Election of the Beadle," which is worth recalling for the number of side-lights it throws upon the subject.

The aged parish beadle, having died suddenly through over-exertion in conveying an intoxicated female to the strong-room of the workhouse, added to a severe cold caught by that indefatigable officer in his capacity of director of the parish engine—an antiquated contrivance like a pump in a box on four low wheels—by inadvertently playing over himself instead of the fire, the vacancy thus occasioned had to be filled by the process of popular election.

Party spirit ran high. There was the official party who claimed patronage of all such offices as a privilege, if not as a right; these were the steady supporters of the churchwardens and overseers, who generally managed to manipulate the rates to suit their own and their friends' vested interests; and there was the parishioners' party, little less culpable, fighting to wrest this power from their opponents, and turn it to their own advantage.

Naturally the latter charged the vestry officials with all sorts of high misdemeanours, as " the mismanagement of the workhouse, and the grinding down of the paupers by diluting their beer, slack-baking their bread, boning the meat, and lowering the soup." They demanded an independent beadle of their own. But the party in power had secured a strong candidate in a man named

To lead Creatures at play in the Church yard with Contempt

BEADLE CASTIGATING THE IDLE APPRENTICE.

(By Hogarth.)

To face p. 294.

Spruggins, who had "ten small children, and a wife."
Had not men with large families always been elected to
office ? Was not the propagation of the human species
to be encouraged—by those who had the exploiting
of them ?

How the election was conducted and how it all ended
are best read in the words of the inimitable "Boz." But
has not the same fertile imagination produced for us the
immortal Mr. Bumble, the fat, choleric, pompous beadle
who overshadowed the young life of Oliver Twist ?
Did not this distinguished official name poor Oliver, as
he claimed to name all the parish children, all the
orphans of the workhouse, who were regarded as nothing
less than infant offenders against the Poor Laws, to be
cuffed and buffeted through the world for presuming
to be born at all ? As he said of all these poor victims
of systematic ill-treatment, "We name our foundlings
in alphabetical order. The last was a S—Swubble I
named him. This was a T—Twist I named him." And
so this officious, over-bearing beadle, the embodiment
of the arrogance once so characteristic of parish
authorities, has become a recognised type, and Bumbledom will stand for all time as synonymous for fussy
official pomposity and incapacity.

It was thus that Bumbledom put its hall-mark on its
foster-children in the workhouse. In the Foundling
Hospital the nameless innocent would seem to have had
a better chance of succeeding to its own. The point is
illustrated by Captain Marryat in his amusing novel,
"Japhet in Search of a Father," the hero of which begins
his adventures as a pretty black-eyed babe, found one
dark night, wrapped in warm flannel within a covered
basket, suspended from the knocker of the Foundling
Hospital. Attached to the living contents of the package
was a note addressed to the governors of the charity,

couched in these laconic terms: "This child was born in wedlock; he is to be named Japhet. When circumstances permit, he will be reclaimed." Japhet he was accordingly named; and very entertaining are the chapters that follow, recounting the numerous adventures which overtook the enterprising foundling in his determined and prolonged search for his unknown parent.

For the realisation of the utter sordidness and callous neglect which characterised the management of the eighteenth-century workhouse, nothing more impressive is needed than the picture presented by the Rev. George Crabbe, "the poet of the poor," in his poem entitled "The Village." This poem, after correction by Burke and Johnson, appeared in 1783; it was a complete and an instant success, and the description of the parish workhouse in it was copied into all the periodicals of the time:—

"Such is that room which one rude beam divides,
And naked rafters form the sloping sides;
Where the vile bands that bind the thatch are seen,
And lath and mud are all that lie between,
Save one dull pane, that, coarsely patched, gives way
To the rude tempest yet excludes the day.
Here, on a matted flock, with dust o'erspread,
The drooping wretch reclines his languid head;
For him no hand the cordial cup applies,
Or wipes the tear that stagnates in his eyes;
No friends with soft discourse his pain beguile,
Or promise hope till sickness wears a smile.

Theirs is yon house that holds the parish poor,
Whose walls of mud scarce bear the broken door;
There, where the putrid vapours flagging, play,
And the dull wheel hums doleful through the day;
There children dwell who know no parents' care;
Parents, who know no children's love dwell there;
Heart-broken matrons on their joyless bed,
Forsaken wives and mothers never wed,

THE ELECTION FOR BEADLE.

Dejected widows with unheeded tears,
And crippled age with more than childhood fears;
The lame, the blind, and, far the happiest they,
The moping idiot and the madman gay.
  Here, too, the sick their final doom receive
Here brought amid the scenes of grief, to grieve,
Where the loud groans from some sad chamber flow,
Mixed with the clamours of the crowd below;
Here sorrowing, they each kindred sorrow scan,
And the cold charities of man to man.

Then, as to the parish doctor—

Paid by the parish for attendance here,
He wears contempt upon his sapient sneer;
In haste he seeks the bed where misery lies,
Impatience marked in his averted eyes;
And, some habitual queries hurried o'er,
Without reply he hurries to the door,
His drooping patient, long inured to pain,
And long unheeded, knows remonstrance vain;
He ceases now the feeble help to crave
Of man, and sinks into the grave."

As the "poet of the poor" Crabbe was slightly anticipated by Dr. John Langhorne, also an excellent and amiable clergyman of the eighteenth century. He pleads warmly for the poor vagrant, whom he recognises as having been—

"Known to no human love, no human care,
The friendless homeless object of despair."

Perhaps (he continues) the child of some slaughtered soldier, born far from England on some inhospitable shore; and the first sad gaze of whose widowed mother—

"Gave the sad presage of his future years,
The child of misery, baptized in tears."

In "An Appeal to County Justices on Behalf of the Rural Poor," a subject highly significant of the times, are some very powerful passages. For the "shivering train" of paupers he asks of the magisterial squire a sympathetic hearing—

> "Nor leave thy venal clerk empowered to hear;
> The voice of want is sacred to thy ear.
> He, where no fees his sordid pen invite,
> Sports with their tears, too indolent to write."

Worse is his indictment of another parish official—

> "But chief thy notice shall one monster claim;
> A monster furnished with a human frame—
> The parish officer!—though verse disdain
> Terms that deform the splendour of the strain,
> It stoops to bid thee bend the brow severe
> On the sly, pilfering, cruel overseer,
> The shuffling farmer, faithful to no trust,
> Ruthless as rocks, insatiate as the dust."

A little further on the farmer overseer is pictured as repulsing the impoverished labourer, who is—

> "sent with insolence away,
> Referred to vestries, and a distant day."

To the fox-hunting justice, more heedful of his sport than his social duties, he presently makes this spirited appeal—

> "Wouldst thou then raise thy patriot office higher?
> To something more than magistrate aspire!
> And, left each poorer, pettier chase behind,
> Step nobly forth, the friend of humankind!"

Yet, after all, what is the climax to the poet's story which inspired this passionate pleading on behalf of the neglected poor ? It is the horror of a sickening discovery in a wretched cottage, where—

> "extended on a bed
> Of naked fern, two human creatures dead !"

They are the shepherd and his wife, victims of the then universal parochial neglect, who have simply "died through want."

Such was the typical tragedy of rural life, which could, and did, sometimes happen under the callous administration of the Poor Laws in the "good old times" of the eighteenth century.

By the beginning of the nineteenth century workhouses were commonly dubbed "bastilles," being regarded by the poor as veritable prisons—the name, of course, being borrowed from that of the State prison in Paris, destroyed by the revolutionary mob in 1789.

A strong and deep-rooted aversion from "the House" has now become characteristic of the self-respecting poor, and many causes have contributed to this result. In the past there was practically no attempt at classification ; and when all were herded together it must have been trying for the sane, the healthy, and the decent-minded to live with the imbecile, the epileptic, and the degraded. The respectable aged poor even have a great horror of the common dining-rooms and the common dormitories. The compulsory cleanliness is only a minor grievance, if one at all.

The problem which called the workhouse into existence is one which, so far, has passed the wit of man to solve. To-day, in London alone, the cost of workhouse inmates amounts to about a million per annum, while it takes more than half that sum to pay the officials.

XXVI

THE SETTLEMENT OF THE POOR

Wages fixed at Quarter Sessions—In husbandry and the handicrafts
—And proclaimed by the Sheriff—Refusers of fixed wages
accounted vagabonds—Wages fixed at lowest limit—Act of
Parochial Settlement, 1662—Requires strangers to give security
against becoming chargeable to the rates—Mobility of labour
destroyed — Yet labour always attracted by capital — All
strangers ordered to leave a parish within forty days—Labourers
hunted from parish to parish—Examples of the law's harshness
—At Bilston (1699)—At Leicester sub-tenants disallowed—A
strange tailor expelled from Lyme—An offence to "harbour a
wife's sister" — Industry strangled — Guarantees given for
imported workpeople—Adam Smith on this oppression—Help-
lessness of voteless labour—A cumbrous law—Legal methods
of acquiring a settlement—Some mean advantages taken of the
helpless and destitute—A Wednesbury subterfuge—A pauper
halved — A gentlemanly agreement to let no cottages to
strangers—Unless they indemnify the churchwarden by a bond
—A law that prepared the mind for inevitable pauperism—
Victimised pauper punished for corrupt officials—A French
view of this law (1810)—The distress after Waterloo (1815)
—Parochial selfishness—Divorces capital and labour — Bad
effect on labourers' dwellings.

THE Elizabethan Acts of 1597 and 1601 were the first
assertion of the principle of a compulsory assessment of
property for the relief of the destitute ; they formed,
faulty and fallible as they were, the basis of a Poor Law
system which was to endure for three centuries. The

next important development of parish particularism was the Act of Parochial Settlement, 1662.

It would now seem that at last the poor were secured against starvation—at any rate in their old age.   But the working of this new Poor Law has to be considered in conjunction with an Act which gave to magistrates sitting in Quarter Sessions the power of fixing the rate of wages in their locality, both in husbandry and the handicrafts.

A statute of the fifth year of Elizabeth's reign, entitled " An Act touching divers orders of artificers, labourers, servants of husbandry and apprentices," repealed all previous statutes of like purpose, chiefly because the wages limited by them were palpably too small, and had been found unanswerable at that time, on account of the great advancement of prices.

The rates of wages were therefore to be settled annually by the justices in sessions assembled.   The rate so settled, having been approved by the Privy Council, was to be proclaimed by the sheriff ; and both the payer and receiver of any higher rate of wages were liable to fine and imprisonment.

The Act proceeded further to outrage the principles of free labour contracting, by declaring that all able-bodied labourers, wandering the country through their refusal to work at the rates thus arbitrarily legalized, were to be accounted rogues and vagabonds, and as such subjected to all the cruel punishments then in vogue.

An enactment as early as the reign of Richard II. had forbidden any person to leave his parish without the consent of the magistrates (p. 106).   Had not English legislators ever before them the pattern and warrant of the great Roman Republic to build up a State on the basis of servile labour ?

That the labourers resented this fixing of their wages

at a bare pittance was not unnatural, and men frequently moved from a district where wages were very low, hoping to better themselves elsewhere. But after the Restoration of Charles II. in 1660, the landowners became all-powerful in the State. They were not slow to employ their strength in Parliament to bring the labourers into complete subjection. This was done by the law of Parochial Settlement, enacted in 1662.

This Act empowered the churchwardens and overseers of a parish to remove from it any new-comer who arrived in the place and occupied a tenement of less than ten pounds annual value, unless he could give ample security that he would not become chargeable to the parish.

As no ordinary labourer had the means to rent a tenement of the annual value of ten pounds, no labourer could give the required security; so the local authorities kept a sharp look-out for the appearance of a new face searching for work and attempting to settle in the place. The man was immediately pounced upon, and required to give an account of himself. If the account was not satisfactory, he was peremptorily sent back to his own parish.

The effect of the Parochial Act was to pen up the labouring classes in their villages and destroy all freedom of movement, all mobility of labour. It was thus the English labourer once more became a serf, and a serf in a far worse position than his forefathers of Norman times, for now he had no land. The artisan, as well as the peasant, was included in this Act, though he afterwards obtained his freedom at an earlier date.

Long before this Act, as we have seen, their own parish was the boundary within which the poor might endeavour to obtain a livelihood; beyond that circle it was again peremptorily ordered they might not pass.

The Act recited that "by reason of some defect in the law, poor people are not restrained from one parish to another; and therefore do endeavour to settle themselves in those parishes where there is the best stock." By the "best stock" is meant the largest amount of capital; in those parishes where there was the best stock the funds for the maintenance of labour were most readily unlocked for the labourers there established. Naturally enough poor people from outside would try to settle themselves there, and a great struggle arose between those who wanted to come in and the authorities who wanted to keep them out.

The method of procedure was for the justices to make an order that within forty days all strangers should leave the parish. Naturally enough the indigent non-parishioners sought to evade the law by remaining in hiding for that period, and then claiming a settlement. To circumvent this, it was decided in 1685 that the forty days should count from the time of making the claim on the overseers.

Looking upon poverty as a crime, or something akin to it, legislators framed every law relating to the poor with Draconian severity; the administrators of those laws, actuated by the same spirit, put them into force with corresponding harshness. Not only were vagrants beaten with many stripes, branded with hot irons, and cast into noisome dungeons, but in some cases they were at this period actually shipped off to the American colonies to work on the plantations as slaves—a subject to which fuller reference will be made in a subsequent chapter.

Even the industrious poor were now driven from parish to parish, like hunted beasts, that they might effect no claim to a settlement. Typical of the attitude assumed, and the action taken by local authorities, is the following resolution passed at a meeting of the churchwardens, overseers, and inhabitants of Bilston, in 1689 :—

> " Forasmuch as some persons by skulking within the Constable-wick have surreptitiously gain'd settlement here, 'tending that they have lived here long enough before ye Act about Settlement did commence in ye reign of King James II., therefore to frustrate such p'tentions in ye future, Richard Cooper and Daniel Whitehouse, Chapell Wardens and Overseers of ye poore, made a search about all ye incomers, ye daye date above said, and they are these yt follow."

Here the names of twenty-two persons are given ; many of these, although in the employment of inhabitants, were forthwith ordered to go to the parishes in which they were born, lest they should obtain a settlement in Bilston, and in the more or less remote contingency of falling into pauperism, become " chargeable" to the rates thereof at some time or other.

The dread that under-tenants might become charge-able to the parish led to a domestic inquisition of a very tyrannous nature. At Leicester a search was made every month to discover fresh under-tenants. At Brighton no new-comer was to be allowed to stay until the con-stable and churchwarden had ascertained that he was possessed of sufficient substance to be unlikely to become burthensome to the town.

A tailor newly come into Lyme was met by a peremptory notice, naming the day for his departure ; and it is recorded of a jury of that place that they even "presented" to the consideration of the Court of Quarter Sessions the case of a man who " harboureth his wife's sister."

It was this monstrous strangulation of the mobility of labour which first made the irksomeness of the system felt. The Act was double-edged, and began to cut into the employers as deeply as into the employed. The spread of manufactures began to be accompanied by loud complaints that while there was an abundance of employment at one spot, the necessary workers could not be procured there, because they were imprisoned in their own distant parishes by a disabling Act of Parliament.

Consequent upon this a system arose whereby employers imported workpeople on the condition that no responsibility for their maintenance should fall upon the parish into which they were brought.

Strangely enough the legislators, writers, philanthropists, and philosophers of the eighteenth century appear to have seen nothing wrong in this denial to the labourer of the right to sell his labour and his skill in the best market, till Adam Smith, the greatest authority of them all, saw the system at its true worth :—

"To remove a man," says that writer, "who has committed no misdemeanour, from the parish where he chooses to reside, is an evident violation of natural liberty and justice, and an oppression, to which the people of England, though jealous of their liberty, but, like the people of most other countries, never rightly considering in what it consists, have for more than a century, together suffered themselves to be exposed without a remedy."

But it may be asked, What remedy had the labourer ? How could he make his resentment felt ?

Unfortunately the labourer had no remedy for this injustice because, having no vote, he was inarticulate and could not voice his wrongs. Moreover, the right to combine in defence of his labour-rights was sternly denied him—to attempt to form a trades union was construed as conspiracy. For some time he had to remain a mere pawn in the hands of the law-makers ; he was as yet a factor of no political consequence in the State.

The Law of the Settlement of the Poor was a cumbrous

piece of machinery which cannot be dismissed without
further reference to a few of its other leading points.
Legal settlement in a parish was acquired by *birth*,
or wherever a child was first known to be, though a
bastard (having, in the eye of the law, no father)
could not be referred to the father's settlement, like
his legitimate children.   When parents acquired a
new settlement, the children always followed the last
settlement of the father, or, after his death, the last
settlement of the mother.   A new settlement might
be acquired by *marriage*, the woman taking her
husband's parish ; by *forty days' unchallenged residence*
in a parish, after delivering a notice in writing to the
overseers of his place of abode and the number of his
family, which notice was to be read in church and
registered ; by having an estate of his own, or *renting
for a year a £10 tenement*—this was the law's discounting
of a man's poverty to which reference has already been
made ; by *paying public rates and taxes*, and serving
for a whole year in any public parish office ; by being
bound to and serving an *apprenticeship* for the learning
of some reputable trade; or lastly, by *being hired and
serving for a year* when unmarried and childless, or
being a widow or widower with children "emancipated"—that is, with children who had found a legal
settlement for themselves—by being, in fact, a servant
without "encumbrances."

Such were a few of the complexities of a law which lasted
well into the nineteenth century, and for two hundred years
exercised the ingenuity of parish authorities and officials
in their anxious attempts to rid themselves of as much
responsibility of providing for the needy and destitute
as possible.   Advantage was taken of all the ambiguities
and uncertainties of the law, and in most places no
subterfuge was thought too mean in dealing with the

helpless poor, to rid a parish of such undesirables who might become a charge on the rates. It is recorded in a local history, that sometime towards the close of the eighteenth century the overseers of Wednesbury purposely omitted to call upon a group of householders to collect their poor rates. This unusual leniency might have been incomprehensible at the time, but the sequel ultimately yielded an explanation that was thoroughly characteristic of the spirit of parochialism. The dwellings in question were on the extreme edge of the parish, and were all occupied by married apprentices to the gun-lock trade—a notoriously improvident class following a very precarious calling. When, as the parish authorities had anticipated, a trade depression suddenly threw the whole of these people out of work, the liability for their maintenance or relief was plausibly repudiated on the ground that their names were not to be found on the rate-book.

In the same locality, where one side of a street is in the parish of Wednesbury and the other in Darlaston, the boundary-line (as was indicated at the customary official perambulation, by the procession, or at least the youthful section of it, climbing across the roof) cut through one dwelling-house. The occupant of this house eventually became chargeable to the rates. But which parish was liable? The point was contested, and in the end it was decided that the unfortunate bedridden pauper was to be saddled upon the parish in which his head was situated as he lay upon his wretched couch, the parish into which his feet stretched being totally exempted from liability. This indeed was almost equal to the judgment of Solomon.

There is a State Paper, dated June 30, 1631, setting forth the special measures adopted for the relief of the poor in the hundred of Nantwich, with the result that in the following year the principal owners of property in the town signed an agreement, which was entered in the burial register as follows :—

"Memd.—It is covenanted, promised and agreed by us the gentlemen and others the inhabitants of this Towne whose names are subscribed. That by reason our Towne is greatly oppressed with Inmates and Strangers continually cominge to reside amongst us without any restraynt, in regard whereof our own poore cannot so well be resieuved [received] as otherwise they might. That from henceforward, wee will not sett or let any of our houses or cottages to strangers dwellinge out of our towne except they shall be such as shall be able to secure the Towne, by bond to the Churchwardens, for the time beinge, from any charge that they or their ffamilies might draw upon ytt."

There was at this period (1630) a fear abroad that the population was increasing so fast that there was some danger of a serious dearth of food occurring in the large towns, and the erection of new houses was actually prohibited in the cities of London and Westminster.

The Law of Settlement but aggravated matters ; it had the natural effect of destroying energy, and it insidiously prepared the mind for inevitable pauperism.

Among the many abuses to which the system gave rise was the conveyance from place to place, at the public expense, of persons who were not "rogues and vagabonds," which became quite a common practice of dishonest constables or other corrupt officials. To circumvent this it was ordered that, before removal, the culprit should be first publicly whipped—a drastic method of ensuring identity.

A large proportion of the money raised for the relief of the poor was expended in shifting the burden of their relief from one parish to another ; a costly staff of functionaries was maintained out of the poor-rates simply to operate the Law of Settlement.

How the Law of Settlement worked was best seen with the eyes of an intelligent foreigner who visited England in 1810. He observed how the poor were repulsed from one parish to another—

"like infected persons   They were sent back," he records, " from one end of the kingdom to the other, as criminals formerly in France, *de brigade en brigade.* You meet on the highroads, I will not say often, but too often, an old man on foot with a little bundle ; a helpless widow, pregnant perhaps, and two or three barefooted children following her ; they have become paupers in a place where they have not yet acquired a legal right to assistance, and are sent away on that account to their original place of settlement."

After the conclusion of the Napoleonic War in 1815 the economic condition was aggravated by the number of disbanded seamen, discharged soldiers, and agricultural labourers out of work, wandering about the country in search of employment. The most natural law of bringing labour into contact with capital, for the beneficial employment of both, was resisted by the working of the Act of Settlement. In the spirit of this Act, agricultural parishes arrived at the determination of employing none but their own parishioners.

" The immediate consequence of this resolution," says an official report, "was the removal of numbers of the most industrious families from homes where they had lived in comfort, and without parish relief, all their lives, to a workhouse to which they belonged "

It was not till 1861 that the first attempt was made to break up these ignorant and selfish laws for the removal of the poor.

One phase of the evil resulting from this Act was the terrible state of the dwellings of agricultural labourers. They were invariably ruinous and filthy, and when landowners and farmers were asked why they did not build houses for their labourers, they replied that "far from building, they would rather pull down such houses."

So farm labourers were frequently crowded into hovels in the adjacent town or village. Cottages were not built or properly kept up in agricultural parishes, because no capitalist would speculate in houses for his labourers, when the most industrious of them might be hurried away at the bidding of the overseer.

How the system of parish particularism struck the popular mind may be gathered from this sample of a topical song or ballad, called "The Parish is bound to find us," which appeared in a musical publication of 1673 :—

"A fig for care, why should we spare?
    The parish is bound to find us!
For thou and I and all must die,
    And leave the world behind us.
The clerk shall sing, the bells shall ring,
    And the old, the old wives wind us;
Sir John shall lay our bones in clay
    Where nobody means to find us."

It was in this spirit, in ballads jubilant, that the vagabond rejoiced in his "mobility"; rejoicing in his unassailable freedom he could mock all the cramping efforts of a narrow parochialism.

XXVII

"ALLOWANCES"

The justices all-powerful—Wages reduced to a scale barely
supporting life—Attempt to relax Law of Settlement (1697)
—Barriers in restraint of the labourer—Severe apprenticeship
laws—Jealousy of trade guilds—The labourer the slave of the
employer—Wages fall and rates rise—The Board of Trade
(1696)—The system of "allowances"—Its iniquitous features—
And demoralising influences—The Berkshire bread scale of
1795—Encouraged grave abuses—The strain upon the poor-
rates — The proposed "Universal Benefit Society" for insurance against invalidity (1786)—The degraded servitude of
"allowanced" labourers.

BY the two great Elizabethan Acts of 1597 and 1601
was introduced systematic rating, for the relief and
support of the feeble poor, for providing the able-bodied
pauper with work, and for the apprenticeship of pauper
children, all under the control of overseers and justices ;
county organisation being called into being to deal with
sturdy vagrants in Houses of Correction. The point to
note is the immense power thus placed in the hands of
the county justices, who had the fixing of wages, and
who were, almost to a man, landowners.

After the passing of the Poor Law the magistrates
reduced the rates of wages steadily from time to time.
In effect this method of administering the law said to
the labourer : "As your old age is now to be provided

for by the ratepayers, we, as representing the latter, shall give you no more wages than will barely support your life and enable you to work for us."

The relief of the destitute was spread over a whole neighbourhood, and all occupiers were compelled to pay poor-rates. But many occupiers, particularly towns-people, were not employers of labour. Therefore employers of labour enjoyed to the full the low rate of wages they paid to their workmen, while at the same time they only paid their share with the rest when it came to the question of relief. As the justices were almost invariably landowners their advantage in screwing wages down becomes at once apparent.

The great mass of labourers generally remained in the locality in which they were born. In 1697 there was an attempt to relax the Law of Settlement; it came to be felt, if not avowed, that paupers were created by the artificial restraints which prevented their seeking employment where there was work to be done, and compelled them to starve upon the parochial pittance where there was no capital to support labour. But the clumsy machinery of remedying the evil would not act, and the common labourer's condition of semi-slavery remained unmitigated.

In the higher grades of labour the barriers which prevented the artificer or the trader from passing out of his first condition into one more eligible were almost as insurmountable. The severe enforcement of the laws of apprenticeship kept a man for ever in the particular pursuit for which he had served seven years of dreary education; and the devices of the Guilds and Companies and City-freedoms created a practical monopoly which it was difficult to overthrow. A small percentage of the more determined and enterprising, the workers who combined courage with ability, certainly did rise to higher levels, but the rise of the commonalty was always regarded with extreme jealousy by the born great.

Apprenticeship being regarded as highly desirable, as early as the year 1600 well-disposed persons had bequeathed money for apprenticing poor children to trade. But the jealousy of the trade and craft guilds standing in the way, it was ordered in 1628 that the overseers might set up any "trade or mystery" for the purpose of apprenticing poor children to "parish labour."

All enactments in restraint of the free movement of labour were bound, in the nature of things, to become as ineffectual as the obsolete statutes for fixing the rate of wages. The general impulse of society towards industrial improvement was sure to free the labourers from these galling restraints, step by step, as the principle of the common interest of employer and employed came to be understood and more honestly carried out.

The working of the Statute of Labourers passed in the fifth year of Elizabeth's reign, which has been commented upon, proved most disastrous. There was the provision by which the justices might arbitrarily fix the rate of wages in any employment; another that limited the number of apprentices who might be employed; a third which forbade any combination of labourers; and, taking it altogether, it practically made the labourer the slave of the employer.

The results were that wages were brought down to starvation point by the justices for their own ends, that the number of the purely labouring class was increased, and that wages had to be supplemented by the poor-rate, which was paid by all occupiers.

There was thus a constant tendency for wages to fall and the poor-rate to go up.

William III. established the Board of Trade in 1696 in

his alarm at the continually increasing amount of the poor-rates. Then grew up an official theory of profitable employment. A weighty memorandum of John Locke, the deepest thinker of the time, contains his opinion that more than half of the people then receiving parish relief were quite able to earn their own livelihood. One-fifth of the population at that time consisted of paupers and beggars.

Towards the end of the eighteenth century the difference between the wretched wages allowed to the worker and the price of food became too great to be longer endured. Unless something were done it was plain that the labourer would starve, and the most grasping landlord could see the inconvenience of that.

So a system of "allowances" sprang up. Instead of freeing labour and giving honest wages, each able-bodied labourer had an allowance made him according to the number of his family. The advantage to the land-owner of such a scheme is manifest. The single man and the childless received no advance in wages. The allowances came from the poor-rates, so that the whole community assisted in paying the wages of the lowest class of labourer, chiefly those engaged in the tilling of the soil.

Allowances were given to the pauper, either for day work or for task-work, but were always considerably less than the wages paid to independent labour. Though the farmers thus shifted the burden of their wages bill on to the shoulders of the ratepayers, pauper labour was found to be dear at any price, so that the farmer was, to an extent, disadvantaged. The pauper, too, was utterly demoralised, for the system was of no benefit to him in any shape.

Under the allowance system, as the labourer in the heyday of his strength and manhood received a part of his subsistence in the form of a parish gift, he naturally enough came to regard the workhouse, the great parish institution, as his ultimate and legitimate home.

Nor was this the only iniquitous feature. The power put into the hands of the justices, who were the arbiters of the labourer's fate under the law, was enormous.

They never hesitated to use that power to their own advantage. A remarkable plan of the Berkshire justices, put forward at Speenhamland in 1795 (and mentioned in chapter xxxiv.), was conceived in a spirit of benevolence, and was readily copied in other parts of the country. It was a system of allowances in proportion to the size of the family, and fluctuating with the price of flour— but the scale was so adjusted as to return to each family the sum which in a given number of loaves would cost beyond the price in years of ordinary abundance.

Naturally this allowance system led to the gravest abuses. Often in a large family the allowances sufficed to maintain the household at least in the bare necessaries of life, and the people refused to work at all. Again, the labourers learned that they could demand relief at the workhouses, even when themselves able-bodied, and the working classes throughout the country became pauperised through and through. They swarmed into these parochial institutions and lived there at ease, and in most places lived very well. A premium was put on pauperism.

"In the workhouses," says the social historian of the period, "the able-bodied men got as much as they could eat." "We never weigh anything," said a governor of one of these workhouses, "and there is no stint, so long as they do not waste anything. Then they have good table-beer and good ale."

The demoralising influence of the parochial system, and the utter dependence in which the people of this country were reared, may be illustrated by a case that was by no means rare, if not, indeed, a typical one. A stripling would marry a girl as ignorant and as helpless as himself. They then looked to the parish to provide them with a house to live in and a bed to lie on, or at least some substantial assistance towards those elemental requisites of married life. Shortly, when an addition to the family was imminent, the services of the parish doctor and midwife were requisitioned. If the child died, as often it did, the circumstances of the parents demanded that it should be buried at the expense of the parish. And so in youth and in age, in health, in sickness, and in death, a pauperised people looked always to the parish—to a soulless, niggardly, and unsympathetic source for all the mere necessaries of existence.

The parish pay-table was approached without shame, for all feelings of repugnance had long since disappeared. People claimed and received their means of living from the poor-rates as a matter of right, and without any feeling of degradation. The consequences of all this were deep and far-reaching. Industry was checked, self-reliance was destroyed, the entire labouring class was pauperised—the effect on the national character was appalling. As William Cobbett said, to be poor and independent was well nigh an impossibility. Poverty was indeed "the mother of many miseries."

The Poor Laws were thus reduced, after two centuries of use and abuse, to breaking-strain, and at last gave way under the vast weight of the expenditure they entailed. In 1783 the poor-rate for England and Wales was about £1,000,000 for a population of 8,000,000 people. In 1833, it was nearly £9,000,000 for 14,000,000 people. In many cases the poor-rate devoured the whole rent of the land, while, in the main, the money went to supporting the idle and vicious able-bodied, instead of the really deserving. The rates naturally went up by leaps and bounds during this period of national pauperisation.

By 1786 the country was thoroughly alarmed at the ever-increasing burden of the poor-rates, and a proposal was made for the establishment of what was called a "Universal Benefit Society." The scheme, broadly, was that every labourer (commencing between the ages of twenty and thirty) earning 10d. a day should contribute to a national fund 2d. a week, and every woman earning £3 a year, 1½d. weekly; and when sick or disabled should receive benefit at the rate of 4s. a week, with 1s. a week added for each child. There were, of course, many other details in the scales, but the chief interest lies in the fact that this was perhaps the earliest proposal for the national insurance of the labourer against invalidity.

The parish servitude which succeeded the feudal servitude imposed the miseries and contumelies of slavery without its exemption from immediate care and future responsibility. It is difficult to conceive a more complete state of degradation than the "allowanced" labourers exhibited in the year 1815, which ended the great war, at whose beginning the annual expenditure on the poor had been two millions a year and was then seven millions; the greater portion of which had been expended during the war years on fostering pauperism, by this system of parish "allowances" in aid of wages.

By 1821, from lessons learnt at such well-managed workhouses as that at Southwell, where the sexes were separated, the inmates classified, the dietary improved, and the institution well and economically conducted, a workhouse test had been established—offer of admission to the "House" being made the test of actual distress.

XXVIII

PAROCHIALISM, A NATIONAL BLIGHT

Failure of parochialism—Which ingrained thriftlessness into the English labourer—National poverty and social stagnation—Crime hand-in-hand with poverty—Colleges of crime and mendicancy—The thief-taker—The "forty-pound crime"—Night scenes in Covent Garden (1820)—"Honest poverty" described by the gentle Elia—Cankering forms of outdoor relief—Partial support to encourage disagreeable idleness—The "roundsman system"—Parish employment—The Labour-rate System—Absolutism of the magistracy.

IF enough has not already been written to exhibit the failure of parochialism, with its narrowness, petty meannesses, and rank injustice, a few more facts may be presented to show the state of the poor, and the condition of the lower orders, at the beginning of the last century.

For two centuries the English worker had been discouraged from any attempt at thrift or foresight; he had been remorselessly and systematically thrust down into a position of hopeless and degrading dependence. The evil effects of the old Poor Laws have not yet been entirely eradicated, and the social reformer is still occasionally disheartened by existing evidences of thriftlessness, by the old and apparently ingrained habits of improvidence, on the part of the poor.

National resources were being constantly depleted by

successive wars, and while the country as a whole was advancing rapidly in commerce and in material wealth social progress always failed to keep pace with it; the inestimable blessings of education having as yet been denied to the masses of the people.

Pitt is said to have been once induced to introduce a Bill for the relief of the poor, through having witnessed the appalling destitution in the Essex village of Halstead, at a time when he believed the country as a whole to be prosperous. But a great War Minister can find no time for social reforms, and the proposal came to nothing.

In the towns crime all too frequently went hand in hand with poverty. The highwaymen who had infested the dark and lonesome roads outside the towns had passed away; they belonged to a previous era. But for a decade or two longer the town streets, left to the comparative safety of feeble oil lamps and decrepit watchmen, were overrun at night time by tumultuous vagabonds. In London and other great cities there were easily to be found houses of evil repute, haunted by vagabonds and criminals, which were variously known as "flash cribs," "shades," or "infernals." These filthy dens were the resort of beggars, thieves, and abandoned women, riotous or drowsy with drink, surrounded by children of all ages, rapidly qualifying for their degrees in the college of crime and mendicancy.

As yet the notion of a preventive police had not dawned; there was only the "thief-taker," who was generally on terms of good fellowship with the thief, sitting and drinking with him till in the fullness of time things were ripe for action. Often enough the two were in league together, working under an organized system of negotiation for the return of stolen property, which bred legions of experienced depredators.

The thief, even when the purloining of five shillings might be a hanging matter, could count on the forbearance of the officer until he committed a "forty-pound crime"—a well-recognized phrase then for an offence for the detection of which the State adjudged a reward of forty pounds, to be paid on conviction. Thievery was fostered under this iniquitous system into a steady advance from small offences to great, till some deed of more than common atrocity delivered the petted criminal into the hands of the wily thief-taker, gloating over the blood-money that had at last fallen into his expectant maw.

Till about 1820 there nightly assembled in Covent Garden Market and other places in the metropolis that afforded a partial shelter to hundreds of men and women, boys and girls, criminals and vagabonds, who continued all through the hours of darkness in a state of shameless profligacy, which is described by a writer of the time "as presenting a scene of vice and tumult more atrocious than anything exhibited even by the lazzaroni of Naples."

Little else was to have been expected from the inefficiency of the police system which then prevailed; a system which left the guardianship of this great city to the parochial constables and their night watchmen. To the latter fell the more dangerous duties of the night-time, for which each watchman was equipped with a staff, a rattle, and a lantern. In the previous century they had been armed with halberts, but as the force was mostly constituted of decrepit old men, it scarcely mattered what weapons they carried. Their most effective work was to disturb the silence of the night by crying the hour :—

> " Past twelve o'clock, and a cloudy morning !
> Past twelve o'clock, and mind I give you warning ! "

MARYLEBONE WATCH HOUSE (1809).

To face p. 120.

The contemplation of honest poverty is scarcely less distressing. The gentle Elia in one of his essays describes the very poor man's home as only the image of a home, with its starved grate and empty larder.

"The children of the very poor," he says pathetically, "have no young times. It makes the very heart bleed to overhear the casual street talk between a poor woman and her little girl, for it is not of toys, of nursery books, of summer holidays, fitting for that age . . . it is of mangling and clear starching, the price of coals and of potatoes."

When, in the early decades of the nineteenth century, stock came to be taken of the past working of the Poor Laws a lurid light was thrown upon the many abuses of which the system of outdoor relief given to able-bodied paupers was capable. The interpretations placed upon the law were as varied as they were demoralising.

This relief was sometimes given in money and sometimes in kind. In the latter case it might take the form, as we have seen, of parish-provided food and clothing, or of payment of house rent, or of exemption from the payment of rates.

When given in money it might be relief without labour ; a small and inadequate sum towards the pauper's support, sometimes given without any condition except that he was to shift for himself and trouble the parish no further. More usually the pauper was required to give up a portion of his time ; he was directed to sit in a gravel-pit, or stand in the pound, or attend a roll-call, or do something equally wasteful of his time and effort, merely to ensure that his leisure should not be a means of profit or of amusement. By Bumbledom the imposition of the most disagreeable conditions was considered an achievement.

Then there was the system of "allowances," of relief

paid in aid of wages, taking account of the number of children in a family, to which full reference has been made elsewhere—a system shown to be disastrous to the wage-earning, the personal freedom, and the character of the labourer.

Another plan was known as the "Roundsman System," and consisted of a contract between the overseers and employers to sell the latter the labour of one or more paupers at a certain price. The difference between this sum and the income sanctioned by the authorities, according to a fixed scale, had to be made up to the labourer by the parish. The pauper labourer was given a ticket to present to the employer, and when signed by the latter it was carried back to the overseers as a warrant for work done.

Sometimes parish employment was given to able-bodied paupers by a more direct method. They were employed on the roads, or in gravel-pits, or in some such forms of unskilled labour, for which they were paid by the parish. The superintendence of the work was invariably very lax, and as it brought the men together in gangs, not unfrequently riots and rick burnings broke out among them. This was the system most disliked by the farmers.

An Act at the beginning of the nineteenth century empowered churchwardens and overseers to acquire land, to the extent of fifty acres in a parish, and to set indigent persons to work upon it. These parish farms had an injurious effect on agricultural wages, and were further condemned in that they tended to social degradation.

In the early years of William IV. yet another method of dealing with the able-bodied pauper was in vogue in agricultural parishes. This, called the Labour-rate System, was an agreement that the ratepayers, each of them, should employ resident labourers in proportion to their rental, to the number of horses kept for tillage, to the number of acres occupied, or according to some such arbitrary scale which was quite irrespective of their real requirements for labour ; or, in default, the ratepayer had to pay the wages of his proportion of labourers to the overseers. This system, however, had to be legalized by a majority of three-fourths of the ratepayers in the parish, and approved by the justices. Of course, in practice, it always worked inequitably ; the labourers could never be distributed proportionately to the various requirements.

It is astounding to recall the amount of misguided ingenuity which must have been given full play to devise all these stupid, wasteful, and demoralising systems of dealing with the able-bodied poor. How much misery in the past England owes to the ineptitude of the bucolic mind it would be impossible to estimate. The poor who fled from the petty tyrannies of parochialism crowded into the towns, only to lose themselves in the purlieus of beggary and crime, and add to the sum of human misery there.

That the State should, in some way or other, undertake the duty of finding work and wages for the people is a Socialistic principle. But all these crude experiments had the effect of unsettling the labour market and spreading the taint of pauperism, chiefly through the machinery and methods employed.

More than one allusion has been made to the enormous powers with which the magistrates were invested for dealing with the poor. From the time of Richard II. the power of fixing the rates of wages had been reposed in the justices ; and this power had been largely increased in the time of Henry V., and authoritatively reiterated in the reigns of Elizabeth, James I., and George II., and was not finally withdrawn till 1824.

In the time of Queen Mary the right of issuing beggars' licences had been reposed in the magistrates ; and they had later been given the power to make the assessments for the relief of the poor; in 1815 they even had the right to order outdoor relief on their own responsibility, and in 1819 the curtailment of relief.   Their authority in the apprenticing of poor children, and other minor matters of a similar nature, need not be mentioned to prove the absolutism of this non-representative body over the lives and destinies of the poor.   And "the poor dance as the rich pipe."

XXIX

THE PARISH APPRENTICE

A constant supply of bastards and foundlings—"The town husband"—Helpless children bound to dangerous trades—No "after-care"—The crime of Elizabeth Brownrigge (1767)—An illustration from Disraeli's "Sybil"—How apprentices were treated at Wolverhampton in 1840—The domiciliary workshop—Climbing boys—Invention of the Scandiscope—Opposed by the Master Chimney Sweepers—Act of 1834 for reconstruction of flues—Blake's "Songs of Innocence"—Climbing boys abolished (1842)—Premiums paid by the parish—Poor parents consigned their children to same hardships—In mines—In cotton mills—The joyless lives of infant workers—Gradual introduction of legislative restrictions—Emancipation of the child slave.

THE problem of dealing with children chargeable to the parish was solved in the readiest manner an unthinking age could devise—they were put out to earn their own living at the earliest possible moment. Both from illegitimacy and desertion, offences which perhaps the systematic impoverishment of the people might palliate, a constant supply of bastards and foundlings was kept up.

The general poverty encouraged immorality among the labouring classes. Bastardy was so prevalent that in some places there was a parish officer known as the "town husband," whose duty it was to collect money from the parents of illegitimate children for the maintenance of the latter.

In no part of the country, east, west, north, or south, was there any dearth of " parish children"; every workhouse had its full complement of them. The workhouse embodied the principle that no man should be idle; and the young found without a trade were promptly apprenticed.

Half the contents of the Wednesbury parish chest, from which every document of value has disappeared, consists of apprentices' indentures ; so carefully were these precious releases from parochial responsibility treasured by the churchwardens of the old-world type. In this part of the country helpless children were frequently apprenticed as colliers, a form of employment which condemned their young lives to the dark and dangerous depths of a coal-mine ; or as gun-lock filers, to slave at the vice in a form of labour that was so arduous, so unfitted to the efforts of a child's immature frame, that the lads invariably grew up round-shouldered and narrow-chested.

The apprenticeship of helpless children to dangerous callings, and the placing of them under the unbridled control of vicious persons, was the first evil but by no means the last. The " after-care" of these children was no one's business ; it sufficed the parish authorities if they were placed out and remained no longer chargeable to the rates. Under a callous system of this kind the sum of juvenile suffering was appalling, and to it may be attributed one of the darkest crimes which ever stained the pages of an English calendar.

In 1767 Elizabeth Brownrigge, midwife to the St. Dunstan's Workhouse, and wife of a house-painter, cruelly ill-used two female apprentices. Mary Jones, one of these unfortunate children, after being often beaten, ran back to the Foundling whence she had been taken. On the remaining one, Mary Mitchell, a workhouse apprentice, the wrath of the avaricious hag now fell with redoubled severity. The poor creature was perpetually being stripped and beaten, was frequently chained up at night nearly naked, was horribly scratched, and her tongue cut with scissors. It was the constant practice of Mrs. Brownrigge to fasten the girl's hands to a rope slung from a beam in the kitchen, after which this old wretch beat her four or five times in the same day with a broom or a whip. The moanings and groans of the dying child, whose wounds were mortifying from neglect, aroused the pity of a baker opposite, who sent the overseers of the parish to see the child, who was found by them hid in a buffet cupboard. She was taken to St. Bartholomew's Hospital, and died soon after admission. Brownrigge was at once arrested ; but Mrs. Brownrigge and her son, disguising themselves in Rag Fair, fled to Wandsworth and there took lodgings in a chandler's shop, where they were found. The woman was tried at the Old Bailey sessions, and found guilty of murder.

The mob raged terribly as she passed through the streets on her way to Tyburn. The women especially screamed "Tear off her hat ; let us see her face ! The devil will fetch her !" and threw stones and mud, pitiless in their hatred. After execution her corpse was thrust into a hackney coach and driven to Surgeons' Hall for dissection ; the skeleton is still preserved in a London collection. The cruel hag's husband and son were sentenced to six months' imprisonment. A curious old drawing is still extant, depicting Mrs. Brownrigge in the condemned cell. She wears a large broad-brimmed gipsy hat, tied under her chin, and a cape ; and her long, hard face wears a horrible smirk of resigned hypocrisy.

Canning, in one of his bitter banters on Southey's republican odes, writes :—

> "For this act
> Did Brownrigge swing. Harsh laws ! But time shall come
> When France shall reign, and laws be all repealed."

The treatment which was frequently meted out to the parish apprentice in ordinary cases may be aptly illustrated by excerpts from Disraeli's novel " Sybil," which contains a graphic description of life among the locksmiths of the Black Country parish of Wednesfield, about the year 1840. After describing the spiritual destitution of the locality, its social and civic neglect, the novelist proceeds to say that at Wodgate (the fictitious name under which he but feebly disguises the " town of locks and keys ") a factory is unknown.

" Here labour reigns supreme. The business of Wodgate is carried on by master workmen in their own houses, each of whom possesses an unlimited number of what they call apprentices, by whom their affairs are principally conducted, and whom they treat as the Mamlouks treated the Egyptians. These master workmen indeed form a powerful aristocracy, nor is it possible to conceive one apparently more oppressive. They are ruthless tyrants , they habitually inflict upon their subjects punishments more grievous than the slave population of our colonies were ever visited with , not content with beating them with sticks, or flogging them with knotted ropes, they are in the habit of felling them with hammers, or cutting their heads open with a file or a lock. The most usual punishment, however, or rather stimulus to increase exertions, is to pull an apprentice's ears till they run with blood. These youths, too, are worked for sixteen or twenty hours a day ; they are often sold by one master to another ; they are fed on carrion, and they sleep in lofts or cellars ; yet, whether it be that they are hardened by brutality, and really unconscious of their degradation and unusual sufferings, or whether they are supported by a belief that their day to be masters and oppressors will surely arrive, the aristocracy of Wodgate is by no means so unpopular as the aristocracy of most places. . . .

"Their plan is to work hard, but not always. They seldom exceed four days of labour in the week. On Sunday the masters begin to drink ; for the apprentices there is dog-fighting without stint. On Monday and Tuesday the whole population of Wodgate is drunk ; of all stations, ages, and sexes ; even babes who should be at the breast ; for they are drammed with Godfrey's cordial. . . . Here is relaxation, excitement ; if less vice otherwise than might be at first anticipated, we must remember that excesses are checked by poverty of blood and constant exhaustion. Scanty food and hard labour are, in their way, if not exactly moralists, a tolerably good police. . . .

"It is not that the people are immoral, for immorality implies some forethought , or ignorant, for ignorance is relative ; but they are animals , unconscious ; their minds are blank ; and their worst actions only the impulse of a gross or savage instinct."

This, then, was the deliberate estimate of a section of the industrial classes and the lives they led in the " hungry forties," as seen at close quarters, and set down in fair round terms, by the great leader of the Conservative Party, at a period when as yet the domiciliary workshop flourished in the land, with its encouragement of irregular hours and the honouring of Saint Monday ; and ere the newly promulgated Factory Acts had had time to organize labour and discipline the workers.

By a law made in 1789 churchwardens and overseers were empowered, with the consent of two justices, to bind any boy eight years of age chargeable to the parish, or any boy found begging, to be apprenticed to a chimney-sweeper, until sixteen years of age. These lads were trained to climb inside chimneys for the purpose of sweeping down the soot with a hand-brush.

At the chilliest hours of the early dawn man and boy would set forth to cry their trade through the dark and deserted streets.

> "With drawling tone, brush under arm
> And bag slung over shoulder,
> Behold the Sweep the streets alarm
> With Stentor's voice, and louder."

Small, undersized boys were preferred, as they could negotiate the flues more easily than big boys ; and it can be safely averred that fewer forms of employment for children of tender age ever offered more objections—the dangers of falling, of becoming stifled or stuck fast, were always imminent, not to mention the dark, sooty, choky tunnel in which every stroke of work had to be done.

While English philanthropists, at the beginning of the nineteenth century, were inveighing against the slave trade of the West Indies, there was being tolerated at home the more cruel "black slavery of white infants." An agitation, however, set in about 1826 for the abolition of the climbing boy and the substitution of a machine-brush called a Scandiscope, to be thrust up the chimney on a jointed stick.

> "Some modern tubes, a brush, a rope
> Are all you need employ ;
> Pray order, maids, the Scandiscope
> And not the Chimney Boy."

The Master Chimney Sweepers, "a respectable body of tradesmen who had risen in their calling by climbing up chimneys," formed a society to oppose the reform, urging that there were many cases in which a machine would be perfectly useless.

At a trade meeting one eloquent speaker said, " Look at the Duke of York's fifty-one new chimneys—most of them run in a horizontal line, then abruptly turn up, so that a machine would be of no more use than if you thrust up an old broom-stick." Another member of the Society admitted that "a few solitary instances of accidents happened" in their trade, as in every other, but that the boys were always as healthy and cheerful as other apprentices.

Now the fact was that climbing boys were often

treated with the utmost cruelty by their masters, and in 1834 a statute was passed regulating the trade, and imposing certain conditions for the construction of flues.

"Hone's Everyday Book" contains the following lines "communicated by Mr. Charles Lamb, from a very rare and curious little work, Mr. Blake's 'Songs of Innocence'" :—

"When my mother died I was very young,
And my father sold me, while yet my tongue
Could scarcely cry 'Weep, 'weep, 'weep !
So your chimnies I sweep, and in soot I sleep.

There's little Tom Toddy, who cried when his head,
That was curl'd like a lamb's back, was shaved, so I said,
'Hush, Tom, never mind it, for when your head's bare,
You know that the soot cannot spoil your white hair'

And so he was quiet, and that very night,
As Tom was a-sleeping, he had such a sight,
That thousands of sweepers, Dick, Joe, Ned, and Jack,
Were all of them locked up in coffins so black.

And by came an angel who had a bright key,
And he opened the coffins, and set them all free ;
Then down a green plain, leaping, laughing, they run,
And wash in a river, and shine in the sun.

Then naked and white, all their bags left behind,
They rise upon clouds, and sport in the wind ,
And the angel told Tom, if he'd be a good boy
He'd have God for his Father, and never want joy.

And so Tom awoke, and we rose in the dark,
And got with our bags and our brushes to work ;
Though the morning was cold, Tom was happy and warm,
So if all do their duty they need not fear harm "

A new enactment in 1840 forbade chimney sweeps to take apprentices under sixteen, and after July 1, 1842, no individual under twenty-one was to be allowed to ascend a chimney. Charles Kingsley wrote his "Water Babies," which deals in a highly fantastic manner with the subject of chimney-sweep apprentices, in 1863.

Such was the old-time system of apprenticeship upon which these illustrations are veritable "light-throwers."

At the period of "binding," the apprentice was invariably a child of tender years, and with each one a premium was paid to the employer, generally of five pounds, though there were some parishes which did not begrudge twice that amount to get rid of their responsibilities. Thousands of these innocents succumbed to the infantile slavery to which they were condemned. They were invariably overworked and underfed, and so ill-treated that death was a happy release to them; and each victim that dropped untimely into an early grave just made way for a fresh apprentice and another premium.

But the conditions of child life prevailing generally among the industrial classes were practically the same all round; and parents, helpless in their poverty, consigned their own children to the same hardships. Children were regularly sold into this form of legalized slavery.

As trappers in the coal-mines or as piecers in the cotton mills children then commenced to work at a remarkably early age. Tiny workers of five years old and upwards were employed in the cotton mills day and night, working shifts of twelve hours each and sleeping in the same beds, turn and turn about, and with no separation of the sexes. Even if the tasks imposed upon these child operatives were of the slightest character possible, everything that goes to make the fullness of real child life was sacrificed —fresh air, play and exercise, education, watchful care, and kindly consideration. Little wonder the Manchester Board of Health in 1796 reported that "factory life was injurious to children." With unremitting toil, performed day after day in an impure atmosphere and amidst dirty surroundings, fevers were rife and mortality was high.

The first amelioration of these conditions was secured, in the face of much opposition, in 1802, when the law demanded the ventilation and whitewashing of mills and the provision of separate sleeping apartments for boy and girl apprentices.

England's great industrial activities commenced about the period in which the last shackles of the ancient feudalism were giving way; to the exploited class, however, it was simply a change of masters, a transfer from the aristocrat to the plutocrat.

But the worker himself cannot be exonerated altogether from the blame attaching to the conditions which then obtained in the industrial world; for among other things he declared that he could not possibly work without the assistance of juvenile and female auxiliaries.

Public opinion, too, so far as it made itself articulate in those days, if not against these child martyrs, was certainly not in favour of reform. It was better, said the many-headed, that children should work than starve; it was better they should be brought up in the school of industry than that they should ramble at large and acquire vagabond propensities; and besides, if their services could not be utilized, trade would be driven out of the country.

And so the evil went on till in 1819 another step forward was taken when the legislature forbade the employment of any child under nine and restricted the hours of labour to twelve hours a day for all young persons under sixteen years of age. But for some years after this, although the adult workers were allowed fifty minutes in the middle of the day for dinner, the children were not allowed a break and had to get their midday meal as best they could.

It was not till 1833 that young persons under eighteen were prohibited from working all night. How public opinion coupled the emancipation of English child slaves with the abolition of negro slavery may be gathered from the works of Tom Moore. An "Epistle of Condolence from a Slave Lord to a Cotton Lord," written by the Bard of Erin, opens with this stanza :—

> "Alas! my dear friend, what a state of affairs!
> How unjustly we both are despoiled of our rights!
> Not a pound of black flesh shall I leave to my heirs
> Nor must you any more work to death little whites."

The last stage in the emancipation of the child slave was the Act which, some half-century ago, compelled factory children to attend school half-time.

XXX

THE PAUPER LUNATIC

Revelations of 1807—Guilty keepers—Bedlam unreformed in 1815
—How patients were done to death—Even under medical
authority—Reforms at Hanwell Asylum—Harriet Martineau's
testimony—The old and the new systems contrasted

IN the chapter on "Bedlams" was described the ancient method of dealing with the insane and feeble-minded. The treatment of pauper lunatics in the workhouses of later times was no improvement on the ancient method. The poor demented creatures were not separated from the sane nor was any special treatment meted out to them ; whether harmless idiots or violent maniacs, they were regarded as unmitigated nuisances and treated with a callousness which amounted in the result to barbarous cruelty.

Sir G. O. Paul, writing to the Secretary of State on the subject of pauper lunatics, in 1807, said :—

"I believe there is hardly a parish of any considerable extent in which there may not be found some unfortunate creature of this description, who, if his ill-treatment has made him phrentic, is chained in the cellar or garret of a workhouse, fastened to the leg of a table, tied to a post in an outhouse, or perhaps shut up in an uninhabited ruin [the writer adds in a note he had witnessed each of these methods], or, if his lunacy be inoffensive, left to ramble half naked or starved through the streets or highways, teased by the scoff and jest of all that is vulgar, ignorant, and unfeeling."

But, it may be observed, these unhappy creatures were not in any of the public asylums, where, it might be conjectured, the treatment would be very different. Let us see. Eight or nine years later a magistrate gave the following evidence before a Parliamentary Committee respecting York Asylum :—

"Having suspicions in my mind that there were some parts of that Asylum which had not been seen, I went early in the morning determined to examine every place ; after ordering a great number of doors to be opened, I came to one which was in a retired situation in the kitchen apartments, and which was almost hid by the opening of a door in the passage ; I ordered this door to be opened ; the keepers hesitated, and said the apartment belonged to the women, and they had not the key. I ordered them to get the key, but it was said to be mislaid, and not to be found at the moment ; upon this I grew angry, and told them I insisted upon its being found, and that if they could not find it, I could find a key at the kitchen fire-side, namely the poker ; upon that the key was immediately brought. When the door was opened, I went into the passage and I found four cells, I think, of about eight feet square, in a very horrid and filthy situation" . . . &c., &c.

The particulars given are too disgusting for further detail. Upstairs he found a room twelve feet by seven feet ten inches containing thirteen women, who at night had no other habitation than the cells described.

It was also stated in evidence that in the same asylum patients had been whipped, kept generally in a filthy state, treated with every kind of personal indignity, and shut up naked in dark cells, though money had been obtained by the keepers for the necessary clothing for them. There further appeared but too much reason to suppose that patients had died in that institution from neglect or ill-treatment.

In St. Luke's Hospital and other metropolitan institutions the management was, at this period, no whit better. At "Bedlam" it was proved, before a Committee, that a great number of the patients were closely chained to the wall, and occasionally handcuffed besides ; that they were left in that state with no other covering than an unfastened blanket ; that the patients in the cells were obliged in winter to shut out what little light the narrow window afforded on account of the cold, all the windows being unglazed. But there is one case which shows as well as a thousand could do the spirit of the system pursued at "Bedlam" up to 1815. In consequence of attempting to defend himself from what he conceived to be unjust treatment on the part of the keeper, William Norris, a patient, was fastened by a long chain, which, passing through a partition, the keeper, by going into an adjoining cell, could draw him close to the wall at his pleasure. Norris, however, managed to muffle the chain with straw from the bed on which he lay, so as to prevent its being drawn through the partition. Then, with the concurrence of the medical authorities, the following proceedings took place. A stout iron ring was riveted round his neck, from which a short chain, about twelve inches long, passed to a ring made to slide up and down an upright massy iron bar, six feet high, fixed in the wall. Round his body a strong iron bar, about two inches wide, was riveted ; on each side of this bar or hoop was a circular projection, which, being fastened to and enclosing each of his arms, pinioned them close to his sides. From this waist-bar two others passed over his shoulders and were riveted to the first, both before and behind. The iron ring round his shoulders was connected by a double link with the shoulder bars. From each of these bars passed another small chain to the sliding ring on the iron bar. This complicated machinery being upon the unfortunate man, he could only lie on his back in bed, or, keeping close to the wall, raise himself to an erect

22

posture.   Not a step forwards could he make, nor could he lie on either side on account of the projections enclosing his arms.   In this state was Norris found by a number of gentlemen visitors, on the 2nd of May, 1815, and in this state had he lived for nine years. He was released, but lived only to the following year; though that was long enough to prove the falsity of the allegations as to his ferocious violence which had been made the excuse for the barbarities with which he had been treated.   " Unius dementia dementes efficit multos."

One of the earliest attempts at the humane treatment of pauper lunatics was made by the county of Middlesex at Hanwell Asylum, near London, when experiments were first made in an enlightened system of specialising.

The first essential was a separate building, of cheerful aspect and pleasant surroundings, and with special provision for every department of the work undertaken. But it was the spirit rather than the practical details which differentiated the new methods from the old.

Harriet Martineau visited Hanwell Asylum in 1834, and states that out of 566 patients then in the house, 10 only were restrained, and the restraint was simply the confinement of their arms as they walked about among the other patients.   But it must not be supposed there were no other modes of restraint, though those about to be mentioned will not injure the reputation of Hanwell for humanity.   " ' Oh, do let me out, do let me go to my dinner ! ' wailed one in her chamber who had been sent there because she was not ' well enough ' for society in the morning.   The dinner-bell had made her wish herself back again among her companions. ' Let me out, and I will be quiet and gentle ! '   ' Will you ? ' was the only answer when her doors were thrown open.   In an instant she dispersed her tears, composed her face, and walked away like a chidden child." Mr. Hill, a pioneer reformer of the Lincoln Lunatic Asylum, recommending treatment of a similar kind in cases of violence, said " a maniac is seldom known to break his word."

"Our patient," he states, " has thus ultimately recovered ; on quitting the Asylum its parting care for his welfare is manifested in the pecuniary assistance rendered to him (from a fund specially provided, called 'The Adelaide Fund') to continue him a little longer in the enjoyment of the comforts he cannot yet safely be without, and keep his mind easy whilst he seeks employment or resumes his natural position."

With respect to the important matter of personal restraint, such as that implied by the use of bands and belts, Mr. Hill was the first to demonstrate their superfluousness ; he reduced his theory to practice in the Lincoln Asylum for three years without a single accident.

" It may be demanded," he remarks, " what mode of treatment do you adopt in place of restraint ? How do you guard against accidents ? How do you provide for the safety of the attendants ? In short, what is the substitute for coercion ? The answer may be summed up in few words, viz ---classification, watchfulness, vigilant and unceasing attendance by day and night, kindness, occupation and attention to health, cleanliness and comfort, and the total absence of every description of other occupation of the attendants·"

In conclusion, then, we have in the one case darkness, chains, and whips, cold, nakedness, and filth, contempt, neglect, utter solitude ; or a society still more mischievous and all generally ending in a deeper, and more confirmed, and more dreadful phase of the disease, if the unfortunates are not in the meantime cut off by a premature death ; in the other we have the opposites of all these. The first faithfully depicts the characteristics of asylums as they were ; the second as faithfully what they now are.

XXXI

FOUNDLINGS

Child murder and desertion—London Foundling Hospital established, 1739—Infants from the country miscarry—The receiving
basket hung at the gate—Institution enlarged by parliamentary
grant, 1754—Identification of foundlings—By coins, trinkets,
clothes, &c.—Infants accepted with £100 and "no questions
asked"—Eligibility, treatment, and training—Notable patrons
of The Foundling—Hogarth—Handel.

IT was to prevent the too frequent occurrence of child
murder, and the exposing of infants in the streets
to perish, that the London Foundling Hospital was
established in 1739 by Thomas Coram, a captain of a
trading vessel, who borrowed the idea from similar
institutions in France and Holland.

A basket was hung at the gate of the hospital, in
which the children were deposited, the persons who
brought them ringing a bell to give notice to the
officers in attendance. In order to forward the "little
innocents" from distant country parts a branch of the
carrying trade was established, and babies arrived in
London in increasing numbers from all parts of the
country. Large sums were, in some instances, paid
for their conveyance, a fact which more than hints at
the social position of the parents; and as the carriage
was prepaid, there was a strong inducement on the part

CAPTAIN CORAM AND THE FOUNDLING HOSPITAL.

To face p. 340.

of the carriers to get rid of their burthens on the way. Many of the infants were drowned; all of them were neglected, and that, in the large majority of cases, was tantamount to their early death. It was publicly asserted in the House of Commons that one man, having the charge of five infants in baskets—they appeared to have been packed like so many sucking-pigs—and happening to get drunk on his journey, lay asleep all night on a common, and in the morning three out of the five were found dead. Many other instances of negligence on the part of carriers, resulting in the death of infants entrusted to them for carriage to London, are on record. Persons were actually tried for infanticide, and would have been hanged, had it not been proved that the crime was committed by the carrier. Even the clothing in which the children were dressed was often stolen on the way, and the babes were deposited in the basket just as they were born. It is reported that one foundling who was received into the hospital at this time, lived to become a wealthy banker in the north of England, and being in after life anxious to make some inquiry into his origin, applied at the hospital, when all the information he could obtain was that it appeared on the books of the establishment that he was put into the basket at the gate perfectly naked.

Any person bringing a child rang the bell and waited to hear if it would be received or rejected on account of disease; no questions were asked as to the parentage of the child, but when the accommodation was exhausted a notice was displayed on the door, " The House is full." At such times mothers balloted for the admission of their little ones, and riots occasionally occurred when large numbers of applications had to be refused. By 1754 the institution had been enlarged to accommo-

date six hundred children. Then Parliament made a
grant of £10,000, and sanctioned the general admission
of children, who were to be trained to be good servants,
or, when qualified, to serve in the King's forces.

In order to safeguard the parents against suspicion of
having foully made away with their offspring, in 1757 a
notice was issued by the governors to the effect that all
persons bringing children should leave some token by
which, in case any certificate should be wanted, it might
be found out whether such child had been taken into the
hospital or not. From that date all the children received
into the institution had some token attached to their
person, and in course of time a goodly collection of these
was accumulated.

Coins of an ancient date seem to have been the
favourite articles used for this purpose of future identification, but there are many things of a more curious
nature. Sentiment was often blended with this effort of
utilitarianism. A playing-card—the ace of hearts—with
a dolorous piece of verse written upon it ; a ring with
two hearts in garnets, broken in half, and then tied
together ; three or four padlocks, intended, perhaps, as
emblems of security ; a nut ; an ivory fish ; an anchor ;
a gold locket ; a lottery ticket. Sometimes a piece of
brass, either in the shape of a heart, or of a crescent
moon, was used as a distinguishing mark, generally engraved with some little verse or legend. Thus, one has
these words upon it, "In amore hæc sunt vitia" ;
another has this bit of doggerel :—

"You have my heart
Though we must part."

Identification was also made possible by preserving the
record of a minute description of the clothing in which

the infant was deposited at the gates of the institution. Sometimes a few doggerel lines were pinned to the clothes :—

> " Pray use me well and you shall find
> My father will not prove unkind
> Unto that nurse who's my protector
> Because he is a benefactor."

While this indiscriminate admission lasted, of 15,000 babes received into the hospital, only 4,400 lived to be apprenticed, a result achieved at an expenditure of £500,000. Parliament, appalled, withdrew its grant. The governors, to recruit their empty exchequer, offered to accept any child accompanied by a hundred-pound note, and "no questions asked"; an amazing system which, for the forty years it lasted, put a premium on the profligacy of the well-to-do classes. After 1801 the regulations for admission improved, though remaining somewhat capricious. The child of a mother's "first fault," or one whose father had just died, or enlisted for a soldier, was easily eligible. The object of the charity was not only to save the life of the infant, but to hide the shame of the mother ; no fee was asked and no recommendation was necessary. No intercourse was afterwards permitted.

Immediately a child was received into the Foundling Hospital it was baptized, and innumerable Miltons, Shakespeares, Nelsons, and Drakes emerged from the social obscurity of the institution. The first male in 1741 was Thomas Coram and the first female was Eunice Coram, so called after the founder of the charity and his wife. The nurslings were then dispatched into the country, where wet-nurses were provided for them, each one having its clothing legibly marked with its name, and a distinguishing mark also hung round its neck on a chain. They were visited and medically supervised during the five years they remained with their foster-parents. Between the ages of five and fifteen they were educated at the hospital, and then the boys were apprenticed and the girls put into domestic service. It may be remembered that Thomas Day, the eccentric author of "Sandford and Merton," selected from the Foundling Hospital one of the two girls whom he resolved to bring up and educate, in the hope that one would prove a model wife; both, it is needless to add, turned out failures.

Before the children are put out very careful inquiries are always made as to the character of the persons to whom they are entrusted. The institution, run on modern lines and in general conformity with modern ideas, now accommodates about five hundred inmates, at an average cost of £27 3s. per head (1897).

Hogarth took a great interest in the Foundling Hospital; Handel was a generous patron. The uncertainty of the origin and destiny of so many of its inmates have made it a fertile source of inspiration to the fictionist. As previously mentioned, Captain Marryat has utilized "The Foundling" (p. 295). The opening scene of Dickens's "No Thoroughfare" is fixed at the gates of this institution, while another scene shows us a veiled lady walking round the dinner-table where the children are seated, making surreptitious inquiries for one of a certain name. Though in the majority of cases the personal history of an inmate might reveal only the sordid and the ignoble, or not infrequently a tale of scandal and human depravity, there was occasionally developed a tinge of romance from some belated or unexpected identification; or, it might be, of touching pathos from the over-credulousness of a mistaken identity.

XXXII

POOR PRISONERS

Ancient practices reviewed—The Jubilee of the Jews—The Draconian code of Athens—Bred revolution—Which Solon averted —Arbitrary powers of creditor over debtor in Rome—Called forth tribunitial protection—English prisoners—The "twopenny ward" and "alms basket" of an Elizabethan jail—Cruelties and extortions of warders—A parliamentary inquiry, 1727— "The Cries of the Oppressed," 1691—"Remember the Poor Debtors !"—Tragic prison incidents—At Liverpool—Lincoln— Appleby—St. Edmundsbury—Placation of jailers—Sponging-houses—"The Humours of the Fleet," 1749—Debtor imprisoned at expense of the creditor—Or in default thereof discharged— Fleet Prison abolished, 1844—Its indictment in "The Pickwick Papers"—The sufferings of prisoners of war.

ERE we judge too harshly the callous and often inhuman treatment formerly dealt out to imprisoned debtors in this country, we should do well to pause for a moment and examine the treatment which was meted out to similar unfortunates by the ancients.

It is notorious in the history of all civilised nations that the power vested in the creditor has been arbitrary and almost uncontrolled.

The Jews had their jubilee, which restored to every man his inheritance ; and the release, which was effected every seven years, when the captive debtor who had been sold into bondage was restored to his liberty.

At Athens, the Draconian code, civil and criminal, was

rigidly severe upon the debtor; so severe that it involved the republic in many alarming commotions. At one time the harmony of society was destroyed, and revolution threatened.

The debtors convened in various parts, and determined by solemn resolutions to elect a military chieftain to lead them on to their purpose, which was to obtain a new division of property—to put to death their creditors, and to new model the government. The creditors had exercised to the full extent the powers which the law had granted for the collection of their demands; the insolvent debtor was reduced to absolute slavery—doomed to the most servile employment—put to the draught, like beasts of burden, in the cultivation of their farms. The sons and daughters of the debtor were sent to foreign countries, and sold into slavery. In this crisis, it was doubtful who was most powerful and likely to prevail, the rich creditors with those who managed their farms and worked the mines of Attica, or the debtors, with those who espoused their cause. It was unanimously agreed to have recourse to an amicable settlement of the difference; and Solon, a man of distinguished talents, virtue, and integrity, was unanimously elected. It is very evident, from the history of Greece at this moment, that the power of the creditor over the debtor was the chief cause of this alarming condition of the commonwealth. The very first act of Solon's administration was to abolish existing debts, and totally to destroy the power of the creditor over the body of his debtor. But he refused to make a new division of property; and every individual was made secure in the enjoyment of his possessions. Both parties submitted to these measures; and thus Solon saved the republic.

In Rome we have the same example. In the best days of Roman liberty the law of the twelve tables existed, containing a system of cruelty, relative to debts, which is a blot upon the human character. After judgment was obtained, the debtor was allowed thirty days of grace; he was then committed to the custody of his creditor, and was loaded with chains, not to exceed fifteen pounds weight. In this condition it was his privilege to be exposed, three times in the market-place, to ascertain if his friends or countrymen would relieve him. If no friendly hand extended relief, at the end of sixty days the debt was discharged with the loss of life or liberty. For, be it remembered, if two or more creditors were so unfeeling, they had the right to divide the body of the debtor, or to sell him into foreign slavery beyond the Tiber. This cruel proceeding was not confined to the worthless vagrant, the idle and dissipated, but it embraced, and actually operated upon, the brave defenders of Roman liberty. This arbitrary power, so barbarously exercised, produced the most dangerous convulsions and alarming disaffection in the Roman commonwealth. The ruin which threatened the very existence of that government was so great, that they resorted to the extraordinary expedient of appointing a dictator who was clothed with absolute power and dominion. The army refused to meet the foes of their country, and the people, *en masse*, refused to volunteer their services to repel even invasion while they saw a Roman citizen scourged by a merciless creditor, and his body bleeding from the severity of the punishment. The tribunitial power in Rome had the same origin: it was the offspring of the despotic power which was vested in the creditor. The people demanded these officers, with power to protect their personal independence.

When Christianity triumphed over paganism the precepts of the gospel forbade the infamous traffic.

In an early chapter (p. 35) it was indicated that the

practice of selling debtors into bondage prevailed in this
country among the Anglo-Saxons ; and throughout the
Middle Ages the treatment of English debtors invariably
bordered on the barbarous, languishing in prison being
the mildest element in it.

In the play of the Elizabethan dramatist, Robert Greene,
entitled "Tu Quoque," occurs a scene between a spend-
thrift who has been cast into jail and his jailer. Says
the latter :—

"If you have no money, you had best remove into some cheaper
ward ; to the twopenny ward, it is likeliest to hold out with your
means ; or, if you will, you may go into the *hole*, and there you may
feed for nothing."

The reply is :—

"Ay, out of the alms-basket, where charity appears in likeness of
a piece of stinking fish."

The reference is to the broken food then commonly
distributed to the poor from the tables of rich men.
Beggars and other recipients who were free might
perhaps have received their portions without loss or
hindrance ; but the allowance to distressed prisoners
confined for debt, and unable to purchase food, had to
pass through several ordeals before it came to them.
The best and most wholesome pieces of food were
systematically filched by the jailer, and sold by him at a
low price to people out of prison. The portion which
reached the prisoner was as inferior in quality as it was
meagre in quantity. In the play just quoted, another
character is a miser who "never saw a joint of mutton in
his own home these four-and-twenty years, but always
cozened the poor prisoners ; for he bought his victual out
of the alms-basket !"

In former times it was a custom in London, if not

elsewhere, for prisoners in the various jails who had no allowance, to depute persons to walk the streets and solicit alms for their support while incarcerated. These persons went round day by day, crying out, "Remember the Poor Prisoners!" and begging of passengers or calling at the dwelling-houses for broken food. For the latter purpose each one carried a "maund" or capacious covered basket, suspended at the back by leather handles, through which the arms were passed. He was also equipped with a round deep money-box having the usual slit at the top, which he carried in his right hand; in the left hand was carried a staff or walking-stick for support.

Often it is the fate of the poor to fall into debt, and for debt to fall into prison. And what the impecunious have suffered in the debtors' jails of this country in times past would almost rival the tortures of the Inquisition. The cruelties perpetrated in these prisons have generally resulted from the easy possibility of making money by the warders and jailers, who showed no compunction in enforcing fees and other illegal charges under all manner of pretences.

Immediately on his introduction to prison the new-comer was promptly subjected to tribute by his fellow-prisoners, who exacted from him a sort of entrance-fee which was called "garnish." If the wretch had no money, there was no compunction about stripping him of most of his clothing, which with the aid of the jailer could be converted into coin of the realm.

> " But, kind sir, as you're a stranger,
> Down your garnish you must lay,
> Or your coat will be in danger—
> You must either strip or pay! "

From the year 1586 poor prisoners in London complained repeatedly of cruelties by warders, even to charges of murder and other high misdemeanours, until in 1727 the House of Commons appointed a Committee of inquiry; but even after this, simpler practices of unwarrantable extortion were continued with little modification until 1844.

Thirty-six years before the inquiries of this Committee, a small volume had been published, entitled "The Cries of the Oppressed"; an engraving in it showed the Fleet Prison as it was in 1691. In the foreground of the view is seen a fashionable visitor, carrying in his hand a bunch of sweet-smelling herbs, held to the nose to prevent the noisome smells of the jail. A gentleman and a lady passing the gates are depicted as charitably placing in the begging-box of a prisoner some coins for the benefit of the destitute prisoners, a number of whom are seen at the strongly barred windows, clamouring for monetary assistance in the accustomed formula—"Pray remember the poor debtors!"

This book, issued by Moses Pitt, himself a deeply injured debtor, was the result of communications addressed to sixty-five debtors' prisons in England. Some of the incidents recorded are truly tragic. At Liverpool a surgeon named Morgan, incarcerated for debt, was ultimately reduced by poverty, neglect, and hunger "to catch by a cat mice for his sustenance," and for complaining of his lot was shamefully beaten by the jailer and loaded with irons.

In the castle of Lincoln an unfortunate debtor, because he asked for the return of a purse of money of which his jailers had deprived him, making him destitute thereby, was "treated to a ride on the jailer's coach," which was a euphemistic way of describing a mode of punishment, in which he was placed on a hurdle in the prison-yard, with his head on the stones, and so dragged about till the pitiless ill-usage left him with impaired intellect.

A PRISONER BEING STRIPPED FOR GARNISH.

RACKETS AND SKITTLES IN THE FLEET PRISON.

To face p. 350.

At Appleby the jail was eight yards by four and a half yards, without chimney or place of ease; prisoners had not the benefit of air, fire, or refreshment; and not unnaturally in the course of years some of them had died of starvation, and some of a "poisonous jail-fever." It was the custom of the jailers to charge high fees for bed and lodging, to force prisoners to buy their food from them at extortionate prices, and continually to demand all sorts of gratuities; and to ill-treat and torture all who failed to gratify their rapacity.

One wretched man in the jail at St. Edmundsbury had thumbscrews put on him, and was then chained on tip-toe by his neck to the wall, for daring to send out of the prison to buy his meals. In many prisons the unfortunate debtor was manacled, sometimes loaded with chains, and almost invariably confined in dungeons that were loathsomely filthy.

Such was the treatment meted out to poor prisoners. On the other hand, for the unscrupulous swindling debtor who could command money with which to placate his jailers imprisoment was quite a free-and-easy sort of existence; as a poem entitled "The Humours of the Fleet," published in 1749, fully informs us. The author describes the dwellers in this "poor but merry place," whose joviality consisted of ill-regulated and noisy companionship; detailing all their amusements, their pursuits, and the manner of conducting themselves in the little walled-up world in which they lived :—

> "Such the amusement of this merry jail,
> Which you'll not reach, if friends or money fail"

That there were occasionally warders of another type is proved by the case of the poet Savage, who died in the debtors' prison at Bristol (1743) and was buried at the expense of his humane jailer.

The debtor was first taken to a "sponging-house," and there charged enormously; if too poor to pay, he was removed to the prison, but subjected to high charges for the commonest necessaries. Even if he lived "within the rules," as the privileged houses of the neighbourhood were termed, he was always subjected to visits from jailers, who would declare his right to that little liberty forfeit, unless their memory were refreshed from time to time by a fee of adequate proportions.

By a Georgian Act of Parliament a debtor, under certain circumstances, could claim his discharge from prison unless his creditor paid him 3s. 6d. a week for his maintenance; and if more creditors than one insisted on his detention they had each to agree to pay him a sum not exceeding 2s. weekly. In 1811 a debtor confined in the Marshalsea prison applied to the court for his discharge, on the ground of his creditor having failed to pay him his sixpences in a legal manner. It appeared that the creditor had tendered him for his week's allowance 3s. and a piece of silver resembling the coin that passes for sixpence; the latter, however, upon a close inspection, proved to be a foreign coin. The judge being of opinion that this was not a tender within the meaning of the Act, which directs that the allowance to debtors should be paid in the coin of the realm, ordered the debtor to be discharged.

The notorious Fleet Prison, abolished in 1844 after existing as a place of incarceration for debtors more than two centuries, has been introduced times without number into nearly every type of fictional literature. Some description of it, as it existed in its latest period, occurs in that greatest of our humorous romances, "The Pickwick Papers."

It will be recalled that Mr. Pickwick, rather than pay the iniquitous damages of his famous breach of promise case, elected to go to prison. On his admission to that abode of recklessness and despair the good soul was aghast, on looking down a dark and filthy staircase which appeared to lead to a range of damp and gloomy stone vaults beneath the ground, to be told that those wretched dungeons were occupied by unfortunate prisoners, who not only lived there, but occasionally died there, too.

"The poor side of a debtors' prison is," says Dickens, "as its name imports, that in which the most miserable and abject class of debtors are confined. A prisoner having declared upon the poor side, pays neither rent nor chummage. His fees, upon entering and leaving the gaol, are reduced in amount, and he becomes entitled to a share of some small quantities of food; to provide which, a few charitable persons have, from time to time, left trifling legacies in their wills. Most of our readers will remember a kind of iron cage in the wall of the Fleet Prison, within which was posted some man of hungry looks, who, from time to time, rattled a money-box, and exclaimed in a mournful voice, 'Pray remember the poor debtors; pray remember the poor debtors.' The receipts of this box, when there were any, were divided among the poor prisoners; and the men on the poor side relieved each other in this degrading office.

"Although this custom has been abolished, and the cage is now boarded up, the miserable and destitute condition of these unhappy persons remains the same. We no longer suffer them to appeal at the prison gates to the charity and compassion of the passers-by, but we still leave unblotted in the leaves of our statute book, for the reverence and admiration of succeeding ages, the just and wholesome law which declares that the sturdy felon shall be fed and clothed, and that the penniless debtor shall be left to die of starvation and nakedness. This is no fiction. Not a week passes over our heads but in every one of our prisons for debt, some of these men must inevitably expire in the slow agonies of want, if they were not relieved by their fellow prisoners."

Some of the prisoners, however—not "them down-hearted fellers" who filled Sam Weller's breast with such well-merited scorn—managed to while away the term of their incarceration pleasantly enough; for in the same chapter we read of the facilities offered by the prison yard for such games as rackets and skittles, the gravelled

23

area bounded by the high brick wall, with the iron *chevaux-de-frise* at the top, making a capital racket-court.

After this withering indictment of the great novelist the Fleet Prison survived but eight years.

By the Bankruptcy Act of 1883 imprisonment for debt was virtually abolished.

Besides prisoners for debt, prisoners of war are, or were, to be reckoned among *les misérables*. In 1810 there were nearly 12,000 Englishmen in French prisons, and their lot was indeed a bitter one, according to the records of the times. It is true we had 50,000 French prisoners in England, and negotiations for exchange had taken place; but Napoleon's terms were that he should release 1,000 of our men in return for 3,000 of the French. He offered to make the numbers equal by releasing at the same time 2,000 allies, on condition that the British nation bore the expense of returning these men to their own homes. Similar difficulties had occurred in the negotiations for the Peace of 1802. Perhaps we did not treat our French prisoners any too well; we left much to be desired in the treatment of our own, for on the 7th of January, 1811, it is recorded that a prisoner "died of cold and want" in the Marshalsea Prison; and of the 320 debtors then in Newgate, those who had not private means had to "live" on an allowance of twopennyworth of bread, when a quartern loaf cost 1s. 3d. But in any case, our French prisoners of war cost us £1,000 a day for provisions, clothing, and superintendence for several years, namely, until the Treaty of Peace was signed at Paris on November 20, 1815. Bonaparte wanted all his money for the sinews of war, and the fate of British prisoners did not concern him; so we read that they were without proper clothing, bedding, or fuel, which must have involved terrible suffering, as the winter of 1810–11 was a severe one.

An appeal for funds to alleviate the sufferings of the British prisoners of war in France appeared in *The Times* of January 11, 1811, and was nobly responded to.

Of the deplorable condition of the criminal prisons, the biographies of John Howard and Elizabeth Fry afford ample evidence. The latter on making her first acquaintance with the interior of a jail, fresh from the pure atmosphere of her own life, asked herself the question, " If this is the world, where is God ? " When she began her gracious mission among the jail-birds, an English prison was an inferno, a dark and filthy cellar, in which were herded together an assemblage of abandoned and shameless creatures, half-naked and often half-drunk, who made the heavy walls resound with obscenity, imprecations, and licentious songs, and who demanded rather than requested charity of visitors.

Newgate was regulated to hold 500 criminals, but in 1813 we find 822 in jail. Hardly any bedding was allowed, no coals and candles, or pails to the debtors. Young and old, criminals, lunatics, debtors, and children, were all herded together ; drink was sold to any who had money, and no limit put to the quantity. The whole system was one of bribery and corruption. "At every session criminals in scores were sentenced to death, and the 'death sermon' in the prison chapel was an almost weekly occurrence. It was a favourite place for sightseers, who used to attend the service and watch the poor wretches herded in the 'condemned pen' round a table on which was placed a black coffin. Even as late as 1833 we are told 'sentence of death was passed on a child of nine who poked a stick through a pane of glass in a shop front and stole some pieces of paint worth twopence. This was housebreaking, and the penalty of housebreaking was death.' After some delay, however, the sentence was commuted."

XXXIII

NEGRO SLAVES IN ENGLAND

English serfdom in 1558—Attitude of the national mind towards
slavery—A national hero as a slaver—First negro slaves in
America, 1619—White men sent as slaves to the Plantations—
To the extent of 15,000 a year—Irish bond servants and political
prisoners—Treatment of white slaves—No rights for " heathen
negroes"—Negro slaves in England—Wear collars (1710)—And
are openly bought and sold—Granville Sharp—Takes up the
case of an ill-treated negro slave—And rescues him from further
molestation (1765)—The philanthropist continues the agitation—
And obtains from Court of King's Bench the historic decision
that "a slave setting foot on English soil is free "—Liverpool's
share in slave trade—Trade abolished 1807.

THE slavery which had prevailed in Saxon times, and
continued in the form of villenage through the centuries,
was not entirely obliterated till the seventeenth century,
though serfage practically ceased in Elizabeth's reign.
Even then, the idea of slavery, as an institution, had not
become so utterly repugnant to Englishmen as it is now,
and many relics of it lingered for a long time afterwards.

In the household orders of the Earl of Derby in 1558
it is set forth that "no slaves shall sitt in the hall, but in
the place therefor appoynted convenyant."

Also "the yeomen of horses, and the groomes of the
stable" were not to suffer a "slave to abyde about the
stables, nor lye in theym, nor in any place about theym."
These "slaves" were white men, natives, and bond-

servants employed in the household. This form of slavery or villenage was, as Blackstone observes, neither strictly feudal, Norman, nor Saxon, but mixed and compounded of both. It was the last dying flicker of English serfdom. And as English serfdom died out, negro slavery began to rear its head.

As set forth in another place (p. 129) the statute 1 *Edward VI.* ordained that all idle vagabonds should be made slaves and fed upon bread, water or small drink, and refuse meat ; should wear rings round their necks, arms, and legs, and should be compelled by beating, chaining, and otherwise to perform the work assigned them, however vile it might be. This statute was repealed 3 *and* 4 *Edward VI.*, cap. 16, as being too infamous. But at least it shows the attitude of the national mind towards the subject of slavery.

In these later times, however, it is in connection with our over-sea colonies that England is brought into contact with slavery ; and the condition of slavery in English colonies is usually associated in the mind of the average reader with a black skin. And in this connection let it never be forgotten that Sir John Hawkins, one of our revered national heroes of the spacious days of Queen Elizabeth, took an active and prominent part in the slave trade between Africa and the West Indies.

It was in the year 1619 the first negro slave was taken into America ; a ship in the August of that year entering the James River, in Virginia, with a cargo that included twenty negroes.

In the early history of the American colonies it cannot be found that any great difference was made between the white slave and the negro. White servants were imported from England and sold openly in the markets like any other merchandise. Until late in the seventeenth century it was quite a common way of getting rid of superfluous prisoners of war to sell them into servitude in the English colonies.

"So usual," writes Bancroft, the historian of America, "was this manner of dealing in Englishmen, that not the Scots only who were taken in the field of Dunbar, were sent into involuntary servitude in New England, but the Royalist prisoners of the battle of Worcester, and the leaders in the insurrection of Penruddock, were shipped to America."

It is estimated that for some years after 1664 not less than 1,500 white slaves were imported every year into Virginia alone. The refuse of the prisons were periodically sent to work on the plantations. The number sent from England to the colonies and the West Indies together at the time numbered quite 15,000 a year. The traffic was indeed very considerable till 1675, when it began to decline.

To furnish labourers for the colonies of Virginia, South Carolina, and Georgia (says Booker T. Washington in his interesting book, "The Story of the Negro" [1]) the almshouses and prisons of England were occasionally emptied; nor was it always the destitute and the outcast that were sold into servitude in the colonies, but some of these unfortunates were persons of quality—in fact, a considerable proportion of the political prisoners were.

"There had grown up a systematic speculation in servants both in England and in Virginia. A servant could be transported to America for from six to eight pounds and sold for forty to sixty pounds. London and Bristol were the chief markets for young men and women, who were sold to shipowners, who transported them to America and sold them."

Our authority quotes an advertisement from an old

[1] T. Fisher Unwin, London, 1910.

Baltimore newspaper—the *Maryland Journal*, the first number of which was issued August 20, 1773—offering a reward of £10 for the recovery of an Irish Servant Man who had absconded from his master ; a full description of the runaway is given, and he is evidently regarded purely in the light of a chattel.

Says Mr. Booker Washington :—

"At other times large numbers of Irishmen were sold into servitude in different parts of America. Because the number of slaves brought to America was so immense, the sufferings which they underwent have made a profound impression upon the world, but from all that I have been able to learn, the sufferings endured by these unfortunate Irish bond-servants during the course of the long voyages to America were frequently as hard as those of the slaves. 'The crowded exportation of Irish Catholics,' Bancroft remarks, 'was a frequent event, and was attended by aggravations hardly inferior to the usual atrocities of the African slave trade'

"In 1685, when nearly a thousand prisoners were condemned to transportation for taking part in the insurrection of Monmouth, men of influence at court scrambled for the convicted insurgents as a merchantable commodity."

There were differences, of course, between the conditions of white slavery and black, though these differences must have been more apparent than real. The chief of them seems to have been that the white servant was supposed to be restored to freedom on the expiry of the term for which he had been committed, while the black servant, unless he could buy himself off, or had his freedom given him by an exceptionally generous master, was a slave for life. It was a provision in George Washington's will, readers may be reminded, that his slaves should be set free. It is also curious to note that in the earlier days free negroes enjoyed the same liberties under the law as free whites, except that they were not allowed to hold persons of white blood as bond-servants.

In the seventeenth century pious and compassionate

persons established funds for redeeming Christian captives held as slaves by Barbary pirates; yet in the reign of William and Mary the Court of Common Pleas held that a man might have property in a negro "because negroes are heathens."

Mention is made in *The Tatler* of 1710 of the metal collars worn by negro slaves; and in the Museum of the Scottish Society of Antiquaries is a brass collar which was worn in 1701 by a criminal—a Scotsman—who, after being condemned to death, was respited to perpetual servitude. At Hampton Court is a bust of the favourite slave of William III—whom history labels as a "champion of English liberty"—wearing a collar and padlock. The ignominy of helotism does not seem to have occurred to the English mind till very late in the day.

English newspapers in the eighteenth century contain frequent references to negro slavery in this country. One enterprising tradesman advertises "collars with silver padlocks for blacks," but most of the announcements have reference to the sales of negroes, and the offers of rewards for runaway slaves. An advertisement of 1720 offers a reward of half-a-guinea for the recovery of a negro slave "branded on the left breast," who had gone away from Limehouse Hole; one of 1761 offers for sale "a healthy negro girl" who has had smallpox, is capable with her needle, and able to perform other domestic duties.

In 1771 a sale was announced to take place at the "Baker's Arms," Lichfield, by John Heely, an auctioneer of Walsall, of a negro boy, eleven years of age, described as of mild disposition, healthy, fond of labour, "and for colour, an excellent black."

Granville Sharp, son of a clergyman and grandson of an Archbishop of York, was an aggressive Christian who earned a foremost place among English philanthropists by leading the struggle against the slave trade; and, incidentally, he was also opposed to the impressment of sailors. One of the earliest cases which attracted his attention was that of Jonathan Strong. This man was a negro slave brought to England by a certain David Leslie, who treated him most barbarously, on one occasion beating him over the head with his pistol so severely that he left him to die, as being of no further use. But he was recovered from his deplorable condition by Mr. William Sharp, a surgeon, and brother of Granville Sharp, who gave a portion of his time to the healing of the poor. The latter also took a great interest in the wounded man's case, and eventually, by careful nursing, the patient became robust and strong again. A little later on, his former master, Leslie, meeting him, at once formed a design to kidnap him.

The negro was seized at a public-house, and conveyed to the Poultry Compter, but without any legal warrant; and while detained here he was sold by Leslie to a man named Kerr, for £30. Granville Sharp promptly intervened, and waited upon the Lord Mayor, who was induced to discharge him in the absence of a warrant; though the case had staggered the lawyers who argued it. As the parties moved out of court the captain of the ship who was to convey Strong to Jamaica went up to the negro, seized hold of him, and said, "Then now I seize him as my slave." Upon this Mr. Sharp placed his hand on the captain's shoulder and pronounced these words, "I charge you, in the name of the King, with an assault upon the person of Jonathan Strong, and all these are my witnesses." The captain, intimidated by the charge made in the presence of the Lord Mayor, and fearing a prosecution, let the negro go, and without further ado he was taken safely away by the philanthropist (1765).

As the agitation of Granville Sharp for the abolition of negro slavery made headway, the public sales of black slaves in this country became fewer and fewer, although it was computed that in 1764 there were 20,000 to 30,000 of them domiciled in England. Most of these had certainly ceased to regard themselves as slaves in a free country; but the matter was brought to a head in 1772 under the following circumstances.

James Sommersatt, a coloured man, had been made a slave in Africa, and sold there. When brought to England by an English master he ran away, but was caught again and put on board ship to be sent to Jamaica. Granville Sharp took up his defence, and Lord Mansfield granted a *habeas corpus*. The decision of the Court of King's Bench was that "as soon as any slave sets his foot on English soil he becomes free." From that date the buying and selling of slaves in this country has been recognised as distinctly illegal.

It should not be forgotten that among the causes which contributed to the rise of the port of Liverpool was the wealth it derived from its once extensive traffic in the slave trade; for no commodity was calculated to yield such a margin of profit as the famous (or infamous) "black ivory." *Notes and Queries* printed in 1865 an English bill of lading, not nearly a century old, which relates in plain and undisguised terms to a consignment of "115 males, 64 females; total, 179 slaves."

An Act was passed in 1807 abolishing the slave trade, the penalty for trading in slaves being £100 for each slave bought or sold; any vessel fitted out in the kingdom, or the colonies, for carrying on the prohibited trade was to be forfeited. Insurances in the traffic were also made illegal. Negro slaves captured in war were not to be sold; they were to be enlisted in the king's service, or bound as apprentices for fourteen years, a bounty being paid their captors in the shape of head money; namely, £40 for a man, £30 for a woman, and £10 for a child. This Act, however, did not abolish slavery in our colonies, nor prevent the removal of slaves from one British settlement to another.

> "Slaves cannot breathe in England; if their lungs
> Receive our air, that moment they are free;
> They touch our country and their shackles fall"

sings Cowper. But before we join in the exultation of the poet let us ponder the next chapter.

XXXIV

THE EXPLOITED CLASS

The romance of exploitation—Mops or Statute Fairs—Method of
hiring farm servants—"Runaway Mops"—Hiring scene from
an old play—Act to ensure farm servants (1405)—Wages and
hours of labour fixed (1563)—All artificers and labourers to be
compelled to serve—Or accounted vagabonds—Statutes against
the combination of workmen—Eighteenth-century combinations—Tailors' wages in 1768—Spitalfields weavers—The
Luddites—Rise of Trade Unions—Suffolk farm labourers in
eighteenth century—The iniquitous Game Laws—Wages on
the famous "Bread Scale" (1795)—Dorset labourers—Shelley's
"Song of the Men of England"—Hood's "Song of the Shirt"
—"Yeast, a Problem"—The problem of the agricultural
labourer—English and Belgian agriculture contrasted.

FROM a variety of causes, chief amongst them being
destitution and ignorance, men allow themselves to be
exploited by their fellows—by those who are cleverer,
or in possession of greater resources. Social usage, and
the laws made by the class with the upper hand, then
conspire to keep them in subjection. The first step
towards emancipation is education, enlightenment.

Man's exploitation of man throughout the ages has
saddened the history of the human race.

> "Man's inhumanity to man
> Makes countless thousands mourn."

Some phases of this veiled enthralment, however, have

not been without a tinge of romance—viewed from a distance.

Mops, or Statute Fairs, at which farm servants were hired for the year, are barely extinct at the present day. At these Hiring Fairs, men and women stood in rows in the public street, ready to treat with proposing employers, some exhibiting bits of straw, or, if a cowman or a ploughboy, bits of whipcord, to indicate their unengaged condition and the line of work they undertook. Shepherds carried a crook, and carters a whip.

The bargaining between these parties was transacted openly in the hearing of gaping crowds, most of the hirer's questions eliciting an "Ees, sur," or a "No, sur," and the whole usually winding up with either, "I conna gue for less," or "Yo'll find me yarn it, sur." Earnest money or a sealing drink concluded the contract, which the law construed for one year, although it might be for a longer or for a shorter period. Many farmers were wary enough to hire their indoor servants for fifty-one weeks only, purposing thus to prevent their effecting a settlement under the old Poor Law.

Statute Hiring Fairs were usually held in the month of September, and in most cases the contract ran from Michaelmas to Michaelmas. In a few localities "Runaway Mops" were held a week or two later, to which repaired all who for some reason declined to go to their new places, and had "run away" from their first bargain; and those who had not yet secured situations.

These farm servants possessed very little worldly property beyond the clothes they wore, and not often too many of those. The day before they left their old situations, when they got their worldly possessions together ready for the move, was commonly called Packrag-day.

An extract from Isaac Bickerstaffe's "Love in a

Village " will serve to illustrate the kind of scene these hirings occasioned in the old time, when even the squire engaged his household servants by the year :—

Hodge. This way, your worship, this way. Why don't you stand aside there ? Here's his worship a-coming.

Countrymen. His worship.

Justice Woodcock. Fy ! Fy ! What a crowd's this ! Odd's, I'll put some of them in the stocks. (*Striking a fellow.*) Stand out of the way, sirrah !

Hodge. Now, your honour, now the sport will come. The gut-scrapers are here, and some among them are going to sing and dance. Why, there's not the like of our Statute, mun, in five counties ; others are but fools to it.

Servant Man. Come, good people, make a ring, and stand out, fellow-servants, as many of you as are willing and able to bear a-bob. We'll let my masters and mistresses see we can do something at least : if they won't hire us it sha'n't be our fault. Strike up the Servants' Medley.

AIR.

Housemaid.

I pray, gentles, list to me,
I'm young, and strong, and clean, you see ;
I'll not turn tail to any she,
    For work that's in the country.
Of all your house the charge I take,
I wash, I scrub, I brew, I bake ;
And more can do than here I'll speak,
    Depending on your bounty.

Footman.

Behold a blade, who know's his trade
    In chamber, hall, and entry ;
And what though here I now appear,
    I've served the best of gentry.
        A footman would you have,
        I can dress, and comb, and shave
For I a handy lad am.
        On a message I can go,
        And slip a billet-doux,
With your humble servant, madam.

Cookmaid.

Who wants a good cook my hand they must cross;
For plain wholesome dishes I'm ne'er at a loss ;
And what are your soups, your ragouts, and your sauce,
    Compared to old English roast beef ?

Carter.

If you want a young man with a true honest heart,
Who knows how to manage a plough and a cart,
Here's one to your purpose, come take me and try ;
You'll say you ne'er met with a better than I,
                        Geho, Dobin, &c.

Chorus.

My masters and mistresses, hither repair,
What servants you want you'll find in our fair ;
Men and maids fit for all sorts of stations there be,
And as for the wages we sha'n't disagree.

In 1405 the aristocracy and lords of the soil, finding
a serious deficiency in the supply of servants and field
labourers, had secured an enactment prohibiting the
apprenticeship of any child to a trade or craft in a
city, unless the parents were in possession of land worth
20s. a year at the least. A proper supply of tillers and
toilers was to be kept up at any cost.

Common field labourers were hired only by the day
or the week, and did not "live in." A statute of the
fifth year of Elizabeth directed that all persons having
no visible effects might be made to work ; it defined
how many hours they were to work in summer, and
how many in winter ; punished all who deserted their
work ; and empowered the justices to settle the wages,
penalising heavily those who exacted and those who
gave more.

Artificers as well as labourers were bound to work
the specified hours, on pain of imprisonment ; and
their wages were fixed by the magistrates, heavy penalties
being imposed, as before mentioned. Special provision

was made for artificers to engage in field labour at hay-time and harvest. Unmarried women between the ages of twelve and forty might be forced into service.

By the law of 1563 all who were whole and mighty in body, able to labour, not having land or master, nor using lawful merchandise, craft, or mystery, and all common labourers loitering and refusing work for such reasonable wage as was commonly given, were to be grievously whipped for a first offence, and for a second were to be burnt through the gristle of the right ear with a hot iron of the compass of about one inch. So ran the phrasing of this imperious enactment.

By the same enactment no person was to be hired for less than a year "in the mysteries or arts of a taylor, shoemaker, tanner, pewterer, baker, brewer, glover, smith, farrier, sadler, spurrier, turner, capper, hatmaker, bowyer, fletcher, arrow-head maker, butcher, cook, or miller." All persons brought up in these trades, if under thirty and unmarried, might be compelled to serve. All persons between twelve and sixty years of age, not being apprentices or lawfully retained in any employment, could be compelled to serve by the year in husbandry. On leaving a situation, each labourer was required to take "a testimonial of liberty to serve elsewhere," and if any employer engaged him without such document, he was liable to a penalty of £5, and the labourer to be whipped as a vagabond.

Later statutes, from the time of Anne, dealt specifically with the workmen employed in the manufactures of woollen, cotton, linen, buttons, gloves, hats, laces, leather, shoes, iron and steel ; many of them of a highly restrictive and fettering tendency—artificers were not to combine together, or to go into a foreign country to work, or send tools abroad; foreign-made leather gloves were not to be imported, while iron and steel goods were not to be exported; in the hatting trade there was to be one journeyman employed to each apprentice; no butcher could be a tanner, and no tanner a shoemaker; and not the least noteworthy feature was the number of offences, as the embezzlement of material served out to him, for which a workman could be publicly whipped.

Till quite recent times the right of combination was denied to workmen; the law generally regarded any such attempt as conspiracy. In the Middle Ages hired journeymen were frequently dissatisfied with their wages, and occasionally combined to resist their employers, but no permanent combination ever lived for any length of time, the rigours of mediæval law being directed against all such efforts. Modern Trade Unions can in no way be regarded as lineally descended from the ancient Trade Guilds, which were combinations of masters and men; to-day the two exist side by side. By the eighteenth century London journeymen had lost all the privileges in which they had formerly participated as members of City Companies.

Prior to 1700 no permanent or continuous associations of workmen had existed for maintaining or improving the conditions of their employment. Soon after this date, however, many of the skilled trades began to combine, as becomes evident by the passing of the Combination Act in 1799, a comprehensive enactment forbidding all such combinations.

This attempt at legislative repression was too late in the day. An independent spirit was abroad, and what could not be done openly was done surreptitiously. Workmen began to meet together, generally in taverns, to establish Sick and Funeral Clubs, or other provident institutions. But at such assemblages it was inevitable that trade interests should be discussed, particularly rates of wages.

In some trades, in which journeymen frequently travelled from place to place in search of work, there slowly grew up a system by which their fellow-workers in each town extended relief to these "tramps"; they were helped on their way, in fact, by means of irregular trade societies.

In 1768 the tailors, a numerous body, and one which could generally contrive to act in combination against their employers, had secured a betterment of their condition by having their wages fixed at 2s. 7½d. a day, working from 6 a.m. to 7 p.m., with a break of one hour in the middle of the day. This rate of pay was considerably higher, and for fewer hours of work, than it had been in the reign of George I. While shoemakers have ever been men of advanced thought—an observer has suggested that there is "something in the smell of leather" which makes them so—the tailors have always held a good opinion of themselves; as Canning tells us, the "three tailors of Tooley Street" who petitioned the House of Commons, styled themselves "We, the people of England."

In 1713 the weavers had created a great uproar, and petitioned against the introduction of French silks. Between 1765 and 1773 great discontent prevailed amongst the Spitalfields weavers. In the latter years Parliament fixed a new rate of wages for them, and from that arrangement the weavers gained some amount of strength, inasmuch as their representatives are afterwards found appearing before the justices who had the fixing of the scale of wages, and making their views respected. No one could follow the trade of a weaver unless he served an apprenticeship of seven years to a weaver or a clothier; no weaver was allowed to have

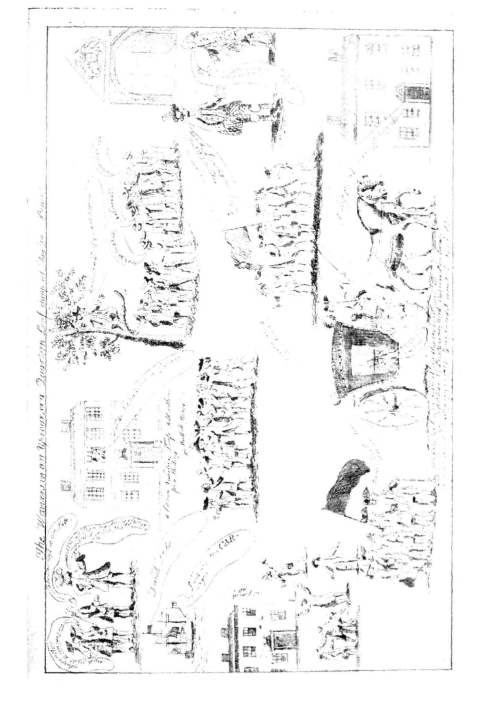

more than two looms in a house in any corporation or market town ; nor might any weaver keep a fulling-mill or engage in dyeing. Such were some of the restrictions in restraint of trade characteristic of the "good old times."

There were, indeed, many forms of restraint in those bygone days of which the poor and the productive classes were always the victims.

The poor, for instance, when difficulties of transport interfered so seriously with the distribution of produce, were always liable to be wronged by unprincipled "regrators," men who "forestalled" the market in some particular commodity ; which could very easily be done by an early purchaser with a little capital. To "forestall" was therefore regarded as a most serious offence ; the law forbade any one to buy and sell wares or victuals in the same market or within four miles of it ; even to buy before the accustomed hour, or to spread a rumour with a view to enhancing the price of any merchandise, was a punishable offence. The statute of 1772 "for repealing several laws therein mentioned against Badgers, Engrossers, Forestallers, and Regrators," boldly declared these laws detrimental to the proper supply of food to the labouring poor

As late as 1800, however, a remarkable case of forestalling came before the law courts. A criminal information was laid against a man named Waddington "for monopolising practices in the purchase of hops." It was alleged that he had invited certain hop-growers to a dinner, at which he had given the toast, " Hops, twenty pounds a hundredweight," and incited these planters to hold back their crops till prices had risen to a high figure. Afterwards, in Worcester market, he had purchased from those in want of ready money all their supply at prices ranging from ten to forty shillings above the prices which were current prior to his appearance.

Prosecuting counsel characterised this forestalling as a "crime of deepest dye." The defendant's counsel argued that he was innocent of any offence, and that if he were convicted the private enterprise of the country would receive a most grievous check and injury. The judge (Sir Simon Le Blanc) remarked severely on the "enormity" of the offence, and the jury promptly found a verdict of guilty. After long delays in goal (where he daily sold a ton of potatoes at a halfpenny per pound for the benefit of his poorer fellow-prisoners) he was ordered to pay a fine of £500, and to be imprisoned for a month.

Perhaps this particular case did not affect the interests of the humbler classes very much; but it is significant that the same year (1800) the clamours against corn-merchants were as violent as in the days of the Tudors, and it is more to the point to record that one of them was convicted before Lord Kenyon of regrating, and similarly punished.

Sight must not be lost of the fact that in ancient times starvation was a real danger to rich and poor alike.

From 1810 trade societies began to prosecute masters who employed "illegal men"—those who had not by a seven years' apprenticeship acquired the right to follow a particular trade. The effect of this was the repeal, in 1814, of these ancient restrictions on craftsmanship.

Here is a curious incident which illustrates the attitude of the law towards the labouring classes as late as 1816.

A sugar-baker having left his employment during a dispute about wages was committed to prison. Upon regaining his freedom he brought an action against the Lord Mayor of London, who had convicted him, "for that he had not received a flogging during his confinement, conformably to the statute in that case made and provided." The complainant won, and was awarded one farthing damages.

A PRISON INTERIOR (EIGHTEENTH CENTURY).

(*See p.* 353.)

FORESTALLER IN THE PILLORY
(SIXTEENTH CENTURY).

Is it generally known that it is little more than a century since the last vestiges of serfdom disappeared from the northern kingdom ?   From about the year 1445 until 1775 the miners of Scotland were bought and sold with the soil. It is stated in the old chronicles that bloodhounds were kept to trace them if they left their employment, and to aid in bringing them back again. By statute law, miners were bound to work all days in the year except Paschal and Yule ; and if they did not work they were to be "whipped in the bodies for the glory of God and for the good of their masters." Not till 1775 was the first law passed in an attempt to better this state of things, but it was 1799 ere the law gave the working miner of Scotland his complete freedom.

Industrial difficulties were complicated in 1811 by the outbreak of Luddism, an organised conspiracy in the manufacturing districts for the destruction of machinery. The name was derived from that of a poor idiot, Ned Lud, who thirty years before, in a fit of irritation, had broken two stocking-frames in Leicestershire. The riots began at Nottingham in the winter of 1811, where, owing to stagnation in trade, many hosiers were out of work. A new frame had just been introduced which, being wider than all former ones, needed less manual labour. The populace were infuriated at this and rioted fiercely. A Bill was hurried through Parliament to meet the difficulty. The breaking of stocking- and lace-frames had been punishable with fourteen years' transportation. It was now made a capital offence. The offences did not cease, but were now accompanied by murders though Luddites not guilty of murder had already been hanged under the new law. Riots grew nearly into insurrection, whereupon greatly enlarged powers were placed in the hands of the magistrates. At York in the November of 1812 many Luddites were convicted and sixteen of them were executed.

For a time the movement was apparently suppressed, but it broke out again at Loughborough in 1816 with renewed violence. Armed bands went about at night terrorizing the neighbourhood. They broke into factories, demolished the machinery, and scattered goods and valuable property to the winds. These ravages were not confined to the towns, for night marches were made with suddenness and secrecy to distant villages. The leaders, who were always disguised, overawed the people, harangued their followers, and conducted their operations with military skill and desperation. A leader was known as General Ludd, his chief lieutenants as Ludd's wives, the rank and file as Luddites.

Before too hastily condemning the conduct of these ignorant and misguided operatives, let us not omit to compare it with the ineptitude of their rulers, who could meet the crisis with nothing more adequate or more logical than the barbarous old rough-and-ready remedy of the death penalty. The fact is, men were not " given to think furiously " in those days ; and on behalf of the operatives may be urged the bitter sufferings to which the whole labouring classes of this country had to submit immediately upon the conclusion of the long and exhausting Napoleonic wars.

> "The poor, inured to drudgery and distress,
> Act without aim, think little, feel less ;
> And nowhere, but in feigned Arcadian scenes,
> Taste happiness, or know what pleasure means."

In 1825 workmen acquired the right of collective bargaining, involving power to withhold labour from the market by concerted action. This was a great step in the emancipation of labour ; but unfortunately it aroused a bitter hostility on the part of the employers, and as the men were aggressive, industrial warfare ensued, till the new era of Trades Unionism (which cultivated a reasonable spirit of mutuality between the two parties to the industrial contract) set in, about the year 1860.

Here we may safely leave the case of the artisan and town labourer. He is now generally so well organized · in his own interests, that he can scarcely be reckoned in the ranks of the "exploited."

Of all the industries to which man has put his hand, agriculture, the most ancient, has ever yielded the lowest grade labourer. And as his industrial condition, so also of necessity has been his social status.

In the middle of the eighteenth century the farm labourers of Suffolk were fed abundantly, but coarsely. They ate their country's rye-bread with their country's stony cheese—"too hard to bite," the poet Bloomfield found it; while the farmer luxuriated in his "maslin bread," half wheat and half rye. The plough-boy's breakfast was brown bread soaked in skimmed milk. Indoor farm servants stipulated that they should not be fed more than a certain number of days in each week with "hollow meat," as they termed rabbit flesh, the cheapest flesh-food procurable.

East Anglia, like certain other parts, swarmed with rabbits; but they were not the property of the person on whose land they were found. As the law then stood no person, except he had an estate of inheritance to the value of £100 a year, might kill game. These game laws were termed by Blackstone "a bastard slip of the old forest laws. . . . The Forest Laws (said this eminent authority) established only one mighty hunter throughout the land; the Game Laws had raised a little Nimrod in every manor." Aristocratic legislators had so perfected these laws that "it required fifty times the property to enable a man to kill a partridge as to vote for a knight of the shire." Tardily and very reluctantly these intoler-

able restrictions were removed early in the nineteenth
century, though at the same time the law against poach-
ing was made more stringent.

In spite of this, however, the ill-paid rural labourer
remained everywhere an inveterate poacher. In Wiltshire and Dorsetshire, where till 1828 twelve thousand
deer ranged Cranbourne Chase, the peasantry poached
systematically.

Starvation wages were indeed responsible for even
greater enormities, as the old Somersetshire chant
enlightens us :—

> "Feyther stole th' Parson's sheep ;
> A merry Christmas we shall keep ;
> We shall have both mutton and beef—
> But we won't say nothin' about it."

In 1795 the Berkshire justices endeavoured to institute
a kind of sliding scale, wages to rise or fall in proportion
as the price of bread rose or fell, with a special
graduation dependent on the size of the family. This
famous "Bread Scale" was argued to be mischievous
by Sir George Nicholls, because "it enabled the labouring classes, who formed the bulk of the people, to obtain
the same quantity of food in a scarce and dear season as
in an abundant and cheap one. This is contrary to the
behests of Providence," opines this authority, "as it
would aggravate the evils of dearth, and neutralize the
blessings of abundance."

Frequent bad harvests at this period caused untold
sufferings to the bulk of the community, and in many
parts tumultuous meetings were held, and riotous proceedings took place. Assuming the price of corn to
be the index of wages, there must indeed have been
great privation among the people of this country at the
close of the eighteenth century.

Even in his hours of greatest abandonment, as at harvest-homes, and such-like rustic merry-makings, the Dorsetshire farm labourer to this day confesses his subserviency in characteristic folk-song :—

> " Here's a health unto our miaster,
>   The founder of the feast,
> And I hope to God wi' all my heart
>   His soul in heaven mid rest ;
> That everything mid prosper
>   That ever he tiak in hand,
> Vor we be all his servants
>   And all at his command."

About 1832, that time of intense political excitement, accompanied by riots, incendiary fires, and machine-breaking, Shelley wrote his " Song to the Men of England" :—

I.

> " Men of England, wherefore plough
> For the lords who lay ye low ?
> Wherefore weave with toil and care
> The rich robes your tyrants wear ?

II.

> Wherefore feed, and clothe, and save,
> From the cradle to the grave,
> Those ungrateful drones who would
> Drain your sweat—nay, drink your blood ?

III.

> Wherefore, Bees of England, forge
> Many a weapon, chain, and scourge,
> That those stingless drones may spoil
> The forced produce of your toil ?

IV.

> Have ye leisure, comfort, calm,
> Shelter, food, love's gentle balm ?
> Or what it is ye buy so dear
> With your pain and with your fear ?

V.

The seed ye sow another reaps;
The wealth ye find another keeps;
The robes ye weave another wears;
The arms ye forge another bears.

VI.

Sow seed—but let no tyrant reap;
Find wealth—let no impostor heap;
Weave robes—let not the idle wear;
Forge arms—in your defence to bear.

VII.

Shrink to your cellars, holes, and cells;
In halls ye deck another dwells,
Why shake the chains ye wrought? Ye see
The steel ye tempered glance on ye.

VIII.

With plough and spade, and hoe and loom,
Trace your grave and build your tomb,
And weave your winding-sheet till fair
England be your sepulchre."

One of the earliest writers to draw public attention
seriously to the unhappy fate of the "sweated" worker
was Tom Hood, whose "Song of the Shirt" voices in a
powerful and moving manner the bitter cry of the
London seamstress :—

"With fingers weary and worn,
    With eyelids heavy and red,
A woman sat, in unwomanly rags,
    Plying her needle and thread.

Stitch ! stitch ! stitch !
In poverty, hunger, and dirt,
    And still with a voice of dolorous pitch
She sang the Song of the Shirt."

Surely the rebuke comes home in the lines :—

> "O ! men with Sisters dear !
> O ! men with Mothers and Wives !
> It is not linen you 're wearing out,
> But human creature's lives."

This modern picture of human misery, all the result of social and industrial oppression, Hood completes thus :—

> " Work—work—work,
> My labour never flags,
> And what are its wages ? A bed of straw,
> A crust of bread—and rags,
> That shattered roof, and the naked floor—
> A table—a broken chair—
> And a wall so blank, my shadow I thank
> For sometimes falling there."

And when grinding poverty had done its work, withering the soul and consuming the body, the wretch's requiem was well sung by Thomas Noel in " The Pauper's Drive," in which occur the familiar lines :—

> " Rattle his bones over the stones,
> He's only a pauper whom nobody owns."

In 1851 the Rev. Charles Kingsley, whose views of social reform were unfortunately in advance of his time, considered the problem of the agricultural labourer the one which called most urgently for public attention. The previous year he had published "Alton Locke," a tale designed to show the evils of competition and the grievances of the artisan class ; proffering as a remedy for these evils the adoption of the associative principle among workmen—the combining of capital and labour ; and he now advocated the application of the same principles to agriculture, in a work of equal sincerity, entitled "Yeast, a Problem." The courage and genius which this clerical writer brought to bear upon these subjects places him amongst the most meritorious men of his time, and reflects honour upon the class to which he belonged.

The history of the agricultural labourer is inseparable from the dolorous story of the poor. Nor is his condition likely to improve very materially until something little short of an industrial revolution occurs—say, until such time as the nation comes to regard him as indispensable to the provision of the Englishman's daily loaf : a position in the national esteem to which he may perhaps approximate as the agriculture of this country gradually approaches to that intensity of cultivation which obtains in Belgium. For is not the present situation of British agriculture anomalous? Belgium has a population of over 500 to the square mile; Great Britain a population of 360 to the square mile. Belgium exports manufactured goods to the extent of £9 per head of its population, while Great Britain's exports of manufactures are of considerably less value per head. Yet Belgium, the soil and climate of which are no better than those of this country, not only supplies its own dense population with food, but has a million pounds' worth left for export. When the English soil is made to support the English people, it is within the range of possibility that the cultivator of the soil may not be so ill-paid as he is at present.

XXXV

SLOW EVOLUTION OF THE ENGLISH RUSTIC

The villager—An ethnological problem—Mr. Balfour's opinion—An original servile class—Saxon laws affecting slaves—The four-teenth-century thrall—Mr. W. A. Dutt's theory—A leavening of Indian blood—The Gubbings—" Inhabiting a Scythia within England "—The Cobbledicks—Their communistic farm—The Doons of Exmoor—Said to be descended from the Danes.

NOTHING is more striking in the study of English society than the wide difference always observable between the rural labourer of the fields and the town workman of the factories, even when the latter is but engaged in the lowest forms of unskilled labour. The slow-thinking of the former is frequently exhibited in his speech, his gait, his uncouth mannerisms.

The village poor live the simplest of simple lives, and their ways of thought are much nearer to those of the primitive man than to the scientific outlook of the twentieth century.

A recent study of life in the English villages, where wages are generally at the lowest level, has revealed that comparatively few families are living below the poverty-standard ; the villagers all possess gardens or have easy access to allotments, and do not depend, as town-dwellers do, solely on the money wages they receive. It is on the social side that village life is so much less favourable than life in the towns. There is little social intercourse; entertainments and amusements are few and far between ; public life is virtually stagnant ; and altogether the daily routine of life is so deadly dull that migration to the towns is constantly going on with devastating effects on the countryside.

The slow process of civilisation which has permitted the centuries to pass by with so little amelioration of the condition of the lowest class of Englishmen, is attracting the attention of the ethnologists. Mere environment does not satisfactorily account for men remaining content in these days with a wage of twelve shillings a week, and conditioned so far below the average plane of English labour. Isolation through difficulties of intercommunication, and consequent intermarriage generation after generation, no doubt tend to the race deterioration which is sometimes found in the remoter villages of East Anglia and the less accessible hamlets of other parts. But the backwardness of rural labour seems to call for the elucidation in other probable causes.

It has been suggested that this slowness is to be attributed to the survival of the prehistoric Iberian element in the country population ; to the incorporation into our civilisation of that element as a servile class, which has always remained the exploited class.

The Right Hon. A. J. Balfour, in a recent speech said that—

"traits of character alone are left of race traces. Reserving any opinion that there may be also physical traits, I ask where the character of the hereditary serf is more clearly to be discerned than in the rural labourer of to-day. Aside of mere character it is not usual to find a rural labourer who is not the son of a rural labourer, and so back generation by generation (see the church registers since Elizabeth) to the times when the great mass of the tillers of the soil were styled 'nativi.' Race gradually became class, but if the agricultural labourer is not descended from the villein with almost

unbroken identity of comparative condition, what is he descended
from ? "

At this time of day the slow development of the
English rustic, whatever its causes, calls more loudly for
the attention of the economists than the theories of the
ethnologists.

From the historical point of view there is nothing
improbable in the rural population of England being by
blood of a different race from the pure Anglo-Saxon
stock.

The Germanic race always included freemen and slaves.
The Anglo-Saxon invader, who before all things was a
warrior, may have brought with him an agricultural or
servile class, and as he extended his conquests, may have
augmented their ranks by adding to them some of the
Romano-British population who failed to offer an effective
resistance to his arms.

Over these slaves he at first had power of life and death.
The Saxon theow had no appeal from, or right of action
against, his master. Prior to the introduction of Chris-
ianity the Saxon laws did nothing to fix or restrain the
power of the proprietor over his slaves ; as we have seen
in an earlier chapter, it was the influence of the Christian
clergy which ameliorated their condition. Then they
began to enjoy the same kind of protection as we now
extend to our horses or dogs. Certain offences against
them were recognised by ecclesiastical canons, for which
were imposed penances of various degrees. The State
followed in the wake of the Church. By the laws of Ina
of Wessex (688–726) slaves were not to be worked on
a Sunday ; a little later the laws of Alfred were made
particularly severe against rape upon female slaves, which
seems to indicate that this offence was a somewhat
common one. But as yet the word of a slave was not
accepted as evidence in a court of law.

The condition of this servile class as Norman villeins was advanced but little, if at all, upon that of Saxon theows. Not only were degrading services required of them, but galling restrictions were still imposed upon them; as we have seen, even the intercourse of the sexes was made a subject of taxation.

When the English minstrel succeeded the Norman troubador, the first native songs did not fail to voice the complaints of the suffering peasantry against the oppression of their lords. The early English poets, too, have depicted the woeful condition of the fourteenth-century thrall or bondman.

> "Now es man gildred in ivels all,
> His aun sin has mad him thrall
> That first was fre sinn I for-tald
> Nu has him Sathanus in wald."

An interesting theory has been broached by Mr. W. A. Dutt—an authority who, as an occasional van-dweller himself, has acquired first-hand knowledge of that curious class of people who for centuries have catered for the amusement of holiday-making England, by providing the fun of the fairs. These showmen regularly travel from one country fair to another, always living apart from house-dwelling folk. Mr. Dutt says the gipsy element in these people is very marked, though not a tenth of them are true Romanies.

"I often think," he continues, "there is also a strong strain of aboriginal blood, inherited from remote ancestors who belonged to that long-headed, dark-haired, prehistoric race which the earliest Aryan conquerors of our country dispossessed of the greater part of it. Leland—who was well acquainted with our show-folk, tinkers, *et hoc genus omne*—says that no writer whatever has yet clearly explained the curious fact that our entire nomadic population, excepting tramps, is not, as we thought in our childhood, composed of English people like ourselves. He suggests that it is *leavened with direct Indian blood, and was old before the Saxon Heptarchy.* Old it certainly is, and I am inclined to believe that, just as the Irish tinkers have preserved for us in Shelta something of the secret language of the ancient Celtic bards, so our peripatetic show-folk, conjurors, fire-eaters, thimble-riggers, and others, are preserving some traits of the character, habits, and *morale* of these Neolithic people who probably at one time cut capers for the entertainment of the Celts, and who eventually as pixies, Pechts, or fairies became credited with supernatural powers."

It is an ingenious and a taking speculation on the part of both Mr. Dutt and the versatile Charles Godfrey Leland.

If the English rustic is not autochthonous, are there any autochthones to be found in this country? Let us examine the subject for a brief moment or two.

History furnishes examples of outcasts who have not taken to nomadism, or yet gone away from their native country; contenting themselves with a self-ex-communication from their more conventional fellows, living a wild, and often a predatory life on the fringe of civilisation.

Such Ishmaelitish folk were the Gubbings mentioned by old gossip Fuller, and alluded to by Kingsley in "Westward Ho!"

As the antiquary, writing about 1650, puts it, their land was the "Scythia within England, and they were pure heathens therein. It lieth nigh Brent. For on the edge of Dartmoor it is reported that some two hundred years since, two bad women, being with child, fled thither to hide themselves; to whom some lewd fellows resorted, and this was their first original. They lived in cots (rather holes than houses) like swine; having all in common, they multiplied without marriage into many hundreds. Their language is the dross of the dregs of the vulgar Devonian. Their wealth consisted of other men's goods; they live by stealing the sheep on the moors; in vain is it for any to search their houses, being

25

a work beneath the pains of any sheriff, and above the power of any constable.   Such is their fleetness, they can outrun many horses.   They hold together like bees ; offend one, and all will revenge his quarrel." The novelist gives a vivid description of an adventure with this semi-barbarous tribe, whose settlement on Dartmoor was as the " territory of a foreign and hostile potentate, who had many times ravaged the dominions and defeated the forces of Queen Elizabeth."

A poet of the time of Charles I. thus describes the Gubbins of the Lydford glens :—

"And near hereto 's the Gubbins' cave,
A people that no knowledge have
    Of law of God or men ;
Whom Cæsar never yet subdued
Who 've lawless lived, of manners rude,
    All savage in their den.

By whom, if any passed that way
He dares not the least time to stay,
    For presently they howl ;
Upon which signal they do muster
Their naked forces in a cluster
    Led forth by Roger Rowle."

Mr. Baring-Gould, in his novel " John Herring," gives an account of their congeners " The Cobbledicks," a clan of half-naked savages who dwelt many years ago, the last of them within living memory, on a spur of Dartmoor, near Cosdon Beacon.   The parent stock lived in the parish of Nymnet, " in an old tumble-down cottage, sans windows, sans doors, sans chimneys, sans floors, sans everything save the cob," or shell of mud walls, and the ragged thatch that but half sheltered it.

These semi-barbarians lived quite apart from their

fellow-beings, with whom they had no intercourse whatever, never entering a village, dealing at any shop, or ever being seen at market, or meeting, or least of all at any place of worship. They were unsociable to the most exclusive degree, allowing no one to pry into their affairs or invade their hovel. On the approach of a stranger to watch a Cobbledick at work or at play, "a yelp called the whole clan together and with howls and curses" they drove the inquisitive visitor away, so pelting him with stones that he was compelled to beat a hasty retreat.

These unnatural savages went about half-naked, the few wretched rags they wore—an old sack with slits in it for head and arms it might be, or a stolen piece of tarpaulin, or something equally primitive and easy of adaptation—were worn more for warmth than decency. When the Cobbledicks wanted anything they went over the moors in search of it ; and the neighbouring farmers, who had heard old tales and hoary traditions of revengeful rick-burnings, were accustomed to leave, for purposes propitiatory, cast-off raiment and other discarded trifles, conveniently hanging on their hedges at night-time.

Their principles were socialistic in that there was no private property in any of their possessions, not even in their garments. The few utensils of their household, and the rude implements with which they tilled their farm, were common to the whole family. The farm, on which they chiefly raised potatoes for a common store, consisted of a stretch of clay land, overgrown with rushes, partly bog, which had been reclaimed from the waste in the dim and distant long ago.

Mr. Baring-Gould states that this strange people were autochthonous, and never had been civilized ; and while they never appreciably increased, they did not die out. The novelist utilises one of them, Grizzly Cobbledick an eccentric even among these abnormalities, as a character in his original and very interesting romance.

The Doones of Exmoor, those picturesque scoundrels made famous by the gifted pen of the novelist, Blackmore—if they ever existed—scarcely come within our purview. They were outlaws, but certainly not among the poor or the oppressed. The varying accounts of them agree in depicting them as terrorising the whole countryside, as living solely by rapine and plunder.

A lady writer has claimed them as a branch of a proud and noble Scottish family, the lords of Doune, who being exiled from Scotland in 1620, settled in the Oare Valley, Somersetshire, and there lived as outlaws till permitted to return to Perthshire, 1699. But Mr. E. J. Rawle, in his recently published work, "The Doones of Exmoor," has denounced the entrancing romance of "Lorna Doone" as a modern fabrication.

This well-informed authority traces the whole genesis of the legend; and if there is one thing he proves to a demonstration it is that the name Doone positively had no existence, either in local records or among the people, till about the eighteenth or nineteenth century. He comes to the conclusion that the tradition is based on nothing more substantial than a local "bogey" tale which has survived generation after generation from the time of King Alfred, when the Christian inhabitants of the land suffered such bitter cruelties, and ofttimes ruthless slaughter, at the hands of the fierce Viking marauders; that the word Doon, in fact, is but a modified form of the name Dane, and has nothing whatever to do with the name Doune, or that of any other seventeenth-century Scottish exile. The only vestige of actuality discoverable is a faint tradition that a fugitive from the battle of Sedgmoor, to escape the hangings of Judge Jeffreys, appropriated the ruins of some wretched huts in the recesses of the Badgworthy Glen—now "the Doon Valley "—finding there a safe retreat in which he reared a considerable family, which managed to eke out a living by committing petty depredations on the district. The "last of the Doones," an old man and his grand-daughter, are said to have perished in the snow, during the winter of 1800. Mr. Rawles' work is exhaustive and convincing.

XXXVI

THE TRAMP

The free rover of the roads—Distinct from the "nark" or town beggar—Finds a profit in children—The workhouse tramp—The tramping labourer—Rules of a "padding-ken"—The submerged caste of out-sleepers—Lodging-house manners—"The Amateur Casual"—The actual experiences of an investigating journalist—The tramp ward described—A Cadger's Begging Map—How the "vagrant train" gets recruited—"The House of Charity."

FEW lives are freer from care than that of the well-seasoned professional tramp. His spirits are as light as his wallet, for he never troubles about the morrow as long as he can beg a meal or a few coppers to-day, and satisfy himself with the covering of a cast-off garment. Confidence in his powers to find a cosy barn for the night, when sufficient coppers for a night's lodging are not forthcoming, carries him forward as far as ever he cares to look ahead.

On the road he can live on stolen apples, blackberries, turnips, or anything that comes ready to his hands.

There is the town beggar, known as the "nark," who has nothing of the gipsy spirit about him, who does not enjoy the freedom of the fields, nor sing the song of the open road. He is quite distinct from the tramp, from the free rover of the roads to whom reference is aptly made in the old play by Fletcher :—

"I'll watch you, what old barn you roost in,
And there I'll smother you all i' musty hay."

The professional roadster, or "turnpike traveller,"
accosts pleasantly; he is generally content with a copper,
and failing that, if of the male persuasion, will ask for a
"pipe o' bacca." What they often ask for is "the price
of a bed," and if unsuccessful have a ready knack of
making themselves cosy in a "skipper" or barn. If they
are successful they are never particularly grateful; nor,
on the other hand, are they ever vindictive.

In uncivilized nations children are looked upon as
sources of wealth to the parents. This view is not un-
recognized among the lower orders of civilized society,
and the mendicant fraternity occasionally borrow children
to assist them in their discreditable calling; finding a
large "family" paraded in rags a valuable accessory to
their professional efforts. It is strange, too, to note how
well children of this class scramble through life; how
seldom they suffer from the numerous infantile ailments
to which other children are subject.

Mendicancy is a disgrace to our civilization, and well-
meaning people help to perpetuate it by giving indis-
criminately, and without the exercise of ordinary
judgment. The tramp is the expert beggar who almost
raises mendicancy to the level of an art; it behoves
society to be particularly wary of him and his arts.

There is the workhouse tramp (of whom more
presently) who is despised by the true gentleman of
the road; the latter regarding him as dull-witted and
spiritless, and utterly contemptible for the mighty stone-
breaking feats he performs on an empty stomach.

In the same grade of society, besides the real beggar,
the nark, and the workhouse tramp, or "spikeranger,"
there is the low-class labourer; all these at times find a

meeting-place in the common lodging-house, or "nedhas ker," as they call it. In the last-named category there is the genuine out-of-work, who is but a timid beggar, on whom the professional beggar often takes pity ; and the casual labourer who does a day's work now and then. ' Among these labourers are to be named the cattle-driver, the odd-job man, and even the navvy. The navvy when earning good money will often stay at a common lodging-house, although never too well liked by the other frequenters. He is described as rough, boorish, ill-natured, foul-mouthed, tobacco-smeared, dirty, and often drunken. If the house is dominated by narks and navvies, they make themselves objectionable by a number of petty tyrannies, as taking up all the fire, pouring their greasy shackles (soup) into every available jug, mug, or cup, and such like practices. The nark is perhaps the more disliked of the two, as he is often in league with the lodging-house keeper, acting as spy and informer, and getting pence and privileges in return for mean little services of this nature. Strictly, the word "nark" means an informer.

Here is a set of rules exhibited in one of these tramps' hotels, technically known among the fraternity as "padding-kens"—

> "Fourpence a night for a bed.
> Sixpence with supper.
> No more than three to sleep in one bed.
> No beer allowed in the kitchen.
> No smoking when in bed.
> No clothes to be washed on Sundays.
> No boots to be worn in bed.
> No dogs allowed upstairs.
> No gambling or Fighting here.
> No extra charge for luggage.
> No Razor Grinders taken in.
> Organ Grinders to sleep in the attick."

These houses are all registered, and open to police inspection at every hour of the day and night. Though fairly sanitary, they are never over-furnished with the means of observing decency, particularly the lodging-houses which accommodate married couples. The most common complaint against them is of their dirty beds, broken crockery, and bad fires.

Below these *habitués* of the "doss-house" there is another, and even a lower, caste ; those votaries of misery to be found at night-time sleeping in the parks, on the benches in deserted thoroughfares, under railway arches, or wherever in the welcome darkness they can cast their weary bodies. This class of men and women are so hopeless, so apathetic, they seldom make the feeblest effort to extricate themselves from their abject condition, content to accept a copper, or other assistance, if offered, and in its absence just keeping body and soul together by eating any refuse food that comes to hand, even the pickings of the gutter.

A generation or more ago a flood of light was thrown on the treatment of the tramp and casual pauper by that prince of journalists, the late James Greenwood, whose adventures in a casual ward of a metropolitan workhouse were printed in the *Pall Mall Gazette*, obtained a world-wide reading for their piquancy, and won the *nom de guerre* of "The Amateur Casual" for their writer.

One cold and particularly inclement January night this personal investigator of low life, "got up" in the disguise of a hulking tramp, in a ragged coat that was much too small for his frame and made to meet over his chest with a bit of twine, a coloured cotton "handkercher" wisped about his neck hangman-fashion, a battered old billycock stuck on his head, his face unshaven and not too clean, and with his hands plunged deeply into his empty trousers' pockets, shuffled his way towards Lambeth Workhouse, to discover by actual experience how the casual pauper of this country was lodged and fed at the public expense.

Presenting his shivering, ill-clad body at the workhouse gate, he was curtly received by the porter, his name and application were unceremoniously taken down by a clerk, and he was then led across a dark and dismal yard to be handed over to the care of an irregular inmate official who went by the familiar name of " Daddy." His experiences, interesting reading as they make, cannot be given in detail here.

In a plain, unvarnished narrative this eminent publicist tells how he bathed in a disgusting liquid which looked more like mutton broth than water, after which he was supplied with a check shirt and a rug, his own clothing being taken from him, tied in a bundle, to which was attached a numbered ticket of which the counterfoil was handed to him, and he was then led, unclad, across the cold, windy yard again to the tramps' sleeping quarters.

This place was an airy, dingy, whitewashed shed, in which some thirty or forty men and boys were lying in a double row on shallow pallets. A dirty, touzled, villainous-looking lot they were, some sleeping or pretending to sleep, some of them squatting up, smoking foul pipes, bandying obscene jokes, or singing snatches of horrible songs.

He had missed his skilly—a watery kind of gruel—through being late ; but his allowance of bread was handed to him by the beneficent Daddy. How to conduct himself without exciting suspicion became more difficult at each stage of the adventure, so much was there from which any man of clean habits and decent mind would shrink instinctively.

Under Daddy's direction he managed to pick out

from a stack of bags stuffed with hay a fairly clean bed; but how to stow himself satisfactory in his rug was a problem he does not appear to have solved throughout the livelong night. A hungry youth very soon relieved him of the difficulty his uneatable lump of "toke" had presented to him.

It does not appear which he found the less endurable, the long and wakeful watches after midnight, when the ward was comparatively quiet, or the earlier hours, ere the exuberant vitality of trampdom had exhausted itself in a conversation that reeked of blasphemy and constantly renewed itself by an interchange of horrible imprecations. A few decent men among them certainly uttered a mild protest, but in the face of such an overwhelming majority of blackguards expostulation was worse than useless.

The night, which to the "amateur" had been one long, sleepless nightmare, came to an end at 7 a.m., when the bags of hay, euphemistically called beds, were stowed away, bundles were served out, and the process of dressing quietly gone through, after which ablutions of a primary kind were attempted at a pail in the yard. Breakfast consisted of skilly and bread; and in return for all this luxurious entertainment a certain amount of labour was demanded.

This work consisted of working a crank which turned like a windlass, one operated by each man, under the eye of a task-master, in the dormitory shed. Each night's batch of casuals was expected to grind four bushels or measures of corn; and a little signal bell near the ceiling rang to indicate the completion of each measure.

Some of the revolting practices of the old casual ward are stated to be indescribable in print; but the revelations made by James Greenwood, after that memorable "Night in a Workhouse," served to bring about in due course a reformed system of management.

The regular tramp hates and avoids the workhouse, his chief aim each day being to beg at least the sum of fourpence which is requisite to obtain him a "doss," or night's lodging in a "padding-ken." Hotten's "Dictionary of Slang" contains the reproduction of a cadger's map of his begging district. It is a curious diagram, which shows not only the roads and streets, but distinguishes them for the purpose of his calling by a number of amusing hieroglyphics. For instance, a dot with a ring round it significantly indicates the danger of being "put in quod" if found begging there; a cross with a ring round it fitly marks the residence of "a religious family"; a plain cross ticks off those who are "no good—too poor"; and so on, all the possibilities of the locality being set forth with a cryptic symbolism of much ingenuity.

The women who tramp the highways are hardened, unsexed creatures, often greater impostors than their male companions whose wives they purport to be.

The vagrant train is to a moderate extent recruited by the inefficient or displaced workman. Being neither an expert at, or enthusiastic for, any form of work, he soon gets pressed down, becomes shabby, tries the tramp ward, and presently blossoms into a tramp proper. But the bulk of this class are moral degenerates; they tramp aimlessly from place to place, or rather they aim simply and solely at the enjoyment of an idle life by preying upon the workers. They voluntarily lead a life which the industrious and self-respecting would regard as one of some hardship, though they manage to intersperse it with a number of vicious pleasures. The "spike-ranger," the thriftless wanderer from one casual ward to the next, has not yet been civilized out of existence.

Every day, in the large cities, girls drop into the ranks of the submerged class, some having fallen into vice, others dropped out of homes, all of them finding themselves suddenly homeless, friendless, and bewildered. Some of them drift into Homes, Shelters, Refuges, Asylums, or other similar institutions; and, let it be hoped, a goodly number of them are speedily reclaimed.

In London, at the corner of Greek Street, Soho, is a useful institution known as the House of Charity, which is a home for every kind of friendlessness and destitution which is not the manifest result of vice and profligacy. It was founded in 1846, and is supported by voluntary contributions, for affording to distressed persons of good character temporary refuge and relief; as patients discharged from hospital and not sufficiently recovered to go to situations; out-patients of hospitals excluded, through want of room, from admission; orphan and friendless girls who have accidentally lost their places; widows reduced to seeking a subsistence for themselves; emigrants who have broken up their homes and await embarkation; and all honest persons in like extremity of a temporary character. Such victims of circumstance, on the recommendation of some one who knows them, are saved the degradation of the tramp ward or the night-refuge. In an earlier institution of this character Thomas de Quincey, as he tells us in his "Confessions of an Opium Eater," found shelter from the streets when he was destitute.

XXXVII

SLUMLAND

St. Giles's—Organised beggars' "walks"—Beggars' Carnival—
Single-roomed tenements—Cellar dwellings—Poor Irish—
"Little Dublin"—Accommodating one thousand persons of
no fixed residence—"Rats' Castle" described by Dickens
—Seven Dials—Monmouth Street and its second-hand shops
—Deptford and "marine stores"—The rag-shop sign—
Ratcliff Highway—"Ragged London," Whitechapel—"Rag
Fair" near the Tower—Petticoat Lane—Westminster
"slums."

FEW large towns, particularly those which boast the
least antiquity, are without their slum areas, their
rookeries, where the poor herd together in filth and
squalor, if not always in misery. Those of London
are typical and historical.

St. Giles's-in-the-Fields is referred to elsewhere as the
favourite resort of the beggar population. In the days
of the Regency the beggar fraternity of this locality
were accustomed to hold a general meeting in the
course of the year, and each day they were divided
into companies, each company having its particular
" walk" or round assigned ; the earnings varied widely,
some getting as much as five shillings a day.

It is related that the Prince Regent, accompanied by
Major Hanger, once attended a beggars' carnival in
St. Giles's. He had not been there long when the

chairman, addressing the company and pointing to the Prince of Wales, said, "I will call upon that ere gemman with a shirt for a song." The Prince, with some difficulty, got himself excused on his friend promising to sing for him. The Major, prepared for the emergency, trolled forth "The Beggar's Wedding, or the Jovial Crew" in right good style, and elicited vociferous applause from the assembly by the performance. The episode ended in the approved and only possible way by the company drinking the singer's health—of course, at his expense—"with nine times nine"; whereupon he responded in suitable terms, and after wishing them "good luck till they were tired of it," departed with the Prince, affording the company time to fix their different routes for the ensuing day's business.

The district was entirely one of lodging-houses, and, squalid as they were, many of their tenants, far from being objects of misery, could truthfully be described as "fat, ragged, and saucy." In entire streets of houses whole families lived and thrived in single-room tenements.

In Charles Knight's "London" we read of "cellars serving whole families for kitchen, parlour, bedroom, and all. Here they cluster like cells in a convent of the Order of La Trappe, or like onions on a rope. It is curious and interesting to watch the habits of these human moles when they emerge, or half emerge, from their cavities. Their infants seem exempt from the dangers which haunt those of other people. At an age when most babies are not trusted alone on a level floor, these urchins stand secure on the upmost round of a trap ladder studying the different conformations of the shoes of passers-by. The mode of ingress of the adults is curious. They turn their backs to the entry, and inserting first one foot and then the other, disappear by degrees. They appear a short-winded generation, often coming, like the otter, to the surface to breathe. In the twilight, which reigns at the bottom of their dens, you can sometimes discern the male busily cobbling shoes on one side of the entrance and the female repairing all sorts of rent garments on the other."

These, of course, constituted the respectable portion of the population. There were others. As the old song hath it—

> "On Newgate steps Jack Chance was found
> And bred up near St. Giles's Pound."

At the beginning of the nineteenth century the dingy region of St. Giles's about Broad Street was distinguished by rows of chandler's shops, low public-houses, cook-shops, and cellars for the accommodation of the poorer Irish, who formed a colony there, which colony went by the various names of "The Rookery," "The Holy Land," and "Little Dublin." The inhabitants of this "Holy Land" were a floating population of about one thousand persons, who had no fixed residence, and who hired their beds for the night in houses fitted up for the purpose. Some of these houses had each fifty beds, if such a term can be employed for the wretched materials of which they were composed; the usual price was sixpence for a whole bed or fourpence for a half one. Behind some of the houses were cribs littered with straw, on which the more wretched could sleep at threepence a head.

Seventeen persons—men, women, and children, married couples and single folk—have been known to sleep in one room. A lodging-house keeper frequently held a number of these dens, and not infrequently managed to amass a fortune in the business.

Most of the Irish were honestly employed, though generally in the humblest walks of industry. But the beggar population, which was equally large, were as a rule much better off, and proverbially extravagant. An anecdote is related of one Alderman Calvert going to a beggar's lodging-house in disguise on a Saturday night, many years ago, to witness a weekly revel of the fraternity. The old alderman was considerably alarmed in the early part of the evening to hear some of the revellers order the landlord to bring for their supper "an alderman in chains." Only when he learnt that a roast turkey with sausages was meant did he recover his equanimity.

Readers of Dickens will remember another class in the low life of London who haunt this locality. The great novelist thus describes a night visit in company with Inspector Field :—

"St. Giles's Church clock strikes half-past ten. We stoop low, and creep down a precipitous flight of steps into a dark close cellar. There is a fire There is a long deal table. There are benches. The cellar is full of company, chiefly very young men in various conditions of dirt and raggedness. Some are eating supper. There are no girls or women present. Welcome to Rats' Castle, gentlemen, and to this company of noted thieves."

Then there is Seven Dials, of which the same master said that the inexperienced wayfarer through their mazes would find himself involved "in streets of dirty, straggling houses, with now and then an unexpected court composed of buildings as ill-proportioned and deformed as the half-naked children that wallow in their kennels."

A celebrated street preacher once referred to a street

26

in old St. Giles's which was famed for its second-hand clothing shops in these terms: "If any of you, my brethren, would have a suit to last a twelvemonth, let him go to Monmouth Street; if for a lifetime, let him apply to the Court of Chancery; but if for eternity, let him put on the robe of righteousness." Dickens tersely describes Monmouth Street as "the burial-place of the fashions."

To Deptford, however, belongs the honour of being the birthplace of the rag and bottle, or "marine store," trade. The locality swarms with second-hand shops, and the trade-sign hanging at the door consists of a black doll. The tradition of its origin states that a woman, travelling abroad, brought back with her a black baby as a speculation, but finding that the article had no value in England, wrapped it up in a bundle of rags and sold it to one of the founders of the trade. The story goes on to say the little nigger was reared at the expense of the parish; that she grew up and married, opened a shop in the same line of business, made a fortune, and became the ancestress of all the dealers from that day to this—her children starting fifty shops, at each of which a black doll was hung out as a sign.

This yarn will not satisfy the antiquaries and other experts. It is more probable the earliest of these repositories of old clothes and other household refuse were successors of the old shops where Indian and Chinese curiosities were offered for sale, and which had a "joss," or Chinese idol, for a sign. To Deptford, in the ordinary way of commerce, rags are brought which have crossed the seas, having found their way from Germany, even from India and Australia, wholesale dealers here selling them to the paper mills which abound near Dartford.

One of the entertaining "Sketches by Boz" is a description of "brokers' and marine-store shops," the following extract from which touches upon the matter :—

> "Imagine, in addition to this incongruous mass [rags, bones, and a heterogeneous collection of dirty and dilapidated old furniture], a black doll in a white frock, with two faces, one looking up the street, and the other looking down, swinging over the door."

And then presently the writer gives a description, in the true Dickensian style, of a marine-store dealer's in the Ratcliff Highway, "that reservoir of dirt, drunkenness, and drabs; thieves, oysters, baked potatoes, and pickled salmon."

"Whitechapel," says Hollingshead, in his "Ragged London" (1861), "may not be the worst of the many districts in this quarter, but it is bad enough." Mayhew described Rosemary Lane (now Royal Mint Street) as inhabited by dredgers, ballast-heavers, lumpers, slop-workers, and "sweaters employed in the Minories," one side of it being devoted to the sale of "old boots and shoes; old clothes, both men's, women's, and children's; a variety of cheap prints and muslins, new, but of the commonest; hats, bonnets;" and a variety of other cheap and second-hand commodities.

"Rag Fair," or Rosemary Lane, is mentioned in a note to Pope's "Dunciad" as "a place near the Tower of London where old clothes and frippery are sold."

Pennant gives a humorous picture of the barter going on there, and says :—

> "The articles of commerce by no means belie the name. There is no expressing the poverty of the goods, nor yet their cheapness. A distinguished merchant engaged with a purchaser observing me look on him with great attention, called out to me, as his customer

was going off with his bargain, to observe that man, 'for,' says he, 'I have actually clothed him for fourteen pence.'"

It was here, we believe, that customers were allowed to dip in a sack for old wigs—a penny a dip.

In the *Public Advertiser* of February 17, 1756, there is an account of one Mary Jenkins, a dealer in old clothes in Rag Fair, selling a pair of breeches to a poor woman for sevenpence and a pint of beer :—

"While the two were drinking together at a public-house, the lucky purchaser found, on unripping the clothes, eleven guineas of gold quilted in the waistband (eleven Queen Anne guineas), and a £30 bank-note, dated 1729, of which note the purchaser did not learn the value till she had sold it for a gallon of twopenny purl."

Every one has read of Petticoat Lane (now Middlesex Street), famous for its *al-fresco* Sunday market, which, says Mayhew, in his " London Labour," is essentially the old clothes' district.

"Embracing the streets and alleys adjacent to Petticoat Lane, and including the rows of old boots and shoes on the ground, there is, perhaps, between two and three miles of old clothes. Petticoat Lane proper is long and narrow, and to look down it is to look down a vista of many-coloured garments, alike on the sides and on the ground. The effect sometimes is very striking, from the variety of hues, and the constant flitting or gathering of the crowd into little groups of bargainers. Gowns of every shade and every pattern are hanging up, but none, perhaps, look either bright or white ; it is a vista of dinginess, but many-coloured dinginess, as regards female attire. Dress-coats, frock-coats, great-coats, livery and gamekeepers' coats, paletots, tunics, trousers, knee-breeches, waist-coats, capes, pilot-coats, working jackets, plaids, hats, dressing-gowns, shirts, Guernsey frocks, are all displayed. The predominant · colours are all black and blue, but there is every colour ; the light drab of some aristocratic livery, the dull brown-green of velveteen, the deep blue of a pilot-jacket, the variegated figures of the shawl dressing-gown, the glossy black of the restored garments, the shine of newly turpentined black satin waistcoats, the scarlet and green of some flaming tartan—these things, mixed with the hues of the women's garments, spotted and striped, certainly present a scene which cannot be beheld in any other part of the greatest City in the world, nor in any other portion of the world itself."

In Westminster, in the district to the south-west of the Abbey, was once a Rookery, a colony of vagabonds, where debtors and felons, beggars, outcasts, and thieves herded together, associating as a matter of course with women of the lowest class, and perpetuating the breed of vagabonds. This was the human warren which originated the term "slum" (see p. 268).

And what populous town is there that cannot (or rather could not, before Improvement Schemes were undertaken) produce one of these quarters in which poverty and misery, vice and disease, found a hiding-place miscalled a home ?

XXXVIII

POOR LAW REFORM

Poor Law Amendment, 1835—Allowances abolished—Parochial settlement retained—Out-door relief—Principle of Less Eligibility—The new "Unions"—Sexes separated—Inmates classified —Growth of sympathetic treatment—Lack of national education felt—The Act of 1870 to arrest race deterioration.

It was found after more than two centuries' working that the Poor Laws were a gigantic failure. Our grandfathers undertook what was virtually a crusade against them. Inquiries of an exhaustive character were made, and the laws, after being carefully overhauled, were amended, though still on palliative lines, and characteristically in accordance with the spirit of the times.

In 1835 the new Poor Law was passed, the outstanding features of which were that it forbade the relief of the able-bodied from the rates ; and that it swept away the cankering system of Allowances. Considering the spirit of the times in which it was passed, it was an excellent law, but at first somewhat severe upon the worker, for wages were still very low and food very dear ; the day of the Repeal of the Corn Laws had not yet arrived.

It is true that the fixing of the rate of wages by Quarter Sessions had been repealed in 1824, as also had the laws against the combining of workmen ; but the very "unsettling" law of Parochial Settlement remained ; nor can it be said that the condition of the labourer was materially improved until, in 1849, the Corn Laws were finally destroyed, and an abundance of cheap food was brought within his reach.

The breakdown of the old system was entirely due to the ruinous pressure put on the resources of the poor-rates by the workless able-bodied. Under the new one it now became the main operative principle, copied from Southwell, Bingham, and one or two other parishes, to relieve the able-bodied only within the walls of a Poor Law Institution.

Discretionary power was given to justices to order the relief of adult paupers who, from old age or infirmity, should be unable to work, without forcing them into the union workhouses.

The new union workhouses were designed to accommodate one hundred to five hundred inmates, housing them with some attempt at classification, and employing as many as possible according to their capacity; they were organized to maintain order among the inmates, to inculcate habits of industry and cleanliness, and to afford opportunities for religious observances.

Two new principles were introduced ; the first was that of National Uniformity, requiring that the relief afforded to each class of paupers should be uniform throughout the kingdom ; the second the principle of Less Eligibility, sought to exclude numbers of those superfluous and undeserving cases which, under the old system, had found a too ready way into the old parish workhouses.

The administrators of the Poor Law Amendment Act started off with high hopes and bright anticipations of the benefits to be secured by the working of the new policy. The first union workhouse to be completed under the provisions of the Act was that erected at Abingdon, and was of a somewhat novel character; in plan the three main buildings met at a centre and formed the letter Y; the external boundary walls running through the ends made the figure of a hexagon; and then dividing walls running out from the three angles of the Y to the external walls, divided the enclosed space into six yards. This was to facilitate the better classification of the inmates. On three sides of the hexagon were large spinning shops and other workrooms; at the foot of the Y was the main entrance, in which the sexes were divided, right and left, for their respective parts of the house.

So far, this kind of material progress was good. But it was not all. Ere scarcely a dozen years had passed it was found necessary to modify the new policy, which was based exclusively on arid theory and doctrinaire principles, by the introduction of a little human sentiment— as was exhibited in the more favoured treatment of children and the sick, and in various other directions where it has been found possible to administer relief more effectively by the aid of human sympathy than through the soulless channels of officialism. Sentiment, through the decades of experiment and doubtful success, has been slowly crystallising into principles.

While this advance was being made, it was palpable that ground was being lost in another direction. So slowly do we recognize the facts of existence. Although the country was found to be growing steadily in material prosperity, an uneasy feeling pervaded the nation that all was not quite right, that something essential was still lacking. The missing something was at last recognized to be a sound system of national education.

Just before the passing of the Elementary Education Act of 1870 it was estimated that in England and Wales there was a gutter population of no less than 350,000 children outside the range of all educational influence. In the large towns these street prowlers were to be met in the busy thoroughfares, some looking dogged and sullen in their pure animalism, most of them gaunt and wolfish. Centres of attraction to these neglected and hungry waifs were offered by any of the public markets, where they might be seen almost any day searching through the muck heaps, and eagerly devouring rotten fruit and other refuse with the avidity of pigs and ducks. The Act of 1870 was but the first step in the arrest of race deterioration—how urgently called for nearly everybody seems to have forgotten.

But the English are a conservative people. The Education Act, like the Poor Laws, still awaits the form of finality.

The Amended Poor Laws of 1835, after three-quarters of a century's trial, have been found full of faults and failings. The recent Royal Commission—or at least the more progressive section of it—has presented a report pregnant with novel and far-reaching suggestions. It practically dooms the workhouse to dissolution, and boards of guardians to extinction.

The new line of thought asks for the prevention of destitution rather than the curing of it. It is urged now that the Poor Law, which is a destitution authority, should distribute some of its work among other authorities which work in a less tainted astmosphere; for instance, that the children should be taken over by the Education Authority before the disease of destitution sets in; and that the indigent sick should be dealt with by the Health Authorities; in other words, that the old principle of deterrence should be superseded by that of prevention.

As society develops and grows more complex we are

continually finding that things which once it was desirable to leave to individual initiative, can, under the changed conditions, be performed with better results by common effort.

Another lesson forced home upon us is the utter futility of money gifts for the assuaging of human misery. The newer modes of alleviation incline to Guilds of Help working in mapped-out areas, and the co-operation of the State agencies with every variety of voluntary effort.

After two thousand years of Christianity, expressed in all the philanthropy of religion ; after centuries of legislation—of laws punitive and reformative, remedial and deterrent—the poor remain with us still, if not in the numbers and the extremities as of old, in an aggregate of destitution and suffering which is at least a reproach to our twentieth-century civilisation. There are still upwards of 800,000 paupers in England and Wales.

In a well-ordered society there would be no rich and no poor. Neither poverty nor riches is essential to human happiness; and in the vicissitudes of life the romance of marvellous happenings attaches quite as much to the one as to the other.

That romance, as these pages have endeavoured to set forth, invariably arises from the direct antagonism of the two views, the human and the Divine. For though the latter has been conveyed in the assurance, "Blessed be ye Poor, for yours is the kingdom of God," the worldly spirit of man has received it with scarce the lifting of his eyes, or the slackening of his pace, in the eternal pursuit of riches.

The aphorism of good George Herbert is beautiful—indeed, if we were Christians we might regard it as being very beautiful—"Man is God's image ; but a Poor Man is Christ's stamp to boot."

Index

UNWIN BROTHERS, LIMITED, THE GRESHAM PRESS, WOKING AND LONDON.

Lightning Source UK Ltd.
Milton Keynes UK
UKHW020154090223
416651UK00002B/496